Managing Educational Costs

Managing Educational Costs

PHILIP H. COOMBS and JACQUES HALLAK

Published with the agreement of Unesco: International Institute for Educational Planning

New York
OXFORD UNIVERSITY PRESS
London 1972 Toronto

Library of Congress Catalogue Card Number: 74-182422

Printed in the United States of America

Preface

During the Second United Nations Development Decade most countries, whether industrialized or "developing," will be facing increasingly pressing financial strain in meeting their enormous and urgent needs in the realm of education.

Both planners and administrators will in future have to take into greater account the economic aspects involved in their plans, and explore every means of improving the efficiency of their educational systems so as to get the best value from existing resources. Experience has proved that an indispensable technique for this purpose is analysis of the costs of education, by means of which it is possible to:

- check the economic validity of educational plans;
- draw up a precise program of expenditure over the planning period;
- estimate both the costs and the real economic consequences of specific projects;
- facilitate decision-making when several alternative possibilities exist for the allocation of funds.

To illustrate these techniques as clearly as possible the International Institute for Educational Planning (IIEP) put in hand, in 1968, a large-scale research project on the uses of cost analysis in educational planning. The aim of the study was to carry out a pragmatic inquiry into actual practice in order to provide planners with a general view of the various ways of using cost analysis and with practical hints on the application of these ways to their own particular needs. Mr. Philip H. Coombs, the former Director of the Institute, was responsible for the technical direction of the work, assisted by Mr. Jacques Hallak, also of the Institute, and with the co-operation of a number of IIEP staff members; the project took over two years and was carried out in three stages.

In the first stage, a methodological note was prepared, laying down the general lines on which the research would be carried out; and as many examples as possible of experiences in this field were considered, from which a diversified sample was selected for study in depth.

The second stage was to gather and analyze the statistical information for each case in this sample, and to compile an analytical report based on the data collected for each case study. For these activities the IIEP was greatly assisted by the co-operation of specialists in the various countries and of international experts, especially those of Unesco.

In the third stage the guidelines and principal lessons emerging from an analysis of all the case studies were summed up in the present synthesis report by Mr. Coombs and Mr. Hallak.

The contents of this report should not be regarded simply as a collation of the results of the twenty-seven case studies (which will be published separately by the IIEP in three volumes). Proceeding from the specific aspects of each particular experience of the use of cost analysis, the two authors have sought, first, to identify precisely the multiple and individual roles of cost analysis and, second, to analyse the past and future behavior of educational costs in relation to the most significant factors of development. Practical outlines for the application of cost studies are also given.

In spite of the wealth of information on which it is based, this synthesis report does not pretend to cover exhaustively all the theoretical and practical aspects of the use of cost analysis. Nor does it attempt, as the authors themselves admit, to "say the last word on the subject." The opinions expressed, furthermore, in so far as they are value judgments, are the authors' own and do not commit anyone else.

The project was financed principally by the United States Agency for International Development (USAID) and the Swedish International Development Agency (SIDA), to whom the IIEP wishes to express its deepest gratitude. The Institute would also like to thank the many officials, educators, and specialists who, both in the countries studied and in the various Departments of Unesco, have unstintingly given us their assistance in bringing this project to fruition.

RAYMOND POIGNANT
Director, IIEP

Contents

An Introductory Explanation

This book is about the economics of education but it is written mainly for non-economists, in particular for people who actually run educational systems, who practice planning, decision-making, and management every day in all sorts of situations, or who are in training for such roles. These people include not only the handful of experts and officials in the nation's capital who make over-all plans and top policies; they also include the much larger number who work where the action is—at the state or district or community level, in individual universities, training colleges, schools and classrooms, in farmer training centers, extension services, work-oriented literacy projects, and in training programs for industrial workers. All these people share responsibility for solving education's Number One Problem today: how to get more and better education from the resources available.

By more and better education we do not mean simply more of the same old curriculum and methods for more people, or a retreat to yesterday's standards. We mean a broadening and continuity of educational opportunities of many sorts for many purposes; the chance for each individual to learn more in each time period, whether in a regular educational institution or outside the formal system; and we mean educational content that is up-to-date, relevant, and useful to each learner in his own particular society.

This conception of more and better education cannot be fulfilled merely by expanding existing educational establishments in their old image. It will require revolutionary changes in existing educational structures, content, and methods to match the evolving needs of individuals and nations in a rapidly changing world, and to fit their pocketbooks as well.

Larger budgets will surely be required, but that is not all. A new set of attitudes toward educational change and innovation by educators and non-educators alike is also required, along with new research and development infra-structures and processes within educational systems to enable them to examine themselves critically, to devise new solutions to their problems, and to engage in a continuous process of self-renewal. The pre-condition for all of this is the modernization of educational management, including a much stronger capability (1) to evaluate the performance of educational institutions against well-defined and up-to-date objectives; (2) to discover ways to improve their efficiency and effectiveness; and (3) to plan their future with these changes in view.

It is these larger considerations that make educational cost analysis today so much more essential than ever before. Cost analysis has no special magic to remedy faulty conditions, but it is a powerful and necessary tool for modern educational management and effective educational planning. It can contribute importantly to getting more and better education from whatever resources are available.

The hard-earned experience of recent years, especially in developing nations where shortages are most severe, provides valuable lessons on how cost analysis can be used as a tool for decision-making, and on the penalties paid when cost analysis is neglected. To illustrate, here are some clear conclusions drawn from actual experiences which are examined later in this book:

- An educational or political leader who promises universal primary education by a certain date without first checking the economic feasibility of this target is bound to end up in serious trouble.
- A decision made to upgrade large numbers of poorly qualified teachers to higher-paying categories through in-service training, without prior study of the cost consequences, can put an educational system on the road to bankruptcy.
- A developing nation that accepts a well-intentioned gift of an expensive new educational facility without first checking what it will cost annually in local resources to operate the new facility may

later find its whole educational program distorted and disadvantaged by this generous gift.

• A university with limited resources that proliferates its program offerings in the name of meeting "international standards" or which opens its doors indiscriminately to all secondary school graduates in the name of social justice can soon find itself producing quite the opposite of excellence and justice.

• A school system that reduces its pupil-teacher ratio in the hope of raising quality, at the expense of its meager budget for textbooks and other instructional materials, should not be surprised if its students end up learning even less.

• Educational leaders who try to meet the need for innovation by superimposing a new technology (such as instructional television) upon the old teaching-learning process will find their expenses increased by the full cost of the added technology, probably without a proportionate improvement in learning results.

These familiar type-cases bespeak two basic truths that will reappear in many forms in the pages that follow. The first truth is that any measure taken to improve educational quality or opportunity without prior examination of its cost consequences can easily prove self-defeating. The second truth is that, in most situations, costs have little meaning or value until they are set against educational results and the results are weighed against the objectives. Costs, in other words, are only one side of the equation that links educational resource inputs to educational outputs and benefits. It is this equation as a whole—and this broader, more systematic way of looking at an educational process—that enables educational planners, evalutors, and managers (broadly defined to include teachers) to improve the efficiency and productivity of any educational activity.

A word should be said here about the aims and scope of this book and about the present state of the theory and practice of educational cost analysis.

Educational administrators have always been obliged to pay attention to costs, especially in connection with budget-making. But costing a budget falls far short of the kinds of cost analysis dealt with here. The investigations underlying this book have confirmed what was already suspected, that educational systems and institutions, even in the most highly industrialized countries, have not been very "cost conscious" in the sense of analyzing their costs for purposes of evaluation, planning, policy-making, and general improvement of their cost effectiveness. Indeed, it comes as a shock to discover how little even the most reputable universities know about where their resources are actually going and with what results. This includes eminent universities that offer sophisticated courses and do pioneering research in computer programming, cost-benefit analysis, organizational theory, and management techniques aimed at improving the planning and management of *other* types of enterprises. The widely held hidden premise appears to be that because education is not sold on an open market and does not have a profit and loss statement like a commercial business it is thereby exempt from the principles of efficiency. But this is a badly mistaken premise.

The lengths to which the IIEP staff had to go in locating a satisfactory international sample of actual cases of educational cost analysis to undergird this book is eloquent testimony to the underdeveloped state of the art and to the need for such a book.

The book's aim, therefore, is to provide a better understanding of educational cost analysis and the important purposes it can serve, expressed in language that is understandable to non-economists who are in a position to put cost analysis to good use. More specifically the book seeks to explain why cost analysis has become imperative in these changing times, how educational costs behave, why they behave as they do, how various educational systems and institutions have actually used cost analysis and with what results, how educational analysts can go about applying cost analysis in their own institution, and how decision-makers can profit from the results.

We hasten to add, however, that this book does not provide the final word on the subject. It is, so far as we are aware, the first book of its kind, but it will certainly not be the last. Theories and methods of educational cost analysis have advanced considerably in recent years and their practical application perhaps even faster, but both theory and practice are still in a relatively primitive state and can be expected to evolve rapidly in the future. Thus we can hope that with each passing year there will be more of value to be said on this subject—including, no doubt, things that will contradict some of what is said in these pages.

As of the present writing there is wide agreement on many points about cost analysis, but there are also some vital frontier issues on which able economists still disagree amongst themselves—sometimes with passion. We will concentrate here mainly on the more settled areas of agreement, but we will also call attention to important unresolved issues, making no pretense, however, at offering theoretical breakthroughs that will resolve them. Our main purpose is to extract such practical guidance as we now can from existing knowledge and practice that can benefit practitioners who need and want such help.

It should be added that in carrying out this effort we have profited much from the generous help of many able economists who contributed to earlier theoretical developments in this field. Their greatest *new* contribution was to put themselves in the practitioner's shoes and to help us demonstrate how theory can be practically applied in the cluttered and imperfect world of reality.

From the start of this project we addressed our attention particularly to the problems faced by developing nations, but it has become increasingly evident that the more developed nations are often quite as underdeveloped with respect to educational cost analysis and have much the same basic problems and needs. Thus, although our illustrations will be drawn primarily from the developing world, we hope that the book will prove relevant and useful to industrialized nations as well. Perhaps the greatest difference among nations in this respect is that the poorer ones are even more handicapped than the richer ones in their lack of essential data and talent for doing good cost analysis. But on the other hand, the poorer nations are sometimes more willing and anxious to try such analysis.

A brief explanation of how this book was produced is also in order. There were four main stages: first, an examination was made of the general literature on the subject; second, a search was made throughout the world for some instructive examples, and twenty-seven cases were finally selected and studied; third, the findings of the first two stages were critically reviewed with many experienced economists and educators; finally, the present book was prepared to synthesize the findings and convey them to practitioners who might find them useful.

The twenty-seven case studies are of particular interest because they involved groundbreaking research and provided the main illustrative materials for this book. These cases are extremely diversified in every respect, as will be seen from Appendix 2. They are widely scattered geographically; they are fairly well distributed by level and type of education or training (the two notable deficiencies being teacher training and non-formal education); they vary in breadth of coverage, ranging from individual projects to entire formal educational systems; and, most important, they illustrate the diversity of uses to which cost analysis can be put.

Broadly speaking, the cases illustrate seven principal purposes which cost analysis can serve: (1) costing and testing the economic feasibility of educational plans; (2) evaluating and improving the allocation of available educational resources (e.g. by principal levels and types of education); (3) weighing the comparative advantages of alternative ways to pursue the same educational objectives; (4) determining both the short and longer-run cost implications of a particular project; (5) estimating the introductory costs and the likely longer-term cost impacts of a major educational innovation; (6) conducting a general search for ways to improve efficiency and productivity; and (7) checking the economic implications and feasibility of special policy decisions before they are made.

The case studies can also be usefully classified from a different angle, according to three degrees of educational change involved: (1) the linear expansion of an existing educational system or subsystem without substantial change in its characteristics (the simplest case); (2) significant modifications of existing educational arrangements aimed at improving the qualitative performance and efficiency of the system, but still without radically altering its form and methods (decidedly more difficult); and (3) fundamental innovations aimed at drastically altering the system's structure, content, and performance, or even creating alternative teaching-learning "systems" to replace or supplement the old ones (the most complex case).

Highlights of the IIEP case studies are presented in Part I and numerous specific references are made to them throughout the rest of the book. The case studies themselves are available for inspection in three companion volumes published by the IIEP. Though the present book stands on its own, many readers will no doubt find it worthwhile to explore some of the case studies at firsthand. The full case studies are also useful for training purposes.

About half of them were prepared entirely by IIEP staff members from original documentation, supplemented where necessary by field visits. The rest were prepared under IIEP guidance by outside consultants with firsthand knowledge of the case in question.

As might be expected, the cases vary greatly in the amount of evidence available, in the simplicity or sophistication of the methods employed, and in the amount they have to teach to others. Interestingly, when we checked the complete cases with experienced people, there was wide agreement that the "thin" cases (in terms of the spareness of data available and the crudeness of the methods used) were often the most instructive, because educators in other countries could most readily identify their own situation with them.

These cases, it should be emphasized, are not offered as models to be emulated. In fact in no few instances the chief lessons are, in a sense, negative ones; the greatest value lies perhaps in the analysis of the shortcomings of the methods used and in the suggestions of alternative methods that *might* have been used. But above all, the cases lend an air of reality to the whole subject. They demonstrate to the hard-pressed and hard-headed administrator who has grown skeptical of abstract theorizing that his colleagues elsewhere, with problems rather similar to his own, have actually made a stab at cost analysis with useful practical results. Hopefully such an administrator will browse through a few of these cases himself and be inspired to try a few stabs of his own.

The book falls into three main parts. Part I, as we said earlier, introduces the reader to the case studies and hopefully will whet his appetite to go further. Part II provides some basic insights into the nature and behavior of educational costs that are prerequisite to the practice of cost analysis. Part III contains what the reader presumably is looking for, a wide variety of guides, practical tips, and precautions on how to apply cost analysis to his own situation. A final chapter looks to the future, at some unresolved issues and challenges and at significant frontier developments in cost analysis that hopefully will enable us all to cope with them more effectively in coming years.

The authors owe a deep debt of gratitude to their IIEP colleagues and others who helped to prepare case studies, to the many governments and education officials without whose generous cooperation these studies could not have been done, and to the friendly critics who did their best along the way to keep us straight and to help us serve our readers well. Full responsibility for what is said in the pages that follow, however, rests with the authors personally and should not be regarded as expressing the official views of Unesco or the IIEP.

Managing Educational Costs

I *Important Needs Being Served by Cost Analysis*

Even though cost analysis is a relative newcomer to most educational systems, abundant evidence of its practical value is already available from recent experience in a variety of countries. In the next three chapters we present highlights of this experience derived from twenty-seven IIEP case studies.

The first chapter tells how cost analysis has been used to test the economic feasibility of educational plans; the second describes how cost analysis has helped to reveal the future consequences of proposed educational reforms and innovations and to appraise the comparative advantages of alternative courses of educational action; the third provides examples of how cost analysis has contributed to improving the efficiency of educational systems. Not all of the stories recounted below are success stories, and in no few instances the final chapter has yet to be written by future events and evidence. But negative lessons often are as instructive as positive ones. In any event, these slices of real experience by real educational systems, we hope, will help to persuade beleaguered planners and administrators that the case for trying cost analysis does not rest on purely theoretical grounds, and will help encourage them too to try this approach.

1 *Testing the Economic Feasibility of Expansion Plans*

Many nations had the disappointing experience in the 1950's and 1960's of setting bold educational expansion targets that later proved unachievable, at least within the original time-frame. Often it was because the targets were unrealistic to begin with. They had not been properly "costed" and checked against a prudent forecast of the resources likely to be available. Even in situations where targets had been achieved *statistically*, the accomplishment was often illusory; though the gross statistics indicated rising enrolments, a different story was told by the high rate of dropouts and repeaters and the disheartening deterioration of quality.

The cases below suggest ways by which targets can be made more realistic and plans brought within the grasp of practical attainment.

Tanzania—Learning by Doing

The IIEP has found Tanzania an unusually fertile laboratory for useful lessons about educational planning, including cost analysis. Tanzania's educational and economic authorities and political leaders (not least of all the President himself, a former teacher) have all along been serious believers in planning and have gone about it in a very realistic, pragmatic manner. They wanted plans that could and would be implemented.

An illuminating blow-by-blow account of how Tanzania's first full five-year development plan for education (covering 1964–69) was hammered out—including the important role played by manpower requirements and the resolution of differences between the educational planners and the economic and manpower planners—is given in two earlier IIEP publications.[1] Two more recent case studies in the IIEP cost analysis series show, first, how important lessons from the First Plan were applied in preparing the next one,[2] and, second, how serious errors can be avoided in projecting future costs by using special methods to forecast teacher costs.[3]

A check-up on how Tanzania's First Plan had worked out in practice revealed the following: (1) broadly speaking, the enrolment targets had been achieved (in fact slightly over-achieved at the secondary level) even though the economy had grown at an average annual rate of only 5 per cent against the postulated 8 per cent; (2) actual recurrent expenditures had not diverged substantially from the projected levels; (3) paradoxically, however, teacher costs per student at the secondary level, contrary to expectations and notwithstanding a decline in the student-teacher ratio from 23.3 in 1964 to 21.8 in 1968, actually fell 5 per cent over the five years; (4) equally paradoxical, the enrolment targets had been achieved despite the fact that capital expenditures and the expansion of facilities had run far below the projected amount.

All things considered, this was a good record of planning and implementation. But how did it happen that recurrent costs per secondary student declined unexpectedly instead of rising, and that

1. A. C. Mwingira and Simon Pratt, "The Process of Educational Planning in Tanzania," in *Educational Development in Africa*, Vol. I, Paris, Unesco: IIEP, 1969; and G. Skorov, "Integration of Educational and Economic Planning in Tanzania," in *Educational Development in Africa*, Vol. III, Paris, Unesco:IIEP, 1969.

2. Nicholas Bennett, "Tanzania: Planning for Implementation," in *Educational Cost Analysis in Action: Case Studies for Planners*, Vol. I, Paris, Unesco: IIEP, 1972.

3. John D. Chesswas, "Tanzania: Factors Influencing Change in Teachers' Basic Salaries," in *Educational Cost Analysis in Action: Case Studies for Planners*, Vol. I Paris, Unesco:IIEP, 1972.

the enrolment targets were met despite the substantial shortfall in the planned expansion of facilities?

The answers lie in certain discrepancies between what was assumed in preparing the First Plan and what actually happened. Secondary teacher costs per student were expected to rise due to (1) an improvement in teacher qualifications and the pupil-teacher ratio, and (2) an estimated 2 per cent annual "incremental creep" reflecting the automatic upward movement of teachers within the salary structure, based on years of service. But three offsetting developments were not sufficiently allowed for: (1) the proportion of Tanzanians joining the secondary teaching force at the bottom of the salary scale expanded from 23.3. per cent (1964) to 48.7 per cent (1968), and this tended to pull down the salary average; (2) a considerable number of long-service, pensionable expatriate teachers (the common label for foreign teachers) were replaced by lower-cost, perhaps less-experienced, short-term contract expatriate teachers; and (3) there was an unexpectedly large influx of teaching "volunteers" and externally financed teachers that cost the Tanzanian budget relatively little.

Four other things happened which threw off the assumptions with respect to capital costs at the primary and secondary level: (1) local communities proved more willing to accept part of the burden of building new schools than had been assumed, which eased the demands on the central government's capital budget; but, on the other side, (2) considerably less external assistance was received for the ambitious secondary school construction program than had been projected; (3) contrary to the assumption of geographically uniform construction costs, these costs ran appreciably higher in outlying areas than in the capital; but (4) to save the situation, the capacity of existing schools, as it turned out, was far from fully utilized (contrary to the planners' assumption), and thus some schools were able to absorb many more students than expected.

Fortunately these misfiring assumptions had not seriously impaired the attainment of the First Plan's enrolment targets, but they pointed to lessons which needed to be applied in formulating the next plan.

The second recent IIEP case study on Tanzania looked more deeply into the important problem of projecting teacher costs. A substantial error made here could seriously throw off over-all cost projections and possibly invite mistaken policies. To make the point, an exercise was done on projecting Tanzania's elementary teacher salary bill for the ten years ending 1979, by two different methods.

The first method, commonly used because of its simplicity, merely takes the existing average cost per teacher and multiplies it by the projected number of teachers required in future years (the assumption being that the average cost per teacher will remain more or less constant). The second method, more complicated but somewhat safer, begins with a breakdown of the present teacher force by the main qualification categories and by years of service (differentiating in the case of Tanzania between Grade A, B, and C teachers and between expatriate teachers in different financial categories). The next step is to project not only the total number of additional teachers required in future years (based on enrolment projections) but also any changes likely to occur in the *composition* of the teaching force, since such changes are likely to affect the average cost per teacher (as developments under the First Plan had demonstrated). Thus, for example, a decline in the proportion of short-term contract expatriate teachers or a rise in "volunteer" teachers from abroad both help to lower the average cost per teacher, whereas a slowing down of the rate of expansion and the consequent "aging" of the teacher force in terms of the average number of years of service works in the direction of raising the average.

When the results of the two methods used in the Tanzania exercise were compared, the simple method was shown to underestimate total elementary teacher costs ten years hence by 17 per cent compared to the more realistic method which took changing composition into account.

This exercise sounds a stern warning to all educational systems to keep a close watch on the changing age and qualifications structure of their teaching staff in addition to its over-all size, and to look carefully before they leap into any major changes of staffing or salary policy.

In this connection, Tanzania itself found it necessary to alter the course laid down initially in the 1964–69 development plan. The aim had been to improve quality by expanding the supply of Grade A teachers (the most highly qualified and expensive teachers) and to phase out Grade C teachers (who were considered under-qualified). But by 1968 the Minister of Education found it necessary to announce a modification of this policy because of its heavy cost implications. The phasing out of Grade C teachers, it was decided, would be postponed; but to ensure improvement of quality, the aim would instead be to staff each full primary school with at least three Grade A teachers combined with five Grade B and C teachers. The implication was that each full seven-grade school would have one supernumerary teacher to serve either as headmaster (or headmistress) or as a home economics or other specialized teacher, and the top-grade teachers could assist and encourage the less qualified ones.

Ceylon—Making the Most of Inadequate Data

Ceylon is another nation that has managed—despite a sparsity of good data—to put cost analysis to good use in testing the feasibility of development plans, in fashioning annual budgets, and perhaps most interestingly, in devising budgetary strategies for improving educational quality and teacher productivity.[4]

The data difficulties in Ceylon are well illustrated by the fact that primary and secondary school costs are inextricably lumped together in the national educational budget accounts, thus making

4. The story is told in a case study prepared by Dr. Jinapala Alles (a high official of the Ministry of Education at the time) and five of his colleagues, in close collaboration with the IIEP staff, entitled "Ceylon: Costing First- and Second-Level General Education," in *Educational Cost Analysis in Action: Case Studies for Planners*, Vol. I, Paris, Unesco:IIEP, 1972.

it all but impossible to distinguish between the unit costs of Level I and Level II. Yet if one is to project the costs of a medium- or long-term plan in which the two levels are scheduled to expand at different rates of speed, it is obviously necessary to separate primary from secondary school costs.

Undaunted, the Ceylonese planners invented an ingenious statistical technique for accomplishing this act of separation. They also managed to segregate recurrent from capital costs per student and to break down recurrent costs into teacher costs and non-teacher costs (e.g. textbooks, teaching materials, and supplies, etc.), which became the basis for their strategy of qualitative improvement. Their unit cost estimates were necessarily rough approximations in the form of crude averages (rural and urban school costs per student remained blended, for example, though there were presumably significant differences between the two). They were further handicapped in projecting teacher costs by the lack of detailed information on the composition of the teaching staff (such as was used in the case study of teacher costs in Tanzania).

Despite these formidable obstacles, however, the Ceylonese planners were able to avoid some potentially serious errors in setting planning targets and to strengthen day-to-day management of the educational system through creative uses of cost analysis.

In connection with preparing an education plan for 1966–70, for example, they conducted a rough costing exercise to test the feasibility of rapidly raising the "participation rate" in primary schools to 90 per cent of the corresponding age group. The conclusion was clearly negative. The analysis showed that even if all other factors were favorable (such as the ability of the construction industry to accelerate school construction, which was doubtful), the necessary recurrent expenditures alone would amount to roughly 7 per cent of the GNP. This was clearly too high to be feasible; thus the participation rate would have to be raised more gradually. In the absence of this costing exercise, policy-makers might conceivably have embraced this attractive but unrealistic target.

One of the most imaginative uses of cost analysis in Ceylon dealt with the search for an effective strategy to improve the *quality* of secondary education, particularly in the sciences, mathematics, and foreign languages. As in many other developing nations, educational quality in these fields suffered from obsolescence and from the lack of sufficient resources for curriculum revision, for new textbooks and other materials, and for in-service refresher training for teachers. One surmises that in Ceylon, as elsewhere, one main reason for the lack of resources for the above purposes was that the pressure of rising teacher salary costs had progressively crowded out budgetary provisions for the very tools that help teachers and students to be more productive—tools such as modern textbooks, laboratory supplies, and the like.

The Ceylonese government's "educational management team" devised a scheme for improving quality over a period of years by building into the budget plan a new sub-unit cost item for "quality improvement" which would rise from 0.7 per cent of the total recurrent funds for secondary education in 1968 to 2.0 per cent by 1977. The new cost item would be specifically earmarked for quality improvement through curriculum revision, more and better instructional materials, and in-service training to make teachers proficient in handling the improved curriculum.

One can only regret that imaginative planning and cost analysis of this variety are not buttressed by a more adequate "information system" to provide basic data that could widen the scope and improve the utility and reliability of cost analysis.

The U.S.S.R.—the Use of Norms and Standardized Budgets

Rapid expansion has become a normal way of life for Soviet education. So also have regularized planning and budget-making, based on the extensive use of cost norms, all the way from the aggregate national level down to the individual establishment. Many aspects of Soviet educational planning can be studied with profit by other nations,[5] but here our interest focuses on the extensive role played by cost analysis and costing norms. Their role in the planning and financing of higher education is described in the first of the studies of the Soviet system included in this series,[6] and they are extensively considered in the second study, which is a comprehensive and fascinating survey of the methods used for estimating the annual educational budget requirements.[7]

The Soviet educational system is highly centralized at the national and republic level. In some circumstances this could lead to the kind of standardization and administrative rigidity that throttles adaptation to local variations and to changing conditions, but Soviet authorities seem to have devised flexible means for substantially reducing this risk.

One important aspect of this flexibility is that educational planning takes place not only from the top down but from the bottom up. The top national planning organization—the Gosplan—produces the over-all five-year plan for the economy and educational system as a whole, then, in conjunction with the National Finance Ministry, translates this medium-term plan into annual budgetary plans. More or less simultaneously, however, each individual university and local school system prepares its own five-year plan and annual budget within the national framework set out by the Gosplan, employing norms and procedures laid down by higher bodies.

In formulating nationwide and republic-wide "macro" educational plans, the Gosplan organization makes extensive use of "information norms" (i.e. non-compulsory norms) based on recent experience. At first, "material norms" for physical resource requirements are applied, showing the number of teachers, classrooms,

5. For details see *Educational Planning in the U.S.S.R.*, Paris, Unesco: IIEP, 1968.

6. D. Chuprunov and L. Tul'chinskii, "U.S.S.R.: Economic Planning and the Financing of Higher Education," in *Educational Cost Analysis in Action: Case Studies for Planners*, Vol. I, Paris, Unesco:IIEP, 1972.

7. V. I. Basov, "U.S.S.R.: Estimating the Annual Budget Requirements of the Educational System," in *Educational Cost Analysis in Action: Case Studies for Planners*, Vol. I, Paris, Unesco:IIEP, 1972.

and so forth required in relation to the projected number of students. These "real" resource requirements are then translated into money terms by "financial norms" (e.g. cost per teacher, per classroom, per square foot of new school space, etc.). The results of these calculations are finally expressed in material and financial aggregates and sector and sub-sector allocations, and finally tested for compatibility with the nation's over-all prospective resource position.

Meanwhile, individual universities and local school systems are hard at work preparing their own "micro" five-year plans and their proposed annual budgets, consistent with their five-year plans and fitted to their own particular needs and circumstances. The individual establishment plans and budgets are subject to detailed review and approval by appropriate higher authorities in light of collective budgetary requirements and restrictions. In making their proposed plans and budgets, individual establishments (over local or district authorities with jurisdiction over a cluster of schools) follow prescribed budget forms and procedures and cost norms. In their case, the norms are for the most part compulsory, not simply informational. Each institutional category (e.g. rural primary schools of a given size, urban secondary schools of a certain type and size, higher technical institutes, etc.) has its own set of norms designed to provide reasonable equality of treatment and uniformity of practice within that category. Geographic differentials are provided where necessary to allow, for example, for differences in heating costs under varying climatic conditions and for incentive salaries for teachers in rural areas. Special costs in any one year, such as unusual repair and maintenance costs in a particular institution, are treated independently of the cost norms and approved case by case.

These norms for individual establishments are given in great detail for virtually every cost component—teachers, fuel and light, custodial services, school meals, books, etc. By contrast, at higher planning levels these "individual" norms are often consolidated into broader "composite" norms.

The individual establishment norms are tied to the most appropriate "costing unit"—which might be an individual student, or group of students, a classroom, a teacher, or a whole school or university. Thus, for example, the "material norm" for the authorized number and grade of teachers or professors is usually tied to the number of students; the norms of salary expenditures are expressed on a per teacher basis; norms for official travel are expressed per administrator or per teacher; food norms are applied per pupil; norms for teaching materials may be on either a per pupil or per classroom basis; while costing norms for heating, cleaning, and yard maintenance relate to the area of the premises.

These individual establishment norms are used not only for planning and budget-making but for management, auditing, and cost control purposes. The plan and budget of each institution is geared to its particular accomplishment targets (e.g. the number of students to be admitted and graduated in a given plan period). If the institution falls short of its target, or if it accumulates excess inventories, for example, its budget is reduced accordingly and funds must be returned (or foregone in the next period).

Varying degrees of discretionary authority to transfer funds within strictly defined limits are given to the heads of universities and school districts, but with this exception: they are under strict injunction to adhere in detail to their approved plan and budget and are subject to disciplinary action if they do not.

Soviet experts point out that these uniform cost norms have several advantages over the alternative method of basing each institution's budget on its actual expenditure experience of the previous year. They believe this method ensures greater equality among institutions and their students; it avoids the perpetuation of wasteful practices in any one institution by setting a common standard of efficiency; and it removes the incentive for individual administrators to "spend up" their whole budget before the end of each fiscal period (on low priority things if necessary) to avoid penalizing their budget position for the next year.

It is a very interesting system, and it evidently works quite well. Two cautionary points are in order, however. First, this relatively sophisticated use of costing norms in the Soviet Union rests on an elaborate information system which delivers reliable, comparable, and up-to-date data of many sorts to all the key decision-making points in the system in ample time to be useful. Virtually all developing nations—and most industrialized ones as well—are still a long way from having such an elaborate information system (though this is no reason for their not moving toward costing norms within the limits of their present information system).

Second, costing norms can be a blessing or a curse, depending on whether or not they are appropriate norms for the particular situation, whether they are kept up-to-date and steadily angled toward improved efficiency in the use of resources, and whether they are competently applied. Sound and appropriate norms have a myriad of obvious advantages; poor ones may simply be a perpetrator and perpetuator of educational rigidity and inefficiency. One gains the impression that Soviet experts and authorities are exercising increasing vigilance to keep their norms from drifting into being a liability.

France—Setting Realistic Expansion Targets

Countries attempting to apply nationwide educational planning will find it instructive to examine how French educational planners have used cost analysis, particularly with respect to capital costs.

France was first among the major Western nations to adopt systematic, nationwide educational planning, starting in 1952, as an integral part of over-all national investment planning for economic and social development. In the ensuing years planning played a central role in the vast expansion that began transforming an old "elitist" educational system into a "mass" system. By 1965, for example, some 39 per cent of young French men and women were in secondary schools in contrast to only 19 per cent in 1950, while 17 per cent were attending universities compared with only 6 per cent in 1950.[8] The large increase in "participation rates" at both the secondary and post-secondary level was accomplished on

8. *OECD Observer*, Paris, August 1970, p. 40.

top of a major expansion required by the sharp post-war rise in births. These factors combined lifted French capital expenditures on educational facilities to 1 per cent of the GNP in the 1960's.

Since French planning has mainly been focused on pysical facilities, it is here that one finds the most useful lessons. Of particular interest to us here is how the French system of planning has managed to set five-year capital expansion targets that were economically realistic and that by and large have been successfully implemented. We can get an idea of how this was accomplished by looking at the major steps involved in preparing the Fifth Plan covering the period 1966–70.[9]

At the outset the General Planning Commission (Commissariat du Plan), which guides and synthesizes the whole national planning process, provided the various sectoral planning committees (including the Committee on School, University and Sports Equipment which handles education) with a "draft outline" showing the broad parameters of the economy's expected growth and the projected supply of investment funds that would be available during the new plan period for government allocation and for the private sector. This "draft outline," even though tentative, imposed a certain realism and discipline on the various sectoral planning committees right from the very beginning.

The educational planners then proceeded to make five-year projections of enrolments for each level and type of education. These enrolment projections were based largely on demographic data and estimates of "social demand," though in preparing the Fifth Plan these "social demand" projections were cross-checked with independent estimates of manpower requirements and, at least in over-all terms, coincided reasonably well.

The planners then determined what *additional* school and university facilities would be required to accommodate the expected

9. Claude Tibi, "France: The Use of Capital Costs in Educational Planning," in *Educational Cost Analysis in Action: Case Studies for Planners*, Vol. I, Paris, Unesco: IIEP, 1972. A more extensive study of French educational planning will be found in Raymond Poignant, *Education and Economic and Social Planning in France*, Paris, Unesco:IIEP (in preparation).

number of students over the five-year period in accordance with physical standards considered by the Ministry of Education to be more or less optimum (e.g. maximum of thirty-five elementary school pupils per classroom; a minimum of eighteen square meters of space per secondary student, etc.).

These physical space requirements were then translated into financial terms, using recent cost experience adjusted for price changes and adapted to variations by type, size, and location of educational facilities. In most cases, costs were ultimately expressed in terms of "cost per student place." Thus, for example, the summary of requirements for 1966–70 included for primary education "790,000 places at 3495 francs [10] each," and for first cycle secondary "923,000 places at 8926 francs each." In higher education programs where student capacity is more flexible, requirements were expressed in terms of cost per square meter rather than per student place. Equipment requirements were similarly determined and costed on the basis of established physical standards and recent cost experience.

This method of calculation, of course, implied a high degree of standardization of educational facilities and programs throughout the nation, which in fact tends to be the case in a highly centralized system such as the French one. Even so, considerable room remained within these "standards" and "norms" for architectural variation and for adaptation to local conditions.

By the method just described, the educational planning group emerged with a total investment requirement of 31.7 billion [11] francs for the five-year period and submitted this recommendation to the General Planning Commission. Then came the hard confrontation with reality. Even though education enjoyed a high priority, the Planning Commission's economic projections showed that there would simply not be this much money available for new educational facilities in the new plan period, considering all the

10. At the time of the case study, the rate of exchange was $1 = 5.55 French francs.

11. Throughout this volume the expression "billion" is used to express one thousand million.

other important economic and social needs to be met. Thus, through a process of negotiation and compromise, the government finally set a ceiling of 25.5 billion francs for "educational investment."

The problem then was how to distribute this cut of roughly one-sixth from the "ideal" requirements among the different levels and types of education. The most expedient method would have been to apply a uniform cut "across-the-board," but this would have implied the absence of any priorities *within* the educational plan. The French educational authorities and planners, however, did have some very definite priorities, which at the time favored primary and lower secondary education. Thus the cuts were distributed unevenly to reflect these priorities, as shown in Table 1.1.

TABLE 1.1.
Final distribution of educational investment funds in French Fifth Plan (1966–70) (in millions of francs).

ITEM	AMOUNT PLANNED BY THE COMMISSION	AMOUNT ALLOCATED AFTER GOVERNMENT ARBITRATION	PERCENTAGE OF REDUCTION
Pre-school	1454	1160	20.2
Primary	2761	2350	14.9
First cycle secondary	8239	7500	9.0
Second cycle, short	1898	1710	10.0
Second cycle, long	2192	1250	42.75
Handicapped children	1250	900	28.0
Higher education	6305	4820	23.1
Boarding and student facilities	2094	1310	37.4
Additional equipment	581	450	22.5
Overseas departments	600	550	8.3
Socio-educational and sports equipment	4340	3500	19.3

Source: Claude Tibi, "France: The Use of Capital Costs in Educational Planning," in *Educational Cost Analysis in Action: Case Studies for Planners*, Vol. I, Paris, Unesco:IIEP, 1972.

This action in turn produced variations in what French planners call the "degree of satisfaction"—a useful index which expresses the ratio between (a) the maximum number of students that could be admitted at any particular level if the optimum standards were fully respected and (b) the number that would actually be admitted according to the enrolment projections. A ratio below 100 per cent implied overcrowding and a compromise of optimum physical standards, at least for the time being. Table 1.2 shows the anticipated impact of the capital budget cuts on the "degree of satisfaction" at each education level at the end of the Fifth Plan (i.e. as of 1970), ranging from 100 per cent at the primary level to only 85 per cent in higher education.

TABLE 1.2.
Projected "degrees of satisfaction" of requirements at the end of the French Fifth Plan (1970).

EDUCATIONAL LEVEL	ADMITTANCE CAPACITY AT THE END OF THE FIFTH PLAN (THOUSANDS)	ENROLMENT FORECAST FOR 1972 (THOUSANDS)	THEORETICAL DEGREE OF SATISFACTION
Pre-school	2116	2116	100.0%
Primary	4949	4949	100.0%
First cycle secondary	2552	2635	97.0%
Second cycle, short	452	463	97.7%
Second cycle, long	688	743	92.6%
Higher education	675(1)	793	85.2%

(1) Allowing for the average number of students absent from the class or lecture hall.

Source: Claude Tibi, "France: The Use of Capital Costs in Educational Planning," in *Educational Cost Analysis in Action: Case Studies for Planners*, Vol. I, Paris, Unesco:IIEP, 1972.

The alternative, of course, would have been to reduce the inflow of students to match the available educational capacity, but French policy-makers as a matter of principle did not wish to restrict enrolments at any level even if this meant temporary overcrowding.[12]

Budget cutting is always a painful process in any country, but there is much to be said for getting the worst of the pain over with *before* the plan goes into effect, while there is still time to apply

12. This "open-door" policy did indeed lead to serious overcrowding, particularly in French universities (the extreme case being the University of Paris), and this was unquestionably one important cause of the student riots which led to the "Events of May" in 1968.

carefully considered priorities, rather than suffering the greater pain that inevitably ensues when a country starts off with unattainable targets and abandons all control over priorities. Whatever may be said about certain shortcomings of French educational planning—and French planners themselves have been its severest critics—it must be given credit for its hardheaded adherence to over-all resource limitations—an important example for others to heed.

Thailand—Cost Analysis After the Fact

The contrast could hardly be greater between industrialized countries such as France and the Soviet Union which are blessed with a relatively rich data base for analyzing the cost implications of their educational targets, and developing nations such as Thailand which are not so blessed, yet are obliged to proceed with caution regarding their future educational costs. The experiences of Thailand recorded in two IIEP case studies are likely to seem both familiar and encouraging to educational authorities in other developing nations.

Several different national agencies had a hand in putting together the educational sector of Thailand's National Economic and Social Development Plan for 1967–71, but none of them had sufficient information to determine prospective costs of the plan. It was only after the targets had been set that a Unesco expert became available to help examine the cost implications. Even then, because of the scarcity of basic data, only a rough-and-ready approach could be used, but this was sufficient to expose several quite important hidden problems.

The first step was to get a clearer idea of what educational unit costs per student were like in Thailand—their general composition, how they varied from one educational level or geographic area to another, what changes had been taking place in them, and why, and how they might be expected to behave in the future. This analysis required considerable ingenuity and detective work, using budget records, sample school surveys, and no small amount of statistical calisthenics.[13]

The next step was to apply these findings about unit costs to testing the feasibility of the educational targets and financial provisions of the 1967–71 Plan, making various necessary assumptions and appropriate adjustments to allow for changing conditions.[14]

The following significant conclusions emerged (which must be viewed with caution because of the imperfect nature of the data and methods that had to be employed):

1. The planned allocation of capital funds for new educational facilities appeared to be, if anything, more than adequate, particularly in light of a recent space utilization study which showed only a 75 per cent utilization rate for many existing educational facilities.

2. Public funds allocated in the plan for meeting recurrent costs of pre-primary, primary, and secondary schools appeared adequate to enable *public* schools to fulfill their targets; but *private* schools, which carried an important share of the load, would require a substantial increase either of fees or public subsidies or both in order to meet their recurrent cost requirements.

3. The Plan had set targets in terms both of *enrolments* and of *number of graduates* for vocational and technical training, teacher training, and the universities. But due to heavy student wastage (i.e. dropouts) and grade-repeating in these institutions, the two sets of targets appeared mutually inconsistent. Although the resource allocations envisaged by the Plan to cover recurrent costs were adequate (or even more than adequate) to meet the *enrolment* targets, they seemed decidedly inadequate to meet the targets in terms of *graduates*. In the extreme case of vocational

13. This initial part of the exercise is described in H. W. Reiff, "Thailand: Educational Cost Analysis," in *Educational Cost Analysis in Action: Case Studies for Planners*, Vol. I, Paris, Unesco:IIEP, 1972.

14. This stage is described in H. W. Reiff, "Thailand: The Use of Cost Analysis in Estimating the Total Cost of an Educational Plan and Testing Its Feasibility," in *Educational Cost Analysis in Action: Case Studies for Planners*, Vol. I, Paris, Unesco:IIEP, 1972.

and technical education, the projected resource allocation for recurrent costs was apparently 88 per cent higher than necessary to meet the *enrolment* targets of the Plan, but some 14 per cent too little to meet the target number of graduates.

This costing exercise, even though tardy, proved valuable to educational authorities in Thailand, among other things in formulating proposals for external assistance. But clearly it could have been much more useful had it played an integral role in the initial process of setting the targets rather than simply testing their feasibility later on. It could have sharpened the issue of priorities *within* the educational system and revealed more clearly the available options and potential trade-offs.

To take an example, the Thai Plan proposed a 30 per cent increase in university enrolments over the five-year period, which, according to the later cost analysis, would require about 40 per cent of the total capital budget for education, not to mention substantially higher recurrent expenditures. The cost analysis also showed that the recurrent cost for one university student was equivalent to the cost of ten secondary students. Had this been clear earlier, it might have raised the interesting question of whether the benefits to the Thai economy of each additional university graduate were likely to be as great as the benefits that would derive from ten additional secondary graduates instead at the same cost.[15] It might also have posed the question whether the cost per university student might not somehow be substantially reduced in order to improve the cost-benefit ratio of universities.

One could not have hoped, of course, given the scarcity of data, to get precise mathematical answers to such questions. Yet such questions are well worth asking in the process of developing an educational plan, and worth weighing in the balance with other considerations when priorities and allocations are being established.

Fortunately, when the Thai Plan was first adopted, the Cabinet wisely authorized the National Economic Development Board to

15. The plan called for a 30.7 per cent over-all increase in Bachelor's degrees, including a 157.2 per cent increase in Humanities candidates and about 124 per cent each in Education and Agriculture.

make such annual revisions and changes as might seem warranted. Substantial revisions were in fact made in 1968, based on more accurate estimates of national income and allowing for a temporary slowdown in the projected economic growth rate (of 8 per cent) caused by the 1967 drought. The moral suggested is that cost analysis is better late than never, but more valuable the earlier it is undertaken—even when the supply of basic data is poor.

Unesco's Asian Model—an Improved Cost Test

A feature of Unesco's drive in the early 1960's to accelerate educational expansion in the developing world was the setting of "regional targets" for Asia, Africa, and Latin America by conferences of ministers from Unesco's member states. The first of these was embodied in the Karachi Plan which called for the achievement by 1980 of universal, free, and compulsory education (of no less than seven years) in the fifteen participating Asian nations. This, it was estimated, would mean an expansion of primary school enrolments in the combined fifteen countries from 62 million pupils in 1960 (8 per cent of the total population) to 238 million by 1980 (20 per cent of the population).

Was this a feasible target? No one could be certain, for the basic data for making such an assessment were very scarce. The rough "costing" which was done suggested that fulfillment of the Karachi targets would require an increase in primary school expenditures per inhabitant in the fifteen nations from $1.70 in 1960–65 to $4.30 in 1975–80. The conclusion was drawn that if the Asian economies grew steadily in the next twenty years and the flow of external assistance expanded substantially, the Karachi targets could be readily achieved. But economists who later examined the matter more closely expressed grave doubts.

Two years later, in April 1962, a follow-up conference in Tokyo reviewed progress under the Karachi Plan, broadened the targets to other educational levels, and requested Unesco, in cooperation with the Economic Commission for the Far East, to aid member states in "establishing long-term perspective plans and in putting together these national plans into a draft Asian model which we will examine when we meet again in December 1965."

Great effort and ingenuity went into constructing this draft Asian Model.[16] Unesco teams visited Asian member states to collect all the pertinent educational and economic data they could find, and a quantitative analytical model was designed and programmed for a computer in Bangkok. The model included twelve interdependent formulas which identified a variety of major factors that influence the performance of an educational system and defined systematically the inter-relationships between these factors. By translating them into unit costs per student (separating capital from recurrent costs), the model made it possible to calculate very rapidly (on the computer) the cost consequences at each level of education of a range of alternative assumptions regarding levels of enrolment targets, pupil-teacher ratios, teacher qualifications and salaries, the provision of textbooks per student, and so forth. In effect, the model could simulate the dynamic future consequences, including the cost consequences, of changes in any of the major "exogenous" or "endogeneous" variables that influence the system's behavior, so long as such changes could be expressed quantitatively. (The system's *qualitative* performance, although not subject to computer analysis, was presumed to be affected by variations in quantitative input factors.)

The model was so designed that it could be applied later to planning in individual countries, but for the moment it was applied only to aggregate figures for three clusters of Asian nations (eighteen of them participating by now), grouped according to economic level and to how quickly they were likely to be able to achieve universal primary education.

The aim of the model was not to establish a new set of targets

16. Following the Bangkok Conference in December 1965 the draft model was revised and published as *An Asian Model of Educational Development: Perspectives for 1965–80* (Paris, Unesco, 1966). A description of the model by two of its main architects is in J. Auerhan and E. S. Solomon, "Asia: Cost Analysis in an Asian Model of Educational Development," in *Educational Cost Analysis in Action: Case Studies for Planners,* Vol. I, Paris, Unesco:IIEP, 1972.

but to test the feasibility of the old ones (which were somewhat revised in light of the findings) and to demonstrate the consequences of various changes in basic assumptions and policies.

In effect, it acted as a teaching machine, demonstrating to top policy-makers at the Bangkok Conference the economic ramifications of their own choice of assumptions and policy decisions. It also showed how, in reverse, changes in rates of economic growth would affect the amount of resources available to education. Thus the model tended to discourage the sort of wishful thinking and pious hopes that so often lead international conferences to adopt glittering resolutions favoring more and better education which soon prove to be utterly unrealistic. In other words, the model contributed to a more informed, disciplined, and responsible kind of choice- and decision-making.

It had no special magic, however. It could provoke thought, but it could not be a substitute for thought. It could clarify problems, but it could not eliminate them. What came out of the model could be only as sound and sensible as the assumptions and data fed into it. Moreover, the model had severe inherent limitations, for like any model it was a highly simplified approximation of reality and could not take account of all the unforeseeable forces that influence the course of educational history in any country. One of its greatest limitations was that it tacitly assumed that the economic systems of Asia would be able to absorb and productively use the greatly increased supply of educated manpower foreseen by the Karachi targets. But this was a dubious premise, for even as the Bangkok Conference was meeting in 1965, the problem of "educated unemployed" was fast becoming a dominant issue of educational and economic policy throughout the developing world. The lesson here, not sufficiently highlighted by the Asian Model, was that educational systems cannot be realistically and effectively planned without taking careful account of the needs and constraints of their economic and social context.

It was estimated, using the model, that attainment of the revised Karachi targets, given the various assumptions adopted by the ministers at Bangkok, would require an increase in aggregate educational expenditures by Unesco's Asian member states from roughly $3.0 billion in 1964 to about $9.4 billion by 1980 (in constant prices). At an assumed economic growth rate of 5 per cent (the middle-level assumption), this would mean a rise in educational expenditures from 3.51 per cent of the Gross National Product in 1964 to 5.10 per cent in 1980, and a change in education's share of total public expenditures from 14.66 per cent in 1964 to somewhere in the range of 14.18 to 16.68 per cent by 1980 (depending on what assumption was made about the "income elasticity" of public revenues).

The foregoing estimates were not put forth as firm predictions of things to come; they were intended as nothing more or less than a rough quantitative indication of the consequences flowing from a given set of expansion targets and corresponding educational and economic assumptions. As such, however, they provided a considerably clearer guide to policy than the original Karachi Conference. And with further testing and refinement, a similar model would someday be usefully applied to individual nations.[17]

Chile—a New Way To Test for a Good Investment

Feasibility testing is important not only for broad educational targets and plans but also for specific projects. The "INACAP" project in Chile provides a good example.[18]

In the late 1950's and 1960's Chile found herself needing an expanded supply of well-trained workmen at different skill levels in various fields to undergird economic development. To help meet this need, the training program of the National Training Institute (Instituto Nacional de Capacitation, known as INACAP)

17. A modified version of the Asian Model was in fact applied to the Spanish educational system with the help of Unesco experts in 1970. This "Madrid Model" became a useful tool for testing the targets of the sweeping Spanish Educational Reform launched in 1969.

18. Lucila Arrigazzi, "Chile: Evaluating the Expansion of a Vocational Training Programme," in *Educational Cost Analysis in Action: Case Studies for Planners*, Vol. I, Paris, Unesco:IIEP, 1972.

had been created in 1960 outside the formal educational system to provide workers in a wide range of fields, including mining, industry, agriculture, and fishing, "with the means and conditions for technical preparation and occupational promotion within the framework of the national plans for economic and social development." The clientele of this new "out-of-school" training program of relatively short duration ranged from young school-leavers with no technical training or experience to relatively skilled workers with substantial work experience.

INACAP grew rapidly and by 1965 was turning out 16,000 "graduates" per year. But judging from available manpower data and estimated future demand, this would not be enough to meet the needs of economic development. Thus Chile decided to approach the World Bank for a capital loan to help expand INACAP's output to 30,000 trainees per year (which would still be substantially below the estimated future need).

The World Bank sent a mission of experts to Chile to appraise the project and to form an over-all judgment of whether it would be a sound investment. The mission made the customary checks on whether the project was well designed, whether the contemplated facilities and equipment made good sense, whether the estimated costs were reasonable, whether the added flow of trained manpower was likely to be absorbed, and whether the nation could handle its own share of the costs and pay off the loan on schedule.

But in this instance the Bank mission went beyond the customary practice and for the first time attempted a "cost-benefit" test of the project in the form of a "rate-of-return" projection. This involved three basic steps: first, estimating all the different immediate and future costs involved in the expansion project (both capital and recurrent, including "income foregone" by workers taking time out to study); second, estimating the cumulative future "direct economic benefits" that would flow from the additional training; and third, comparing the benefits to the costs and calculating a "rate of return" on the total investment.

In a later chapter of this book we will examine the practical problems entailed in such a rate-of-return study, and the reasons why the conclusions of such studies should be interpreted and applied with caution. The point for now is that studies of this sort, even allowing for their limitations, can provide a useful cross-check on conclusions reached by other analytical routes.

This is, in fact, how the rate-of-return study was prudently used in the INACAP case. The estimated rate of return proved to be so high that, even with considerable discount to allow for possible error, the investment still seemed well warranted.

2 *Costing Educational Reforms, Innovations, and Alternatives*

If educational planners only had to worry about expanding the present educational establishment in its old image, their life would be much simpler. But in fact, they must also worry about *changing* the old order so as to improve the efficiency and productivity of education, and they must constantly be on the lookout for alternative ways of doing things that might constitute an improvement over the *status quo*. Planning for change is a good deal more complicated than planning for simple expansion, but it is also a good deal more rewarding—as some of the cases summarized below demonstrate.

Ivory Coast—Introducing New Media on a Wide Scale

There is a widespread interest throughout the world in harnessing the great teaching potential of new educational media, particularly radio and television, to spread and improve education and to help solve educational problems that defy conventional solutions. Apart from the intricate pedagogical questions that arise in considering such innovations, however, the down-to-earth issue of costs and financial feasibility finally comes to the fore and is often the decisive factor.[1] A number of educational sys-

1. For a broad discussion of this matter, based on numerous case studies, see W. Schramm, P. H. Coombs, F. Kahnert, and J. Lyle, *The New Media: Memo to Educational Planners*, Paris, Unesco:IIEP, 1967.

tems have been seriously burned by failing to face these cost considerations early and squarely.

The Ministry of Education of the Ivory Coast, having learned from the experience of others, took a different approach that was both cautious and bold; it decided to undertake one of the world's most extensive educational television projects to date, but only after a systematic examination of the likely cost consequences.[2]

Like other newly independent African nations, Ivory Coast had accepted the recommendations of the Unesco Addis Ababa Conference (1961) and set its sights on achieving universal primary education by 1980. Although the statistics registered progress toward this goal by the mid-'sixties, three serious problems begged for attention. First, a high proportion of youngsters who started primary school dropped out along the way, and of those who finished many had repeated one or more grades. This constituted a serious waste of scarce resources. Second, one of the main effects of rural primary schooling, the Ministry felt, was to encourage able young people who were potential leaders of rural development to migrate to the cities, often to join the ranks of other unemployed school-leavers. Third, because of the highly academic orientation of the traditional French-type primary education, most youngsters who completed it were anxious to go on to the equally academic secondary school. The resulting burgeoning pressure on secondary schools was over-straining the nation's sparse resources and threatened to flood the market with secondary graduates far in excess of the foreseeable manpower needs of the economy.

Ivory Coast decided to attack this lethal combination of problems along three main lines: (1) by planning a radical revamping of the curriculum to fit the realistic needs of an economy that

2. The methodology and results of the preliminary cost analysis are contained in a document published by the Ivory Coast Ministry of Education entitled *Programme d'action pour le développement de l'enseignement du 1er degré en Côte-d'Ivoire*, Abijan, 1968. This document is critically analyzed in Ta Ngoc Châu, "Ivory Coast: The Cost of Introducing a Reform in Primary Education," in *Educational Cost Analysis in Action: Case Studies for Planners*, Vol. II, Paris, Unesco:IIEP, 1972.

was destined to remain predominantly agricultural for a long time; this, it was hoped, would make primary education more relevant and useful to rural young people, and help to dampen both the rural-urban migration and the demand for secondary education; (2) by creating a new type of non-formal post-primary education with a work-oriented bias to serve the many primary school finishers who could not go on to secondary school; this, it was hoped, would relieve the pressure and boost the productivity of their primary education; (3) by making extensive use of educational television to accelerate the introduction of the new primary curriculum, to lend support and provide improvement and on-the-job training to the many poorly qualified teachers, and to help serve the new non-formal secondary program.

To test the feasibility of the proposed new primary program, including the cost implications of using television massively, a special cost analysis and financial feasibility exercise was conducted with the help of Unesco experts. It included the costing of various alternatives, particularly with respect to the qualifications level of teachers to be used, the size of classes, and the amount of teaching materials to be used in conjunction with television. At the same time a hard look was taken at the smaller-scale television experience of other countries—particularly Niger, El Salvador, and Samoa—in search of useful clues.

The initial costing exercise revealed the following:

• Under the present (unsatisfactory) conditions—with an overall pupil-teacher ratio of 47.1, with about half the teachers poorly qualified, and with only meager supplies of teaching materials available—costs per enrolled pupil averaged 13,500 CFA francs.[3]

• The next best and cheapest alternative (but probably the least desirable pedagogically), involving the extensive use of "assistant monitors" (the lowest grade of teachers) in conjunction with television, and keeping the pupil-teacher ratio at 47 to 1, would cost an estimated 11,400 CFA francs per student (not including television costs).

3. At the time of the case study, the rate of exchange was $1 = 278 CFA francs.

• A pedagogically more attractive but also more expensive alternative was to use only assistant teachers (better trained than monitors) and to reduce the pupil-teacher ratio from 47:1 to 44:1. This, it was estimated, would involve costs of 17,154 CFA francs.

Separate calculations of television costs were made which could be added to the above estimates. They included production, transmission, and reception costs (but excluded capital costs, which were expected to be defrayed by external funds) and showed a marked variation by audience size, reflecting the "economies of scale." These estimates ranged from 7800 CFA francs per student for an audience of only 5000, down to 930 francs for an audience of one million.

After weighing these alternatives, the Ivory Coast government decided to opt for the highest-cost one. Its reason presumably was to ensure the attainment of acceptable quality results and to give the daring television venture maximum chance of success. This decision was not made blindly, however; it was made only after the projected costs had been compared to the official projections of financial resources likely to be available to primary education for a number of years in the future. This initial feasibility test showed positive results.

"Second-guessing" this initial costing exercise some months later, the IIEP case study team concluded that the project's feasibility would depend heavily on whether the Ivory Coast economy maintained a high growth rate and on whether teacher salaries remained stable or rose with the economy. If teacher salaries and other recurrent costs could be held constant at the 1967 level (a rather dubious possibility) and if domestic and foreign resources were forthcoming in the amounts projected by the educational plan, then the program seemed to the IIEP analysts just barely feasible. But if input costs were to rise substantially or if the growth of the economy were to falter for a substantial period, then the program might find itself in financial trouble. Even these eventualities would not need to be fatal, however. If the program were otherwise functioning satisfactorily and producing good results, the worst that could happen would be an enforced stretching out of the 1980 goal of universal primary education by a few extra years.

Ivory Coast has since gone ahead with this bold project, thereby making itself an exciting educational laboratory which all the world will watch with keen interest. And even without waiting for the results, it has already set a good example for others by seriously and systematically costing alternative courses of action before making the most important educational decision of its young career.

Madagascar—
Giving Every Rural Youngster a Chance

In the early 1960's most developing nations, inspired by the Unesco regional targets, committed themselves to achieving universal primary education within twenty years or less. But many soon discovered that the practical problems involved, including the costs, were more formidable than they had bargained for.

The leaders of Madagascar were anxious to pursue the goals set forth in the Addis Ababa Plan in 1961. But they sensed from the outset that a strategy of straightforward enlargement of the existing primary system not only was beyond their economic reach but would not really fit their needs. And yet they attached high importance to spreading educational opportunity as rapidly as possible, particularly in rural areas where the bulk of youngsters lived and where educational deprivation was most severe. What was needed, however, was a low-cost education of a type more related to the lives of these youngsters than was the traditional French curriculum then in operation. These realistic considerations led to the Malagasy Education Reform of 1962 and soon to an educational Plan for the period 1964–68.

The reform had four main features: (1) *a reorientation of the primary school curriculum* to bring it into harmony with the needs of day-to-day life in rural Madagascar; (2) *adoption of a "first cycle" (four-year) primary school for rural areas* in place of the traditional six-year school prevalent in urban areas; (3) *creation of a new category of first cycle teachers* requiring only nine years of schooling plus one year of special pedagogical training at a new type of center; and (4) *a new pattern of financing* under which provincial governments (whose budgets were already seriously strained) would continue to bear the main costs of the conventional six-year schools in urban areas, while rural communities (with heavy central government aid) would bear the costs of the new four-year "first cycle schools."

By reducing primary schooling from six to four years and staffing these rural schools with lower-cost teachers, Madagascar would have a realistic chance of achieving universal primary education within twenty years—or at least so it seemed at the time, for this crucial choice had to be made without benefit of systematic cost analysis. The 1964–68 educational Plan was founded on this premise.

By the last year of the Plan impressive progress had been made, but sizable implementation difficulties had thrown the expansion off schedule. At this point the now-strengthened Educational Planning Unit of the Ministry of Education undertook three analytical studies to determine the basic causes of the delay and, more importantly, to clarify the feasible options and best course of action for the Second Plan period, due to begin in 1968–69.[4]

Because of the shortage of basic data, these three analytical studies used very crude methodologies and assumptions throughout; there was no other choice. Nevertheless, they revealed several important facts which led to a stretching out over a longer time span of the original targets and to putting the Second Plan on a more realistic track. A serious lag in teacher supply was identified as the most crucial bottleneck slowing progress. This meant that the creation of new training centers would have to be expedited

4. These studies and their findings are discussed in the case study by Ta Ngoc Châu, "Madagascar: The Role of Cost Analysis in the Introduction and Implementation of the 1962 Reform of Primary Education," in *Educational Cost Analysis in Action: Case Studies for Planners*, Vol. II, Paris, Unesco:IIEP, 1972.

in the next Plan period. A further cause of delay, however, was that the Reform had left the initiative for starting new schools in the hands of local rural communities and many of them—particularly the poorer ones—had not taken the initiative. This suggested that the central government might have to share more of the initiative itself.

The studies also revealed that the potential savings inherent in the Reform, although still very substantial, would actually be smaller and slower to be realized than had seemed likely earlier in the absence of a detailed cost analysis. This was mainly because: (1) the training and retraining of teachers to handle the new curriculum would be more costly than anticipated, and (2) the substitution of lower-salaried "first cycle" teachers in the first four grades of the existing six-grade schools would have to await the retirement of more highly qualified and higher-salaried teachers presently teaching in these grades.

Finally, the studies showed that the intended relief to provincial government budgets under the 1962 Reform was proving to be less than expected. The continued rapid expansion of primary enrolments in urban and semi-urban areas had in fact raised still higher the percentage of provincial budgets required for education.

With these findings in hand, the policy-makers of Madagascar were in a better position than earlier to shape a realistic course toward eventually giving every rural youngster a fair educational chance.

Norway—Examining Policy Alternatives in Extending Compulsory Education

Norway's problem in the 1960's was not how to achieve universal primary education, but how to extend its duration, from seven years to nine years—which the Norwegian Parliament had voted for in principle in 1959.

Implementing this decision, however, was a more complicated affair than an outsider might think, due to the unique structure of Norwegian education, particularly in rural areas where the impact of the decision would be greatest. (A number of urban communities had already introduced nine-year compulsory education.) It meant among other things a reformulation of the lower secondary school curriculum in order to make it relevant and useful for *all* students, including those who would not go further up the academic ladder. Moreover, it meant creating a new type of nine-year school for rural communities which would combine elementary and lower secondary education. One question was whether these new type schools should be relatively small and widely dispersed (as the traditional primary schools had been) in order to be close to the students, or more centralized to attain economies of scale and probably better pedagogical results. The choice would greatly affect class size, teacher requirements, and cost per student.

The matter was further complicated by strong political pressures coming from the Norwegian Teachers' Association and other educational groups to reduce maximum class size from thirty to twenty-five, to reduce the normal teaching week for teachers, and to limit the number of overtime teaching hours (at extra pay).

Obviously the total cost of extending compulsory education—and the speed with which it could be accomplished—would depend on what decisions were made with respect to such major policy variables. In the final analysis, it would be up to the Parliament to make these decisions, but it was the responsibility of the Ministry of Education to give the Parliament the clearest picture it could of the options available and of their respective cost and pedagogical implications.

With this in mind, the Ministry developed a series of "cost models" designed to reveal the interdependence of various crucial factors of choice and to compare the respective consequences of these choices for the total financial and teaching requirements involved in extending compulsory schooling.[5] Figure 2.1 shows the

5. The models and findings are discussed in Olav Magnussen, "Norway: The Use of Educational Cost Models in Planning the Extension of Compulsory Education," in *Educational Cost Analysis in Action: Case Studies for Planners*, Vol. II, Paris, Unesco:IIEP, 1972.

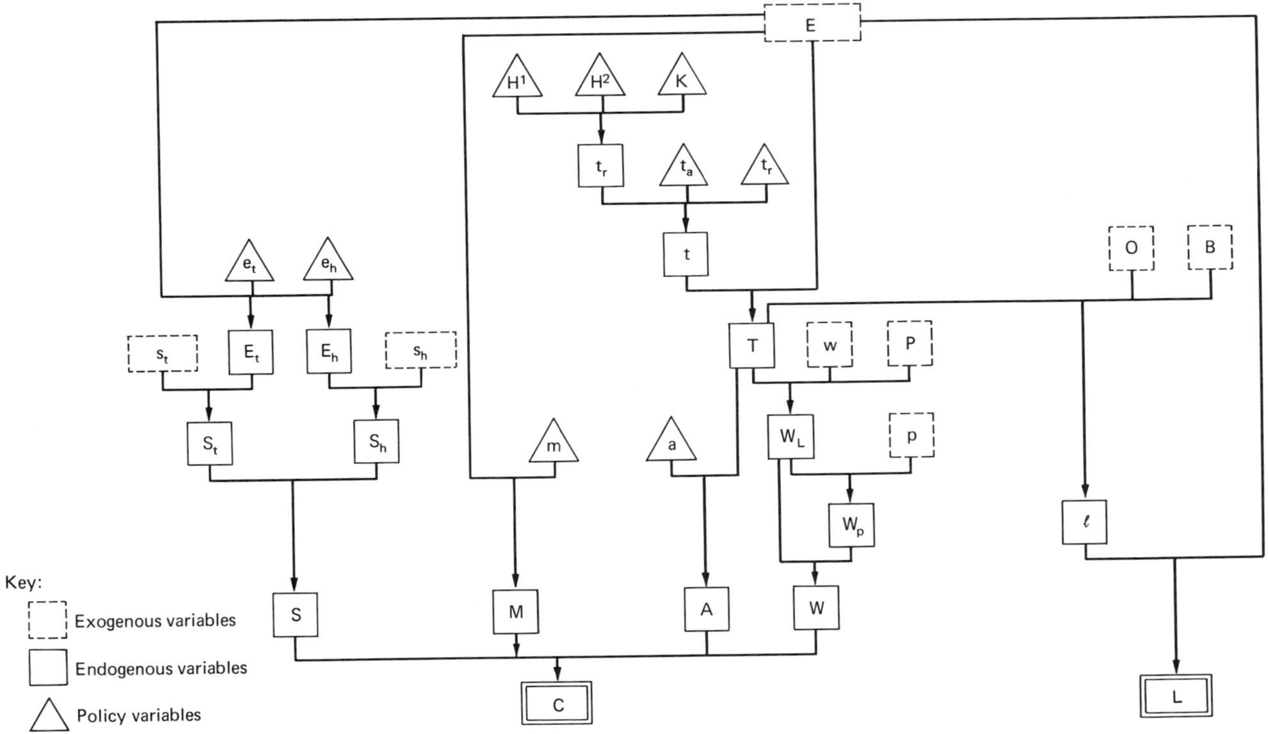

FIGURE 2.1.
The functioning of the model.

functioning of the model. After certain values of the policy variables and the exogenous variables have been selected, to correspond with alternative policy decisions, the equations are solved to give the four components of current expenditure (W, S, M, and A) and thus total current cost (C) and total teacher requirements (L). The model provides separate subtotals for each of the six sizes or types of primary school (grades 1 to 6), and lower secondary schools (grades 7 to 9).

These computational models could handle a wide range of assumptions in various combinations, but for policy-making purposes it seemed best to reduce the parliamentary presentation to three illustrative sets of assumptions, considered by the Ministry to be within the range of practical feasibility. These three alternatives were labeled the "most expensive," "cheapest," and "realistic" (middle-range) options.

The calculations showed: (1) that the number of teachers required in 1975–76 ranged from 24,930 for the "cheapest" alternative to 37,980 for the "most expensive," with an in-between figure of 29,160 teachers for the "realistic" alternative, and (2) the corresponding total current cost estimates for 1975–76 (capital cost estimates were not included) were: for the "most expensive"—1710 million Norwegian kroners;[6] for the "cheapest"—1190 million kroners; and for the "realistic alternative"—1340 million kroners.

The models also demonstrated that, of all the policy variables, total costs were most sensitive to changes in assumptions regarding class size. This particular finding later played a significant role in the parliamentary policy debates and final decision.

The basic principle of showing policy-makers their main options and the corresponding cost and financial implications is fundamental to rational educational management and planning in all countries. Even though most developing nations would not have sufficient statistical data to apply as elaborate cost models as were used in Norway, there is no reason why simpler models

6. At the time of the case study, the rate of exchange was $1 = 7.14 Norwegian kroner.

could not be improvised to serve this purpose, fitting whatever limited data were available.

Barbados—Whether To Extend a Team-Teaching Experiment

Perhaps because of necessity and because they are less encumbered by deeply imbedded educational traditions, developing countries often display greater educational daring than most developed nations. In that spirit, Barbados undertook in 1965 a five-year experiment in team teaching, helped financially by the Ford Foundation and professionally by the Harvard Graduate School of Education.

Well before the five years were up, the educational authorities of Barbados wisely began facing up to the crucial question of whether the experiment should be extended to all elementary schools or terminated. Though the initial results seemed encouraging on the surface, the decision, to be made rationally, would have to be based on the combined results of a pedagogical evaluation and an examination of cost prospects which were an integral part of the experimental design.[7]

The Barbados Team-Teaching Project (BTTP) covered five schools: three of the five-to-fourteen age group, and two of the five-to-eleven age group. Each school had on an average 650 children and four teams of four teachers each, giving each team responsibility for about 160 children. The experiment's budget had been set at U.S. $297,500 for the five years, covering overhead expenses, personnel, special training, and related developmental costs. Since teachers are normally trained to teach in isolation and to be, as it were, jacks of all trades, special stress was laid on retraining the Barbados teachers to work effectively as members of a teaching team.

7. The cost analysis is described in Richard M. Durstine and Barclay M. Hudson, "Barbados: Marginal Costs for Marginal Decisions—the Case of Team Teaching," in *Educational Cost Analysis in Action: Case Studies for Planners*, Vol. II, Paris Unesco:IIEP, 1972.

Team teaching, for those not familiar with it, is based on the notion that teaching requires a range of skills, that each teacher has his own particular strengths and limitations, that pupils learn most when each teacher concentrates on what he or she does best, and that less experienced teachers can learn from able, more experienced ones. Working in teams with a division of labor, teachers can bring their combined strengths to bear on a group of students, which can be redeployed in various-sized subgroups during the school day for different learning purposes. The more clerical and housekeeping chores can be taken over by paraprofessional personnel, thereby freeing the professionals to concentrate on teaching.

The cost analysts from Harvard studied actual expenditures to date and then proceeded to make a projection of how costs would probably behave if the team-teaching program were continued and expanded after the five experimental years were over. They chose a "marginal cost" approach which focused not on the over-all average cost per student but on the added cost resulting from team teaching.

An analytical model was developed for the purpose, flexible enough to handle a range of alternative assumptions about the future and to be applicable with minor modifications and at low cost to other situations apart from the BTTP project.

The model first described the main cost elements of the BTTP project, distinguishing between (1) the normal or regular costs of running the schools in the projects; (2) the additional permanent costs due to team teaching; and (3) the strictly developmental (non-repetitive) costs of mounting the pilot project, including the ancillary costs of evaluation and related research.

Applying these factors to the future, the model gave the following conclusions (among others):

• If five additional schools were teamed each year, about 60 per cent of all primary pupils would be under team teaching by 1978 and all of them by about 1990 (the total number rising from approximately 3300 in 1968 to 30,000 students in 1978).

• By 1978, the extra costs per pupil resulting from team teaching would have fallen sharply from E.C. \$27 [8] under the pilot project to \$7, due mainly to the spreading of overhead costs(such as field supervision) over more schools and to the elimination of "starting up" costs (such as overseas training and technical assistance).

• There would be a steady decrease in the proportion of costs allocated to field supervision and training in the United States, from about 55 per cent to about 17 per cent, and a simultaneous increase in the proportion going into materials and teacher aides (from 18 per cent in 1965–67 to 70 per cent by 1978).

• Total operating costs of team teaching—which were approximately E.C. \$90,000 in 1968 for five schools teamed—would rise to only \$220,000 in 1978 for ten times this number of schools (50).

The analysis also identified a variety of "trade-offs" at equivalent costs which would be available to decision-makers if the project were continued and expanded. The cost model showed, for example, that a one-week teacher workshop would be roughly equivalent in cost to (1) the reduction of the supervisory load from five to four schools per supervisor; or (2) additional equipment and supplies worth E.C. \$400 for each of ten schools; or (3) one additional trained teacher (year's salary) for the project as a whole. Similarly, one week's visit by an overseas consultant would be roughly equivalent in cost to (1) an additional teacher aide for the project as a whole; or (2) additional equipment and supplies worth E.C. \$175 for each of ten schools; or (3) an additional \$0.45 per pupil for materials.

These cost conclusions standing alone were not a sufficient basis, of course, for deciding whether to extend team teaching. But, combined with the findings of the pedagogical evaluation, they would provide the educational policy-makers of Barbados with an unusually good cost-effectiveness basis for making their decision. And if the decision were positive, they would have a variety of detailed operational options to choose from within fixed budgetary limits.

8. At the time of the case study, the rate of exchange was \$1 = 2 East Caribbean dollars (E.C.\$).

Poland—Reforming the Teacher Training System

Most nations have lately been obliged to modify their teacher training systems to meet the need for more and better qualified teachers. Few, however, seem to have gone about it as systematically as Poland did, by examining the comparative costs and advantages of each of the various possibilities.[9]

Up to 1955, new primary school teachers in Poland were prepared in teacher training schools at the secondary level which took in primary school leavers (eight years) and gave them five additional years of instruction (total of thirteen years). In 1954 a new type of teacher training institution was introduced (the *studiow nauczycielskitch*, or SN) to improve teacher qualifications and expand the supply. The SN admitted graduates of general secondary schools and gave them two additional years of preparation (for a total of fourteen years).

Subsequently, earlier graduates of the old teacher training schools were obliged to upgrade themselves to the new SN level by in-service and special training courses, and in 1965 it was decided to phase out the teacher training schools altogether. But since school enrolments were continuing to expand rapidly, some substitute means had to be devised to meet expanding teacher requirements after 1970, when the last graduates would emerge from the old training schools. Different people had quite different ideas, and so groups of pedagogical and economic experts were asked to examine the pros and cons of various alternatives in order to give top policy-makers a clear picture of the options.

Four main alternatives were appraised on the basis of social, economic, pedagogical, and other practical criteria. The economic appraisal began with an analysis of the costs of existing teacher training programs, then projected costs for defined levels of teacher

9. This summary is based on K. Podoski, "Poland: The Role of Cost Analysis in Planning a Teacher-Training Programme," in *Educational Cost Analysis in Action: Case Studies for Planners*, Vol. II, Paris, Unesco:IIEP, 1972.

output through 1975 for each of the alternative approaches. The resulting estimates, as those who made them pointed out, had two serious shortcomings: they assumed no change in future price and wage relationships (an unlikely prospect) and they were confined to recurrent costs (though admittedly capital costs could vary substantially between the alternative approaches). These shortcomings, however, were not so serious as to nullify the value of the estimates for decision-making purposes.

The costing exercise revealed wide cost differences among the four alternative systems of teacher training for the period 1970–75. The Polish educational authorities, however, also took into account various pedagogical and feasibility criteria; as a result, they finally chose the second highest cost alternative as the most practical solution. This did not mean that they ignored the cost considerations; it simply meant that, taking all aspects into account, the two lower-cost alternatives did not seem as practical to implement nor as pedagogically effective; thus they chose to pay the higher price for better and more certain results. The important point is that they made this decision with their eyes wide open, and the fact that they opted for the costlier alternative obliged them to make a strong case for it on non-economic grounds.

Brazil—Diversifying Secondary Education

Another common need faced by most educational systems in recent years has been to remodel their traditional academic, university-oriented secondary schools so as to provide a more relevant and useful education for students who terminate their formal schooling at this stage.

The State of Rio Grande do Sul in Brazil confronted this problem in 1967 when it was invited by the federal government to submit a proposed reform plan that would be combined with approved plans from three other states and submitted to the United States Agency for International Development for partial support (additional support coming also from the federal government of Brazil).

Several qualifying conditions were specified by the federal government. First, the reform plan would have to embody a new "first cycle" secondary school curriculum that included practical arts, and a new "comprehensive" type of "second cycle" school that would give students a broad view and choice of vocational and academic fields. This requirement gave no difficulty to the State of Rio Grande do Sul since its own State Council of Education had already decided to move in this very direction.

The second requirement was that all top state officials must be of one mind on the proposal; it would need the endorsement not only of the State Secretary of Education and the State Council of Education but also the Governor. This, too, presented no problem.

The third qualifying requirement, however, was more difficult. It was that the state must commit itself (1) to spend no less than 40 per cent of its own total educational budget on the proposed secondary reform; (2) to devote no less than 20 per cent of its total public budget to education; and (3) to increase its education budget by at least 2 per cent every year. Before the state could undertake such a serious financial commitment, it needed not only to ascertain the cost implications of the secondary reform proposal itself but to assess these implications in the broader context of over-all educational development and financial prospects—otherwise it might end up "robbing Peter to pay Paul."

The difficulty was that the state's education problems were by no means confined to secondary schools. At the time, for example, nearly half its elementary teachers were underqualified and only 15 per cent of the children who entered primary school completed the full cycle. Unless primary education was also strengthened, it might do little good to strengthen secondary education. The problem of improving and expanding teacher supply was a formidable one at both levels, and there was a perennial scarcity of financial resources for all state functions.

There was little time for making this complex cost and financial assessment for the proposal had to be submitted within six months. But before the costing could be done, an over-all educational plan (already in the process of preparation) would have to be completed and a detailed design worked out for the new secondary school scheme. It is hardly surprising, therefore, that methods and data employed in the costing exercise were rather crude and not altogether satisfactory.[10]

To start with, enrolments had to be projected and targets set. This was done with the aid of two models: (1) a so-called "cultural model," based on estimated social demand and alternative assumptions about promotion rates at various grade levels, and (2) an "economic model" which brought manpower requirements into the calculation of enrolment targets.

The next step was to establish some over-all limits on the assumed amounts of real and financial resources that would be available for each education level during the plan period. The limits for secondary education took into account the qualifying conditions prescribed by the federal government and assumed the availability of substantial external assistance.

Detailed questions then had to be answered regarding secondary education. For example, what would it cost per year for each student enrolled in each type of school? What would be the total recurrent costs? What would be the capital requirements to build and equip new schools and to repair, maintain, and modify existing ones? Who would pay for what, and how much?

On the basis of the whole analysis, the state decided to confine its request for external aid to capital expenditures, and to limit the scale of the new secondary project to what could be done within the recurrent expenditure budget likely to be available from domestic resources. In actuality, the prospective availability of teachers, not simply money, became a major determinant, and this was a major factor in the federal government's later decision to trim the state's proposal somewhat. The cost analysis also became an essential element in the subsequent negotiations between the federal government and U.S. AID.

This costing exercise proved well worth the effort, but one sus-

10. R. C. Fachin, "Brazil: Costing an Expansion Programme for Secondary Education—the Case of Rio Grande do Sul," in *Educational Cost Analysis in Action: Case Studies for Planners*, Vol. II, Paris, Unesco:IIEP, 1972.

pects that its even more important long-range benefit might prove to be that it put the State of Rio Grande do Sul seriously into the business of educational planning and cost analysis, once and for all.

India and Colombia—Testing the Returns on Educational Investments

The broadest issue of choice faced by nations with respect to the costs of education can be compressed into two simple questions: what share of the nation's total resources should be allocated to education? how should this amount be sub-allocated amongst the different levels and types of education?

The logic of these questions is clear enough, but there is no tidy formula for getting precise quantitative answers. Ideally, according to economic theory, a nation's resources should be allocated—as between education and other uses, and within the educational enterprise itself—with a view to achieving the highest marginal social and economic benefits from additional expenditures. Thus, if an extra million dollars spent on education, all things considered, would benefit society more in the long run than the funds spent, say, on expanding industry, then the money should go to education. And if this "investment" would yield larger benefits if spent on more primary rather than more secondary education, then it should be allocated to primary education.

The basic logic of this cost-benefit way of thinking is impeccable; indeed, planners who do not think this way are not rational planners. But thinking by this logic and applying it arithmetically are two quite different matters. How does one actually measure the costs, and harder still, the likely cumulative benefit of all sorts, of each alternative mode of expenditure? Reliable data for doing the arithmetic are hard to come by, and even then a good deal of speculation about future developments must be done, especially when it comes to forecasting "benefits." There is the further complication of differentiating between the *private* rate of return and the *social* rate of return. These admitted difficulties, however, have not deterred a number of economists from attempting "cost-benefit" studies in several countries—or to be more precise, "rate-of-return" studies (which are only one particular kind of cost-benefit study). One of the IIEP case studies examines three rate-of-return studies which apply to India.[11]

These studies were essentially exploratory and not intended to play an immediate role in decision-making. And all shared the inevitable difficulties and shortcomings inherent in any such study at this early stage in the development of methodology. Nevertheless, they can serve useful purposes. For one thing, they draw attention more sharply to the basic determinants of educational costs and benefits, thereby inviting consideration of possible ways to influence these determinants favorably. In addition, they provide deeper insights into the linkages between educational and economic development and thrust up provocative hypotheses that can be profitably explored.

One of the three Indian studies seeks to explain the causes of unemployment among university and secondary school graduates by analyzing labor market mechanisms and estimating social and private rates of return to educational investments.[12] The authors estimated that even with the most narrow definitions of unemployment, there were at least half a million totally unemployed graduates in India in 1967. They tried to discover why such surpluses persisted despite the growth of the economy, and whether, in view of them, education was still "a paying proposition" either for individuals or society.

On the basis of their historical analysis of the *private* (as distinct from the social) rate of return, the authors concluded that

11. Maureen Woodhall, "India: The Use of Cost-Benefit Analysis as a Guide to Resource Allocation," in *Educational Cost Analysis in Action: Case Studies for Planners*, Vol. II, Paris, Unesco:IIEP, 1972.

We call attention also to another very interesting cost-benefit study prepared for the World Bank which was completed too late to be examined in the IIEP series: H. H. Thias and M. Carnoy, *Cost-Benefit Analysis in Education: A Case Study on Kenya* (November 1969), Report No. EC-173.

12. M. Blaug, P. R. G. Layard, and M. Woodhall, *The Causes of Graduate Unemployment in India*, London, Allen Lane, Penguin Press, 1969.

"educated unemployment has worked to reduce the earnings of the educated, exactly as predicted by economic theory, but the decline has never been fast enough to reduce the incentives to acquire still more education. Supply has moved consistently ahead of demand, so that the educated unemployed, as a fraction of the stock of educated manpower, has remained relatively constant."

The second Indian study[13] was concerned only with the issue of resource allocation, specifically with two questions: what should be the total amount of financial support for education at all levels to ensure such goals as economic growth, social cohesion, and national security? how should this total be distributed among different levels and types of education? The key finding of this study, namely, that the rate of return on education compared unfavorably with the economic return on equivalent capital invested in industry, might tempt one to conclude that the heavy Indian investment in education may be slowing rather than accelerating the economy's growth by diverting resources from more productive uses. It is precisely at this point, however, that one needs to be extremely cautious about leaping to conclusions without a great deal more evidence. The reasons why are discussed in a later chapter on cost-benefit analysis.

The third Indian study[14] also dealt with the relative profitability of investment in human and physical capital. Its main finding again was that "the economic return to investment in physical capital is higher than the economic returns to investment in secondary and higher education." (Primary education looked relatively better than higher levels.) The author concludes, however, that rather than re-allocating resources away from education, planners should seek ways to increase the economic profitability of education by improving its efficiency and productivity. "I suspect that . . . many actions can be taken by educators

13. A. M. Nalla Gounden, "Investment in Education in India," *Journal of Human Resources*, Summer 1967, pp. 347–58.

14. A. C. Harberger, "Investment in Men Versus Investment in Machines: The Case of India," in *Education and Economic Development*, ed. C. A. Anderson and M. N. Bowman, Chicago, Aldine Publishing Co., 1965.

to raise the economic productivity of their students without in any way detracting from the cultural and other advantages of the educational process. The key, I think, is to recognize that education *is* an investment. . . . A really serious effort to understand the economic consequences of different detailed types and classes of investment in education would help greatly to improve the contribution that education can make to economic progress."

Another cost-benefit study, applying to education in Colombia,[15] found the highest social and private rates of return on secondary education, the next highest on primary, and extremely low returns on higher education. No comparison was made with returns elsewhere in the economy, though this was implicit. Here, as in all the Indian studies, the benefits and rates of return were based solely upon the "direct economic benefits" and excluded all indirect economic and non-economic benefits.

Though one does well to avoid taking literally the precise rate-of-return statistics in any such studies, the rank order of returns on primary, secondary, and higher education, and particularly in Colombia's case, the strikingly low returns shown for university education, may well find support from other evidence. A separate study of Colombia's future requirements for high-level manpower, for example, had concluded that "although the economy evidently 'needs' additional high-level manpower, if additional human resources are supplied they will not be currently utilized." This distinction between manpower "needs" and actual market "demands" is important for educational policy-makers to be clear about, or else they may direct the system into serious overproduction of high-cost specialists which the economy is unable to absorb.

In the case of Colombia there is evidence to suggest that the two main effects of further rapid expansion of higher education

15. This study, done by T. P. Schultz of the Rand Corporation for U.S. AID, is reviewed in Maureen Woodhall, "Colombia: The Use of Cost-Benefit Analysis To Compare the Rates of Return at Different Educational Levels," in *Educational Cost Analysis in Action: Case Studies for Planners*, Vol. II, Paris, Unesco:IIEP, 1972.

might be, first, to force the social rate of return even lower (possibly into a negative position), and, second, to further stimulate the already substantial "brain-drain" of Colombia's university graduates into the higher-paying labor markets of North America and Western Europe. In other words, emigré graduates may manage to secure a high *private* rate of return overseas on their Colombian education while at the same time the nation itself, and those graduates who remain at home, experience a low *social* and private rate of return.

If we assume for the sake of argument that this is a correct diagnosis of Colombia's situation, then what are the options for policy? One obvious option would be to shift the allocation of educational resources toward more productive forms of education —particularly middle-level technical training—which showed a relatively high return, or else to shift resources from education into some other field. The case for both these solutions would be greatly reduced if yet another approach were vigorously pursued—namely, taking strong measures to improve the internal efficiency of higher education, thereby reducing its cost relative to its benefits, and similarly strong measures to make the content of higher education more relevant to the real needs of Colombia, thereby boosting the benefits themselves. (Similar action would, of course, be appropriate at all other levels of education.) Still another line of attack, complementary to the last one mentioned, would be to work on the economy itself to eliminate dislocations and rigidities that inhibit the generation of employment and the better utilization of the nation's educated manpower.

3 *Getting the Most from Available Resources*

In coming years educational systems everywhere will find themselves increasingly squeezed between resource scarcities and rising unit costs, for reasons we will discuss later. Thus they must pursue two simultaneous courses of action: (1) search for supplemental sources of revenue, and (2) find ways to improve their internal efficiency. Cost analysis, as the cases described below demonstrate, is an indispensable tool for the second course of action.

There are many potential ways to improve both the economic and educational efficiency of educational systems—for example, by introducing modern teaching media, by utilizing facilities more fully, by freeing teachers from clerical and housekeeping chores to spend more time actually teaching, by giving both teachers and students better tools and materials to work with, and by enlarging small classes and educational institutions to more optimum size.

Taking advantage of such potential economies, however, is often difficult. The actions required tend to upset established routines and create inconveniences. Worse still, the more unconventional changes and innovations often appear to some devout believers in old pedagogical doctrines as insidious heresies. In all events, cost considerations alone seldom are sufficient for reaching decisions to alter the *status quo;* these must be weighed against the likely pedagogical consequences (which are rarely as easy to estimate as costs) and against practical problems of acceptance and implementation. Putting schools on a double-shift basis, for example, or raising the pupil-teacher ratio from twenty-five to twenty-eight, or increasing the number of lectures and reducing the number of small seminars in a university, all such changes can improve the cost picture, but whether these gains will be outweighed by pedagogical losses must be carefully considered. Inevitably the final decision involves compromises and trade-offs among a range of considerations.

The cases outlined below illustrate a diversity of ways in which educational systems have used cost analysis in search of greater efficiency. Not all are success stories, but all have useful lessons to impart.

Uganda—Cutting Costs Instead of Targets

We would epecially recommend as "required reading" the IIEP case study of the making of Uganda's Second Five-Year Plan, because it gives an unusually full and realistic picture of the practical problems involved in adjusting targets to resource limits, in part by introducing changes and new economies into established educational practices.[1]

A Working Party on Education and Manpower was set up jointly in April 1965 by Uganda's Ministry of Education and Director of Planning to map out a comprehensive five-year education program within the framework of an over-all economic development plan. The Working Party was instructed to take account of the educational aspirations of the people, the manpower needs of the economy, and the resource allocations indicated by a tentative "perspective plan."

Realizing that there would be a tight squeeze at best for education, despite the favorable priority it enjoyed, the Working Party chose "minimum" enrolment targets right at the outset, barely

1. Nicholas Bennett, "Uganda: Educational Cost Evaluation," in *Educational Cost Analysis in Action: Case Studies for Planners,* Vol. III, Paris, Unesco:IIEP, 1972.

sufficient at the secondary and university level to fulfill the manpower requirements shown by a recent study, and holding down primary enrolments to what would be possible with no expansion of the supply of trained teachers and with no increase in unqualified teachers.

The initial rough costing showed, however, that even these minimum targets would exceed the resource limits set by the perspective plan. By 1971, annual recurrent costs would reach about 289 million shillings [2] against a resource target of 240 million (coincidentally the same target as for recurrent costs in 1971). Therefore the Working Party set about looking for possible cost savings, preferably ones that would be sufficiently conventional to avoid arousing opposition.

They found little possibility for reducing recurrent unit costs at the primary level. Here the planned elimination of supernumerary headmasters would lower unit costs, but an expected rise in the proportion of qualified, higher-paid teachers would offset this saving.

At the secondary level a similar set of countervailing forces was foreseen—a cost-reducing fall in the proportion of high-cost, expatriate teachers by 1971 would be almost offset by a cost-increasing rise in the proportion of boarding school students (from 50 per cent to 70 per cent), leaving a possible net reduction of 4 per cent to 5 per cent in unit costs per student. This, however, was far too little to bring resource requirements and supplies into balance.

Therefore the Working Party proposed an increase in average class size in secondary schools (within the limits of prevailing standards) by expanding undersized classes and providing for a 10 per cent "excessive" intake which would be offset by absentees and dropouts. They also proposed a change in the academic calendar, shifting the long holiday from December-January to July-August to coincide with the home leave of expatriate teachers, thereby eliminating the customary 10 per cent "over-staffing" to provide

2. At the time of the case study, the rate of exchange was \$1 = 7.14 Ugandan shillings.

for teachers on leave. The most dramatic recommendation was to put technical schools on a "sandwich" system, with two shifts of students each alternating between six months in school and six months practical employment experience.

At the university level where there was conspicuous under-utilization of both faculty and facilities, the recommendation was to raise enrolments by 60 per cent with no increase in administrative and other overhead costs and only a 35 per cent increase in library and departmental non-teaching costs.

The foregoing recommendations, it was estimated, would produce a significant lowering of costs at all but the elementary level. Specifically, over-all recurrent costs (for 1971) would be cut by 12.2 per cent from the initial estimate of 289 million shillings to 259 million, but this was still in excess of the 240 million target. Capital costs would decline from the earlier estimate of 265 million to just over 200 million, safely below the 240 million shillings target.

So far so good, but when the above minimum enrolment targets and economy measures were submitted to the government, they were considered *too* minimum to satisfy the nation's aspirations and practical needs. Thus the Working Party was asked to go back to work and calculate the implications of (1) aiming for universal primary education by 1974; (2) a 25 per cent increase in the earlier minimum intake targets for lower secondary schools; and (3) a 20 per cent boost in intakes to the university.

Plainly these higher targets could not be fitted to the resource limitation targets. They would require a combination of much more drastic economy measures than those thus far suggested and a substantial increase in education's allocation at the expense of other sectors. Hence the Working Party proceeded to devise several more radical schemes for reducing unit costs, based mainly on drastic changes in the academic calendar which would permit more students to be processed through existing facilities, with a less-than-proportionate increase of teaching staff and costs. When costed out, however, even these extraordinary measures would not produce the needed cut in costs, especially since the "cushion" of unused capacity had been largely used up by the first round of less radical cost-reducing proposals. For example, allowance had already been made to use technical schools year round and to put two students rather than the customary one in university dormitories. And instead of fewer expatriate teachers, there would now have to be more.

These radical cost-reducing measures were tested only for their cost implications by the Working Party, who left it to others to assess their pedagogical consequences. It was largely on the latter grounds that the government finally decided to hold these measures in abeyance, neither approving nor rejecting them, until their pedagogical efficacy could be more thoroughly explored and perhaps tested out experimentally. The government did decide, however, to raise the primary education targets somewhat above the original "minimum" level, though postponing the goal of universal primary education beyond 1974. It also decided to adopt the higher targets for secondary and university education which the Working Party had been asked to study.

This made it inevitable (and because of the costing exercise, the government was well aware of this) that the tentative resources allocations set for education in the original perspective plan would have to be substantially increased at the expense of other sectors. The target for capital expenditures would have to be raised from 240 million shillings to 370 million shillings, and for recurrent expenditures in 1971 from 240 million to about 280 million.

The capital requirements seemed especially dubious and it was not long before the cost-reducers were back at work again, this time classifying educational capital projects into priority categories so that some could be given a prompt go-ahead, others postponed, and still others dropped altogether for the time being. Further revisions were made in the Plan during its period of implementation. By 1968, two years after the Plan had started into action, the prospect (as seen by the IIEP investigators) was that actual capital outlays for the five-year period might fall about 100 million shillings below the 370 million peak estimate, thus not too far from the original target. No attempt was made to forecast what the recurrent costs might be in the Plan's final year.

A particularly interesting part of the Uganda story was the planning for Makerere College, then a component of the University of East Africa (jointly supported by Uganda, Kenya, and Tanzania).[3] The essence of this story is that two separate groups with two quite different outlooks each undertook independently to project Makerere's budget. One group, the government Working Party mentioned above, had a wide-angle view of the national economic situation and was mainly concerned that the university should produce, at least possible cost, the manpower needed for the nation's development. The other group, made up of university people, took a narrower and more specialized view. Though conscious of the university's manpower training responsibilities, its members were mainly concerned with promoting the institution's academic excellence and its status in the international academic community. They were more conscious of the resources needed than of the limitations on the resources of the economy.

Not surprisingly, the government Working Party emerged with substantially lower budget proposals for Makerere than did the university group. This necessitated a process of delicate negotiation, since the university, though largely tax-supported, was semi-autonomous and anxious to stay that way. It soon became clear to the University Grants Committee, which presided over the negotiations and served the entire University of East Africa, that the three constituent colleges were using different budget terminology and categories, making it impossible to compare, or even add up rationally, their separate budget proposals, much less to assess their soundness. The Grants Committee therefore laid down some common budget concepts and required the three constituent colleges to rework their budgets on this basis. It also required them to apply certain staffing and other norms earlier recommended

3. Nicholas Bennett, "Uganda: The Use of Cost Evaluation in the Planning of Makerere College," in *Educational Cost Analysis in Action: Case Studies for Planners*, Vol. III, Paris, Unesco:IIEP, 1972.

by an international expert group and accepted in principle but never actually applied by the colleges. The ultimate result was the approval of a budget for Makerere, acceptable to both the Grants Committee and the government of Uganda, which fell in between the levels initially proposed by the two groups.

In addition to the experiences reported above, an IIEP team conducted a special study, in cooperation with the Ugandan Ministry of Education, of non-teacher recurrent costs in a sample of secondary schools, based on an examination of individual school accounts.[4] The object of the study was to learn how the schools actually used the block grants made to them by the government for non-teacher costs (the government paid their teachers directly) and to discover whether there were any interesting behavior patterns in these costs. The results of the study, it was felt, provided some useful clues to future economies. We will have more to say in later chapters about this study.

United Kingdom—Better Schools for Less Money

Much has been written, but mainly for architects, about the United Kingdom's outstanding post-war school building program. The IIEP case study reveals the story of the key role played in this program by new techniques of cost analysis.[5]

Britain faced a major school-building emergency after the Second World War. Thousands of new classrooms were urgently needed to replace those damaged or destroyed by war, to deal with the post-war bulge in the child population as well as an extension of compulsory school attendance up to fifteen years of age, and to meet the needs of a shifting population and new communities. Conditions, however, were extremely tight. The construction

4. John Chesswas and Jacques Hallak, "Uganda: Behaviour of Non-Teacher Recurring Expenditures," in *Educational Cost Analysis in Action: Case Studies for Planners,* Vol. III, Paris, Unesco:IIEP, 1972.

5. Maureen Woodhall, "United Kingdom: The Use of Cost Analysis To Improve the Efficiency of School Building in England and Wales," in *Educational Cost Analysis in Action: Case Studies for Planners,* Vol. III, Paris, Unesco:IIEP, 1972.

industry was overloaded and so also was the public budget, under a severely strained post-war economy.

The first attack on the problem was a crash program that produced nearly 7000 prefabricated school "huts" between 1945 and 1949. Meanwhile, a search was mounted for longer-term solutions, beginning with a comparative study of recent school-building costs in various communities. This study revealed wide variations of cost per square foot—ranging from 42 shillings [6] to over 78 shillings for primary schools, and from 43 to 68 shillings for secondary schools—but it failed to explain the cause of the variations. Clearly there was need for a new methodology for comparing the costs of schools differing in size, design, and location, and for setting norms by which the reasonableness of any new school proposal could be judged.

The old method used in soliciting tenders (bids) for new schools had been to prepare a "bill of quantities" which broke down estimated costs according to the building crafts involved, such as carpentry, plumbing, masonry, and painting. This sort of breakdown was of little help, however, in trying to explain why some schools cost more than others; a more functional type of breakdown was needed.

The first obvious step was to separate site costs (land purchase and preparation, utility services, etc.) from construction costs, since it was evident that site costs varied greatly from one school to another, probably much more so than construction costs, and local school authorities usually had less latitude for affecting site costs than construction costs. The next step was to relate construction costs to a series of "elements" common to most school buildings (from which came the name for this new costing technique, "Elemental Cost Analysis"). Typical of these functional elements, for example, were: (1) *enclosures* (including the foundations, outer walls, roofs, and exterior windows); (2) *space division* (including interior walls and partitions, floors, internal

6. At the time of the case study, the exchange rate was £1 = 20 shillings = U.S. $2.80.

doors); and (3) *fittings* (desks, laboratory benches, sanitary fittings, cupboards, etc.).

This new breakdown of construction costs provided a much more meaningful basis for identifying and explaining the differences in costs of schools. It also opened new avenues for rationalizing school construction methods and ultimately for controlling school construction costs and inspiring economies.

Once it had a clear picture of the behavior of school costs and had discussed the matter at length with school authorities and architects, the Ministry of Education, in 1950, for the first time established "cost limits" on all proposed new schools. This rather drastic step (in terms of British traditions) was taken because the economic situation was such that either school construction costs had to be reduced or else fewer classrooms built. But the aim was broader than simply cutting costs; it was to build, at the least cost, schools that would meet acceptable physical standards and performance specifications. Unless tied to such standards and specifications, costs would have little meaning. Guy Oddie, who played a central role in the effort, explained it this way: "Economy in school building means securing the *appropriate* standards for the lowest outlay, and the search for economy must therefore concentrate not on the reduction of standards but on the reduction and elimination of all that is unproductive or underused." [7]

The Ministry of Education's cost limits were set with a goal of reducing actual school construction costs over the following two years to a level 25 per cent below the 1949 average, and it worked. One reason why it worked was that the limits were set in a manner which left considerable scope for ingenuity on the part of architects as well as room for choice by local education authorities. This was accomplished by expressing the limits in terms of "cost per student place" and requiring conformity with certain performance specifications, but allowing them to be met in a variety of alternative ways. Thus, for example, the minimum lighting

7. G. Oddie, *School Building Resources and Their Effective Use: Some Available Techniques and Their Policy Implications*, Paris, OECD, 1966.

standards were set not in terms of so many square feet of window area but in terms of the minimum lighting intensity to be achieved within classrooms. The net effect was to allow wide latitude to architects and local authorities in deciding how best to deploy total space (for example, as between teaching space and non-teaching space), and how best to meet the various performance standards.

Later on these cost limits, which were applied at the point when specific building plans came to the Ministry for approval in advance of construction, were further developed into a system of "cost controls" applied during and after construction to ensure that the limits were actually observed.

There was another whole side to this cost-reducing story, however, which involved fundamental improvements in the techniques and efficiency of school construction, stemming, interestingly enough, from some of the more experimentally-minded local authorities themselves, and strongly encouraged by the Ministry. The basic idea was to design standardized *components* for school buildings (not to be confused with standardized schools) which could be mass-produced at progressively lower unit costs. After such components had been designed and tested out, neighboring local education authorities joined together voluntarily in "bulk purchasing" consortia in order to achieve the economies of scale. This still left them with wide flexibility of school design, but with considerably reduced costs.

The net effect of the various measures described above was to reverse the sharp rise in school construction costs between 1946 and 1949. Even as construction costs elsewhere in the United Kingdom continued to climb, school costs fell appreciably from 1949 to 1952. Thereafter they began rising again, but at a considerably slower rate than construction costs generally.

Another significant result may seem paradoxical at first. Between 1949 and 1959 the *total* area per student place in new school buildings grew smaller, but the amount of *teaching* space per student actually increased. The explanation is that, through careful consultation with teachers, architects discovered that they attached highest priority to getting more teaching space—as distinct from "non-teaching" space such as offices, corridors, entry halls, and so forth. This priority grew stronger as more flexible and individualized methods of teaching were introduced into British schools which required both more space per child and the flexible redeployment of space throughout the school day. Thus the architects, while trimming over-all space per student, also traded off non-teaching space for greater teaching space—which rose from a typical average of only 40 per cent of total space in new buildings in 1949 to more than 67 per cent by 1955.

The British experience just described has all the evidences of a genuine success story. In the twenty years from 1946 to 1966, during which Britain's school age population rose by 2.1 million, 4.2 million new school places were created which are widely regarded as functionally better than the conventional pre-war types. By rough estimate, the total construction cost would have been £1.6 billion if traditional methods had been followed. Instead, the actual cost was just over £1.0 billion—a dramatic saving by any standard.

*Canada—
Improving the Management of University Resources*

A Systems Research Group at the University of Toronto developed some new techniques during the 1960's for using simulation models to help university managers improve planning and the utilization of resources. What is especially interesting about these models is that they were intended not merely for theoretical exercises but for practical use by decision-makers. Among other applications of these models, a particularly interesting one concerned the expansion and restructuring of medical education at Toronto.[8]

8. Jack B. Levine, Richard W. Judy, and Richard Wilson, "Canada: Comprehensive Analytical Methods for Planning in University Systems—Planning a New Health Sciences Education Complex," in *Educational Cost Analysis in Action: Case Studies for Planners*, Vol. III, Paris, Unesco:IIEP, 1972.

In late 1966 the Faculty of Medicine invited the help of the Systems Research Group to plan a new health sciences education complex. The aim was to increase each annual class of medical students from 175 to 250, strengthen graduate studies and research, introduce innovations into the curriculum and teaching methods, provide a larger role for the medical faculty in the teaching hospitals, and institute improvements in staffing and remuneration policies. There were a number of alternative ways of approaching these objectives, and the basic problem was to find the best combination within the framework of prospective resource limits and other constraints. Working in close collaboration with a new Health Sciences Function Unit, headed by a vice-president of the university and responsible for planning the new complex, the Systems Research Group fashioned a series of analytical models designed to assess the costs and effectiveness of various alternatives. With the aid of the models and a computer it was possible to calculate quickly the input and output implications of different potential practices and arrangements —measured not in monetary units but real resources, such as the number of teachers, student contact hours, patients served, time available for research, and so forth. Where appropriate, these real resource and performance measures could later be converted to financial terms. Prompt answers could thus be given to such practical questions as the following, which were posed by the medical education planners:

- What changes in departmental staffing are implied by a given expansion of the undergraduate and graduate programs within stated budgetry limitations?
- Is the total departmental income that could be expected in a given set of circumstances compatible with the corresponding salary and other operating costs?
- How many resident medical interns of various types can be adequately trained within a specific program given the existing number and types of hospital beds?
- How many undergraduate and graduate trainees can a given size and type of faculty support?
- If instruction were organized around an examination of dif-

ferent human physiological systems rather than by conventional departments, for 250 students per class how would this affect the number of student contact hours required of the faculty as a whole and of different sub-groups of the faculty?

By weighing the evidence thus provided to them on comparative costs, practical feasibility, and likely benefits of various alternative patterns, members of the Health Sciences Function Unit were able to reach decisions on the new program in which they and others could have a higher degree of confidence.

Members of the Systems Research Group, looking back on the experience, estimated that the savings achieved by this means of planning the new health sciences education complex outweighed the costs of the analytical exercise by a factor of 100 to 1.

The types of simulation models and operation research techniques devised and applied by the Toronto group would appear to have useful application to a wide range of higher education institutions in other countries, including developing countries.

Morocco—a Profitable Fact-Finding Expedition

When the educational officials of Morocco decided to request the World Bank to help on financing a large expansion of secondary education, they found themselves handicapped by lack of facts about costs—and here the Bank was bound to ask searching questions. What were the costs per student in secondary schools—the capital costs and the recurrent costs—broken down by major components? What were the variations in unit costs among different schools and what accounted for them? How did costs differ by size of school? How was existing school space and equipment actually used? By what norms and criteria should the estimated costs of new schools be judged? Without a clearer understanding of how secondary school costs actually behaved and how space and equipment related to different uses and to the number of students, it would be extremely difficult for Moroccan educational authorities to make sound plans and to present convincing proposals for the secondary expansion program.

A fact-finding expedition was therefore undertaken with the

help of Unesco technical assistance experts to try to answer the questions posed above.

The investigators soon discovered that central budgetary and other records were quite inadequate to their purpose because (as is usually the case) they covered up individual school variations in composite totals and averages. Also, the original design plans on file for existing schools had not been kept up-to-date to show subsequent extensions and modifications of space use. A firsthand investigation of a cross-section sample of one-tenth of Morocco's 230 secondary schools was decided upon, cutting across rural and urban, day and boarding, large and small, and other categories of schools. In each case an effort was made to estimate the total cost per student, broken down by major components, and to determine the use of space and equipment.[9]

When the results were assembled and subjected to comparative analysis, the conclusions were both disappointing and illuminating: disappointing because they revealed few clear-cut statistical patterns, correlations, or trends; illuminating because they threw light on the reasons why. Different schools had been built and equipped at different times, meeting widely diverse local conditions and reflecting whatever standard specifications and doctrines prevailed at the time. Many had since been added to or otherwise transformed; each was now operating under its own special circumstances of student demand, overcrowding or underutilization of staff and facilities, and so forth. In short, there was nothing uniform about them and no simple basis for comparing their costs and performance.

This, in itself, however, was a valuable discovery. It emphasized the need for using well-conceived norms to guide future construction, operations, and planning, for establishing better criteria to appraise the efficiency of each school's performance, and for pursuing economies in school construction by standardized components. The study also provided a more realistic picture of

9. J. Proust, "Morocco: Costs of Public Secondary Education—Analysis of the Results of a Governmental Survey," in *Educational Cost Analysis in Action: Case Studies for Planners*, Vol. III, Paris, Unesco:IIEP, 1972.

how facilities and space were actually used, which differed considerably from the picture suggested by school plans on file at headquarters.

Perhaps of greatest value of all, quite incidental to the study's initial purpose, was obtaining a profile for the first time of the actual composition of unit costs and the relative importance of the various components. The study had started out being preoccupied with capital costs (of special interest in regard to a World Bank loan), but what it demonstrated was that, without gainsaying the need to economize on capital costs, in the long run recurrent costs are of much greater importance.

Chile—Using Teachers to the Best Advantage

In 1968, secondary level technical education in Chile was suddently confronted by what seemed an insurmountable problem, arising from an unexpected financial roadblock combined with curriculum and structural adjustments called for by the Chilean Education Reform of 1965.

The problem in brief was this. In January 1968 the Ministry of Education's Planning Office, in consultation with the directors of Chile's 115 state-run secondary technical schools, concluded that there was need for an immediate expansion in the number of classes in these schools, from 1218 to 1411, or about 16 per cent, this largely because of a change-over of school grade classifications under the Reform. Presumably, their total teaching staff would have to expand even more, since the 1965 Reform also required a reduction in hours for technical school teachers. All this obviously had major budgetary implications. But within a month the horrible truth emerged that, because of financial stringencies in the government's over-all fiscal position, the 1968 budget for secondary technical education could be no higher than in 1967.

Confronted by this dilemma, an analytical advisory group under the Directorate General for Education launched a hasty expedition for facts—facts about the number and size of classes in each school, the number of teachers, and how they were spending their time as between teaching and non-teaching duties. The returns from this quick survey opened the door to a prompt solution of the problem. They showed, first, that over 13 per cent of the total available teacher hours (at the reduced working week) were being devoted to non-teaching tasks, and, second, that a large proportion of classes were well below the official maximum size and could absorb considerably more students without impairing educational effectiveness. The problem then became one of deploying the increased student load to the undersized classes, and redeploying the under-utilized teachers to the classes and the schools where they were most needed. What was required, in short, was not more funds but better management of the resources already available.[10]

Finding out why this large, hidden cushion of under-utilized classroom and teaching capacity existed was perhaps as important in the long run as solving the immediate problem. The explanation was that the Ministry's information system was totally inadequate to providing the up-to-the-minute data needed for the efficient deployment of teachers and classroom space, especially under rapidly changing conditions. Moreover, the traditional methods of recruiting, employing, assigning, and reassigning secondary technical teachers were also inadequate to cope with the new situation produced by the Education Reform.

It seems a fair guess that, having gone through this experience, which fortunately had a happy ending, the Ministry would take the necessary remedial steps and not again be caught with its basic facts and teacher-assignment procedures in disarray.

U.S.S.R.—More and Better Education for Fewer Rubles

Leaders of the Soviet Union have always believed strongly that education for all citizens was an essential investment for rapid

10. Lucila Arrigazzi and José de Simone, "Chile: Improving Efficiency in the Use of Teachers in Technical Education," in *Educational Cost Analysis in Action: Case Studies for Planners*, Vol. III, Paris, Unesco:IIEP, 1972.

economic and cultural development. This belief found expression in the enormous expansion of Soviet education between the end of the Second World War and the early 1960's. That education was, indeed, a good investment, despite the heavy burden it placed on the Soviet economy, seemed reaffirmed by Professor S. Strumilin's estimate that 23 per cent of the national income in 1960 was attributable to the increased educational qualifications of the Soviet labor force, and by Professor V. Zhamin's similar estimate of 27 per cent applying in 1962.

As Soviet educational and economic planners looked ahead in the early 1960's, however, some formidable problems loomed on the horizon. They had customarily paid close attention to the external productivity of education by doing their best to match educational output to the evolving manpower needs of the economy. But they had not given as much attention to the *internal* efficiency of education and other cultural organizations as they had given, for example, to issues of efficiency in agricultural and industrial production. Economists who began probing into the matter concluded that this neglect "partly contributed to the uneconomic, wasteful use of material and money which has taken place."

Several problems were converging which signaled the need for greater attention to educational efficiency. One was the high cost and doubtful quality of small rural schools, a problem which would grow steadily more serious as migration to the towns thinned out the population in many rural areas, and even more as the government sought to extend compulsory secondary education into rural areas. A second problem was the steady growth of university-level part-time study in many specialized fields, whose heavy costs and uncertain benefits seemed in need of reexamination.

Attitudes changed sharply on the whole question of educational efficiency after the Plenary Session of the Central Committee of the Communist Party in September 1965 emphasized that using resources economically in education was just as important as in physical production.

It is interesting to see how cost analysis was used to diagnose the two efficiency problems mentioned above, and how Soviet policy-makers responded to the diagnosis.

CONSOLIDATING SMALL RURAL SCHOOLS

The problem of small-scale rural schools with high unit costs, often accompanied by inferior pedagogical results, is common to all nations with large, widely dispersed rural populations. We saw this in the Norwegian case earlier. The same problem plagued a high proportion of secondary schools in the United States for many years and led to a strong "school consolidation" movement. Thus the facts about the Soviet situation should be of wide interest.[11]

In the ten years from 1958–59 to 1968–69 about 25,000 small rural primary schools had been closed in the Soviet Union, particularly in declining population areas, at an estimated net saving of 65 million rubles.[12] But this did not keep pace with the growth of the problem. By 1968–69, over 70 per cent of the primary schools had forty or fewer pupils (nearly one-third had twenty or less) and the average enrolment of primary schools, which in 1940–41 had been seventy-seven, was now only forty-one pupils. This meant in practice that the typical rural teacher had to handle several grades simultaneously, and, not surprisingly, the learning results were considered inferior. Costs, however, ran in the opposite direction: the smaller the school, the higher the cost per student. Nationwide, the mean average recurrent cost per pupil was 50 rubles, but the unit cost for small schools ranged from 100 to 250 rubles.

Previously the problem was largely concentrated at the primary level, but in the future it would grow geometrically if "mini" secondary schools became scattered over the landscape pursuant

11. V. I. Basov, "U.S.S.R.: Estimating the Annual Budget Requirements of the Educational System," in *Educational Cost Analysis in Action: Case Studies for Planners*, Vol. I, Paris, Unesco:IIEP, 1972.

12. At the time of the case study, the rate of exchange was $1 = 0.89 rubles.

to the policy of universal secondary education. It would be economically out of the question to provide tiny high schools with a full-fledged curriculum, a full complement of teachers, and a full supply of laboratories, teaching aids, and the like.

As the result of cost analysis and pedagogical studies, a basic strategy involving three related lines of action was adopted in 1965 to cope with the foregoing situation (with the expectation, however, that many years would be required to implement this strategy fully).

First, as rapidly as possible, selected rural primary schools would be enlarged, while others serving the same area would be closed. (The construction of new schools, as distinct from the extension of existing ones, would be limited to developing areas where population was expected to grow.)

Second, free transportation would be guaranteed to all children living more than three kilometers from a primary school. Pursuant to this policy, by 1968–69 the government had already increased its annual expenditure on school transport to about 30 million rubles.

Third, new eight-year and secondary schools for rural students would as a rule be constructed with boarding facilities (financed from social allocations for housing) to serve children from distant areas beyond the feasible reach of daily transportation.

Soviet economists and educators were confident that this combination of actions for increasing the size of rural schools would "lead to a considerable improvement in the quality of teaching, the rational use of teachers, laboratories, workshops and gymnasiums, and more efficient use of monetary resources."

PART-TIME HIGHER EDUCATION

The Soviet educational system has been relatively unique in affording generous opportunities for higher education to younger people who have left full-time schooling for employment. Such part-time education is provided through evening courses, correspondence, and increasingly through instructional television, usually with periodic visits to campuses or special centers for direct instruction and examinations. The standards applied are the same and the certificate or degree earned in this fashion is indistinguishable from full-time day study.

In the 1960's these popular off-campus programs accounted for roughly half the total enrolments in university-level engineering in the Soviet Union and in similar specialized fields.[13] They had long been highly valued and encouraged by the government for several reasons: they kept open the avenues of self-advancement for able and ambitious young people; they enriched the nation's manpower and thus its productivity; and their costs were assumed to be relatively modest compared to full-time study. As evidence of the latter assumption, the coefficients used by the Ministry of Education for calculating "full-time equivalent students" in higher education equated costs of one full-time (day) student to four evening-course students and to ten correspondence-course students.

These earlier assumptions regarding the costs and benefits of part-time study came under serious questioning by the mid-1960's, the more so as new studies by economists shed fresh light on the subject. Their cost estimates took into account, for example, the fact that the dropout and failure rate was nearly 50 per cent for part-time students, and that 20 per cent of the correspondence students took two extra years to complete a five-year course. Allowing for these and other factors, they reached the conclusion that the direct cost per year of a correspondence student was not one-tenth (as previously assumed) but one-fourth the cost of a full-time student.

But even this greatly increased cost figure did not reflect the full costs to the economy of part-time study. To it should be added, for example, the subsidy from employers for release time to study and for transportation to correspondence centers for consultation and examinations. All in all, it was clear that the real costs of part-time education were considerably greater than had commonly been assumed.

What about the benefits? These could not be precisely quanti-

13. V. Zhamin and B. Remennikov, "U.S.S.R.: Comparative Costs and Efficiency of Full-time and Part-time Education," in *Educational Cost Analysis in Action: Case Studies for Planners*, Vol. III, Paris, Unesco:IIEP, 1972.

fied but several relevant considerations stood out. On the positive side, there was clear evidence that many—though not all—part-time students had improved their knowledge and skills and thus their productivity on the job, especially those who took applied courses bearing directly on their work. Indeed it had not been unusual for part-time students to be promoted to positions of higher responsibility in their factory, school, or other enterprise, even before finishing their course of study. But, on the other hand, the record showed that part-time students as a whole performed significantly less well than day students on theoretical courses such as physics, chemistry, and mathematics. Moreover, there was doubt that those who took courses *un*related to their employment, whether theoretical or practical, had significantly improved their productivity. Beyond this, allowance had to be made for the fact that the older a part-time student was, the fewer remaining years of active work he would have for the social investment in his extra education to pay off. Weighing all these factors together, the following conclusions seemed warranted: (1) the costs of part-time higher education were greater and the average benefits lower than had previously been assumed; (2) the cost-benefit ratio was highest on applied subjects closely related to the student's employment and lowest on theoretical studies and subjects remote from the student's employment; (3) the younger the age of the student, the higher the cost-benefit ratio.

The investigation just described persuaded authorities that full-time education had proved on the average to have significant comparative advantages over part-time, both economically and in the quality and effectiveness of the results. This led them to two decisions. First, planners were asked to give relatively greater emphasis to the development of full-time education. (As a result, in 1968 the intake of full-time students rose to 51 per cent of total new enrolments against 49.2 per cent in 1967, and this upward trend was expected to continue.) Second, emphasis in the curriculum for part-time study would thereafter be given to practical studies; offerings in theoretical studies (e.g. astronomy, radiophysics, mathematics, etc.) would be de-emphasized and reduced; and preference would be given to applicants choosing courses closely related to their work, and in fields where manpower needs were greatest.

Earlier, in discussing another Soviet case study concerning the use of norms and coefficients for budgeting and planning purposes, we made the point that such devices are very useful so long as they fit realities and are constantly kept up-to-date. The experience just cited is a good example of norms (and underlying assumptions) which in fact did not fit reality but which, when exposed to more systematic analysis, were overhauled with important consequences for policy.

Hungary—Confronting Forecasts with Accomplishments

If there is one country where a large effort is devoted to ensuring consistency between long-term, medium-term, and short-term objectives, it is certainly Hungary. Similarly, in that country, particular care is taken in integrating educational plans into the general economic plan, especially after the distortion which appeared during the last twenty years in the form of a surplus of specialists trained for certain occupations, while a heavy shortage of high-level manpower was found to exist in other sectors.

As a matter of fact, the amount of the appropriations which can be earmarked for educational expenditure is established in the medium-term plans as a function of the requirements in the long-term plans and the financial possibilities. Separate estimates are made relating to the investment outlay (covered by the so-called "accumulation fund") and the operating expenses (covered by the "consumption fund" of the national income). The annual plan for educational expenditure, the aim of which is to ensure the attainment of the targets of the medium-term plans, is prepared within the framework of the national budget. At all events, cost analysis and estimates are essential in the whole process of educational planning in Hungary.[14]

14. L. Falugévi, "Hungary: Programming Annual Current and Capital Expenditure During the Planning Period," in *Educational Cost Analysis in Action: Case Studies for Planners,* Vol. III, Paris, Unesco:IIEP, 1972.

More specifically, in the first place, in working out cost estimates, the Hungarian planners use "cost norms" and "indicators." An indicator relates to the number of pupils to receive instruction in a type of educational institution; a cost norm expresses the annual cost forecast on the basis of an indicator. Secondly, the planning of educational expenditure in Hungary takes into account the effects both of quantitative factors (changes in enrolments) and of qualitative improvement of educational systems. For these purposes, a mathematical cost model was worked out and applied to estimate the distribution of expenditures by level and type of education in preparing the Five-Year Plan 1966–70. Naturally the results of the models are considered as being "mechanical" and have to be adjusted to take into consideration principles of economic, social, and educational natures.

In this respect, a comparison between forecasts and accomplishments in the Plan has been undertaken; it shows the usefulness of careful cost analysis in the achievement of accurate and realistic planning. An analysis of the trend of the indicators of the distribution of the cost and expenditure for primary, secondary, and higher education respectively shows that the authorized program allocations approved for the respective years do not differ significantly from the planned targets, the differences varying only between 1 and 3 per cent. While this result in itself has no general significance, it illustrates both the need to prepare the annual budget in consistence with the mid-term plan and also the essential role cost estimates play as indices of achievement of the Plan.

Hungarian planners felt that although their methodology of costing had proved quite efficient, there was still a need for improving it; research was therefore started on a number of topics, e.g. on the need to introduce: cost-benefit analysis, methods for analyzing the possibilities of reducing unit costs and total costs, methods for integrating regional differences in planning educational expansion, techniques to take into consideration the possible consequences of price and salary variations in working out the annual budget program and especially the medium-term plans, etc.

II *The Anatomy and Behavior of Educational Costs*

To talk sense about educational costs, we must start with a rational way of viewing them, an understanding of how they behave, and a knowledge of the major forces that determine them. We must also be familiar with several different concepts and meanings of "cost" as they are used in cost analysis and be able to label them correctly to avoid confusion and muddled thinking. The purpose of the following three chapters is to introduce these essentials, which will be elaborated later.

Some readers who are already well-grounded in the economics of education will find that the next three chapters cover familiar territory and warrant only a quick scanning. Others, however, who are less familiar with economics, and are perhaps even disquieted by the term, will find these chapters helpful, we hope, as a necessary preparation for coming to grips with their own problems of cost analysis, a matter dealt with in Part III. We want to reassure these readers right now that even if their specialty is literature, pedagogy, or philosophy, and not economics or mathematics, they should have no serious difficulty comprehending the ideas presented in these chapters.

4 *Education Viewed as a "System"*

The term "educational system" to most people means the formal educational system—the hierarchical structure of institutionalized, full-time educational activities stretching from the primary school through the university. In this book we will sometimes use the term to mean also (1) any sub-system within the formal structure, however small (such as elementary or secondary education, an individual school or university, or even an individual classroom or particular course of study), and (2) any "non-formal" yet systematic teaching-learning process aimed at particular objectives but conducted outside the formal system (such as an extension service for farmers, an on-the-job training program for industrial workers, or a work-oriented literacy program).

Educational systems have been called by that name for generations, yet they have rarely been *treated* as systems. Everyone tends to look at them in piecemeal fashion and to contrive piecemeal answers to their many problems, as if each problem existed in isolation. This is hardly surprising if we picture the busy school administrator who spends his day keeping one step ahead of the urgent notations on his desk calendar:

Authorize equipment purchase for new technical school.
Meet with teachers on salary schedule.
Prepare proposals on curriculum reform.

Draft Rotary Club speech on "Education's Contribution to Economic Growth."
Look into plan for television instruction.
Review next year's budget proposals.
Answer charges of waste by Taxpayers' League.

As he doggedly attacks these, item by item, it is possible to overlook the fact that each is part of a seamless web; if you do something substantial about any one of them, it will have repercussions of some sort on the others and almost certainly on educational costs.

We need, therefore, a way of looking at educational costs through a wider-angle lens which enables us to see the system as an integrated, dynamic whole, revealing the relationships among its interacting parts and between the system and its socio-economic environments.

The best way to achieve this is to use the framework of a "systems analysis." By this we do not mean a sophisticated mathematical input-output model programmed for rapid calculation on a computer. We mean something simpler, a *conceptual* analytical framework, defined in ordinary words but founded on the same logical concepts as the mathematical model.

Five Key Elements of an Educational System

Viewed through the lens of a systems analysis, any educational system can be seen to have the following five cardinal features (depicted schematically in Figure 4.1).

1. *Objectives.* The attainment of these is the system's only reason for existing and its only warrant for commanding a share of the scarce public and private resources. There are usually a number of educational objectives in any given situation and often they are in competition with one another, making it necessary to set priorities and mediate conflicts. They range from very general and ambiguous goals for the system as a whole (such as "producing good citizens," "developing liberally educated leaders," and "supporting national development") to more specific aims relating

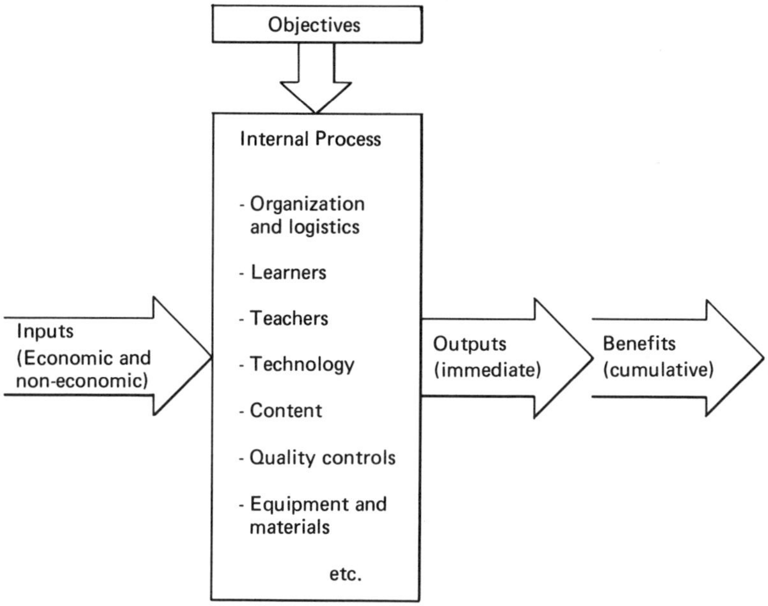

FIGURE 4.1.
Conceptual view of an educational system (or sub-system).

to particular sub-systems (such as "mastering long division, fractions and decimals," "learning the basic principles of physics," "developing automobile repair skills," and "developing simple proficiency in a foreign language").

Not infrequently an educational system's *stated* objectives differ considerably from its *actual* objectives as inferred from its day-to-day behavior. In a developing country, for example, an officially proclaimed goal may be to acquaint young people with the history, culture, and geography of their own country and region, whereas in fact pupils may spend inordinate time trying to master the language and learn about the history, culture, and geography of a distant metropolitan nation from which their own country has only recently gained its political independence. Another proclaimed aim may be to develop the capacity of young people to examine problems rationally and reach their own solutions, whereas in fact they may spend most of their time memorizing somebody else's solutions.

The important point for our present purpose is that if an educational system is not clear about its objectives and priorities, it lacks any rational basis and starting point for appraising and improving its performance, for planning its future, or for making good use of cost analysis for these purposes. Like a ship at sea without a compass, it has no clear notion of where it is going or how to get there.

2. *Outputs*. These include all the residual learnings, skills, insights, attitudes, styles of thinking—all the developed aptitudes and capabilities—that a student carries away from the educational system beyond what he brought to it initially from home or elsewhere. The outputs, in other words, are the "educational value-added" to the student by his exposure to the particular educational process.

Logically, therefore, these outputs cannot be adequately assessed simply by a standardized examination applied uniformly to all students at the end of the process, especially if they entered the process with widely differing family and cultural backgrounds. Some students who do only fair to middling on the final examinations may well have gained more, relative to where they started from, than some who come out on top. Moreover, the key question is not simply how much the students learned, as revealed by final examinations, but how well their actual learning matches the objectives of the system, and how well the objectives themselves match the real needs of the students and the society. Unless there is a reasonably clear idea about these relationships, then all talk about the efficiency, quality, and productivity of the educational system is little more than empty rhetoric.

3. *Benefits*. The ultimate purpose of an educational system is not simply to produce immediate educational outputs and value-added in the sense just described, but to generate longer-term benefits resulting from these immediate outputs. These benefits

take many forms, both economic and non-economic, individual and social.

The individual, for example, may benefit by getting a better job and higher lifetime earnings, by a more satisfying family life, by adding richer cultural and civic dimensions to his existence, by a greater sense of participation in the world around him. The society at large may benefit from higher production of better living standards, by an enlarged supply of effective leadership at every level, and by the enrichment of its culture through the release of greater creativity in more people.

If the society or the individuals were not reasonably confident of obtaining substantial benefits such as these, they would be foolish indeed to spend so much time, effort, and money on the educational system. What the benefits actually turn out to be, of course, is another matter which depends not only on what the educational system itself does but on the behavior of the economy and society as well.

4. *Internal process.* To produce outputs and longer-term benefits, an educational system must have appropriate ways of doing its work. It must have pedagogical methods or technologies; an organization, structure, and logistical patterns; ways of orchestrating its many components and moving parts; means for judging and controlling the quality of its products and for assessing its own performance. Not least of all it must have a curriculum whose content is well related to the objectives of the system and to the needs and future lives of the students. All these constitute its internal process.

Many people, including many educators, often seem to operate on the assumption that there is only one available process for doing education's work properly (that is, the *present* way of doing things). But there are, in fact, many alternative processes, some surely better than others.

5. *Inputs.* These are the various resources and components required to enable the process to function, starting with students and teachers but also including instructional materials, physical

facilities and equipment, and supplies of various sorts. The amounts, quality, and combination of inputs needed depend not only on the number of students to be served but on the nature of the process, of the objectives, and of the students themselves. *These inputs constitute the system's costs,* whether they are expressed in physical (real resource) terms or in financial (monetary and price) terms.

The Meaning of Efficiency and Productivity

These five features of an educational system and the relationships between them permit us now to define precisely what is meant by educational efficiency and productivity, terms which all too often are used vaguely and ambiguously.

Internal efficiency is the relationship between a system's outputs and the corresponding inputs that went into producing them.

Thus defined, an educational system's internal efficiency is expressed by its cost-effectiveness ratio (measuring effectiveness in this context by the system's immediate outputs as distinct from its ultimate benefits).

There are many potential ways to improve an educational system's efficiency, as we saw from some of the case studies and will see from other examples later. Generally speaking, they fall into three categories, according to the degree of change required in the present system. (1) Efficiency may be improved by changing the amounts, quality, and proportions of inputs, or by utilizing present inputs more intensively, without basically altering the system's existing form and technology or "production function." Examples would be: a change in the pupil-teacher ratio or the qualifications "mix" of teachers; the enrichment of instructional materials per pupil; the fuller utilization of buildings and equipment. (2) Going a step further, efficiency may be increased by modifying the system's basic design substantially, involving the introduction of distinctly new components and technologies (such as team teaching, instructional television, "programmed" self-instructional materials, or language laboratories). (3) A more radical approach to improving efficiency would be to design a brand new alternative "teaching-learning system" that differs radically from the conventional one. One could visualize, for example, creating a new system of home or on-the-job instruction involving correspondence and radio, self-instructional materials, and simple do-it-yourself laboratory kits and exercises.

It does not follow, of course, that *any* changes or innovations will improve efficiency; some may do quite the opposite. If 10 per cent more inputs are added per student, for example, and their learning improves by only 3 per cent, this may seem to be a successful change, but efficiency has actually declined because the costs have increased proportionately more than the outputs, worsening the cost-output ratio.

External productivity is a related but different concept from internal efficiency, the difference hinging on the distinction made earlier between immediate outputs and ultimate benefits.

An educational system's external productivity is the relationship between the cumulative benefits derived from it over a given period and the corresponding inputs used earlier (i.e. the costs or "investment" incurred) in producing these benefits. This relationship is what is meant by an educational system's *cost-benefit ratio* (or the benefit-cost ratio), a matter we will discuss more fully in Chapter 10.

Paradoxically, an educational system can have high internal efficiency yet low external productivity. This happens, for example, when an educational system spends its time and resources efficiently teaching the wrong things—wrong, that is, in terms of the real needs of the particular students in light of their environment and future prospects. (Requiring all Eskimo children to learn ancient Greek or tropical agriculture would be an extreme example.) It also happens when a system turns out far too many expensively trained specialists of certain types and too few of other types relative to the economy's manpower needs and demands. The first specialists may have been well trained, but if there are no jobs open in that field, the investment in their training will produce few benefits. The same resources devoted to training more of the scarce-type specialists would be far more productive.

Thus the relevance and "fitness" of what an educational system teaches students at a particular time and place has a major bearing on the system's ultimate productivity. Of course, there are also other determining factors that are external to the system, such as the ability of the economy to make efficient use of the nation's supply of educated manpower and the presence or absence of complementary forces of economic development. For example, human resources are plainly an essential ingredient for achieving a "green revolution," but if the other essential ingredients are missing (such as ample supplies of water, new seed strains, fertilizer, credit, and price supports), the educational efforts devoted to developing the necessary human resources for improved agricultural and rural development may be largely wasted. The ablest graduates of rural schools may simply head for the city, there to join the ranks of the educated unemployed, rather than becoming leaders of a rural and agricultural revolution. Education is a very important part of every "development package," but it is still only a part and cannot produce miracles in isolation.

We will consider later some of the practical problems encountered in trying to measure educational efficiency and productivity. One should have no illusions about the formidable difficulties involved. But the value of the systems approach just outlined does not stand or fall on whether it can be applied with caliper precision. It can be useful even in situations which defy all quantitative measurement. It is simply an intelligent way to approach educational problems, a way that forces one to ask the right questions and to examine the most critical relationships before reaching a final decision. Indeed, when a human activity *cannot* be measured precisely, there is all the more need to approach it with a systematic method of analysis which will focus attention upon and invite careful judgments about the critical issues and relationships *in lieu of* precise measurements.

Different Ways of Expressing Educational Costs

As we observed at the outset, and as our discussion of systems analysis demonstrates, educational costs standing alone have little meaning. It is only when they are seen as a critical link between the inputs of an educational system and its objectives, outputs, and benefits that they become a revealing indicator of how efficiently and effectively the system is functioning. And it is only with the aid of this larger perspective that cost analysis becomes a powerful tool for improving the performance and planning the future of any educational system.

At this point, however, we narrow our focus to study the nature of educational costs. In the ensuing chapters we will be using several different ways of expressing and measuring costs, and to avoid confusion it will be well to clarify these right here.

Resource costs vs. money costs. Educational inputs are expressed in terms of *real resource costs* when they are measured in physical units (e.g. number of teachers or teacher hours, number of textbooks, square feet of floor space, etc.). They can also be measured in terms of their monetary value and expressed as *financial* or *money costs.*

Total expenditures for a given budgetary period are a rough but useful indicator of the real resource inputs used by an educational system during that period, particularly when the expenditures are subdivided by categories of inputs (e.g. teacher salaries, other staff costs, instructional supplies, maintenance and repairs, board and room, construction of new buildings, etc.). We say *rough* indicator advisedly because official budgetary accounts invariably both overstate and understate the real situation, for reasons and in ways we will examine immediately below and in later chapters. The immediate point is that all budget figures and statements of expenditures should be used with extreme caution and discernment.

Current vs. constant prices. In periods of inflation, total expenditures expressed in the current prices and wages of each year convey an exaggerated impression of the increase in real resources going into education. For example, the 1970 budget may be twice as large as 1960 in financial terms, but if the prices and wages paid by education have risen 50 per cent in the interim, then real resources have actually increased by only one-third. To get to this truth it is necessary to convert the expenditures for each year into constant prices, that is, the price and wage structure prevailing in a selected "base year." This is done by applying a "deflator," based on an appropriate "educational price index" which shows how much prices and wages for educational inputs have moved up each year. To take the above example, if 1960 were selected as the base year it would be given an index value of 100, 1970 would have a value of 150, and the deflator would be $^{100}/_{150}$. Applying this deflator to 1970 educational expenditures (of say, $200 million in current prices against $100 million for 1960), the deflated figure for 1970 (in constant prices) would be only two-thirds of $200 million, or $133 million. Thus the *real* increase of 1970 over 1960 has been only one-third, not 100 per cent as the unadjusted expenditure figures imply.

Capital vs. current costs. It is also important to know whether the expenditure figures include capital outlays or cover only current costs. The distinction, though somewhat arbitrary, is highly important and is based on the length of service of various resource inputs. Current costs, by and large, relate to personnel services and to "consumable" supplies that are rendered or used up within one fiscal year and therefore must be regularly renewed (hence they are also called "recurrent costs" or "operating costs"). *Capital costs* relate to more durable items (land, buildings, equipment, etc.) that render useful services over a period of years if properly maintained (hence major repairs and maintenance are, strictly speaking, also capital costs since they prolong the useful life of capital items). Initial capital outlays (e.g. for a new university) involve large lump-sum expenditures (often financed by loans or grants) and may bulk large in total educational expenditures for a particular year. But when capital items are amortized over their useful lifetime and charged to each year of service, capital costs turn out to be only a modest fraction of total annual costs and of total cost per student.

The term total costs, properly used, means current *plus* capital costs for a given period.

Unit cost per student. This is a very handy measurement for many purposes, such as comparing costs as between different educational levels, institutions, geographic areas, or time periods. Unit cost per student is simply the total expenditure in a given period either for the whole system, or, more likely, for some particular part of it, divided by the number of students in the same educational category. Thus, for example, by properly breaking down over-all expenditures one can compute and compare unit costs (per student) as between rural and urban primary schools, primary and secondary schools, secondary general and secondary technical schools, institutions of different sizes, various university programs, and so forth. Such differentials provide important insights which are concealed by broader averages.

Unit costs are most often expressed in terms of per student *enrolled,* but for some purposes it is useful to calculate the unit cost per student *graduated.* Costs can also be related to a variety of other definable units such as teachers, schools, and space areas. The important thing is to know at all times precisely what "unit" is being measured, and to remember that it is an *average* figure for a defined group which may not be precisely accurate for any one member of the group.

Factor costs. These are simply the prices paid by education for its various "factors of production," that is, for its various resource inputs—teachers, supplies, equipment, and buildings. Since the prices of different inputs often behave quite differently and are determined by different forces, it is important to examine and treat them separately when projecting future costs. Factor costs may be expressed either in real or money terms, or in current or constant prices. But to be meaningful they must be tied to explicit physical and qualitative standards, such as a Grade A teacher, a square foot of floor space, or a gross of 8 × 12 writing tablets.

* * *

We apologize if this chapter has seemed a bit theoretical, but perhaps it will seem less so in retrospect as we apply the systems concept and the various definitions presented above to real life circumstances in the chapters that follow.

5 *The Determinants of Educational Costs*

In order to give sound guidance to policy-makers, educational planners must be able to make reasonably accurate forecasts of future educational costs as well as resources needed and resources likely to be available. To do this, they must understand the main determinants of educational costs and revenues, how these operate, how their future behavior can be forecast, and which of them are subject to control by educational managers.

Systems analysis can help planners to sort out and examine these various determinants and to shed light on the future by diagnosing the past. Any such diagnosis reveals the dynamic nature of these determinants. All sorts of factors and forces, constantly changing, combine to determine what it costs to put a youngster through school, his older brother through the university, or his father through a part-time training program. In similar manner, many dynamic factors determine the size of the revenues available to support these educational activities. It is evident, therefore, that educational planners should guard against the simplistic assumption that costs will remain constant or that revenues will grow at a steady pace—assumptions that could put their forecasts wide of the mark and mislead policy-makers into serious error.

In this chapter we will examine mainly those cost determinants that lie outside the educational system, beyond the immediate influence of educational authorities. We will look more closely in later chapters at the internal cost determinants, but a preliminary word about them is in order here. The internal determinants are closely allied to the technology employed by education and to the policies adopted, especially regarding the payment, deployment, and utilization of teachers.

The fact that education uses a highly "labor intensive" technology involving heavy human resource inputs and relatively small physical inputs explains why more than 60 per cent (and sometimes as much as 90 per cent) of total educational costs is often accounted for by staff costs. This in turn explains why a decision to reduce the size of classes and the pupil-teacher ratio, or to upgrade the qualifications profile of the teaching force, or to improve the terms of employment of teachers, can send the unit costs per student soaring upward. From one of our Soviet Union case studies we learn, for example, that a nationwide change in average class size in elementary schools by only one student would raise or reduce the budget by 17 million rubles.[1]

So much for now about internal cost determinants; let us turn to an examination of the external ones, principally by observing their behavior in recent years and considering the implications for the future.

In the two decades from 1950 to 1970, total educational expenditures in most nations, rich and poor, rose remarkably, by five to tenfold. This meant that educational outlays typically grew two or three times as fast as national incomes and total public expenditures. Accordingly, education's percentage share of the Gross National Product and of the total public budget in many countries doubled or trebled during this period. Figure 5.1 illustrates what happened in ten sample countries in fifteen years from 1950 to 1965.

What were the main causes of this unprecedented increase in educational costs? How are these determinants likely to behave in future years? And what are the implications for educational planning? It will be convenient to examine these questions under

1. V. I. Basov, "U.S.S.R.: Estimating the Annual Budget Requirements of the Educational System," in *Educational Cost Analysis in Action: Case Studies for Planners*, Vol. I, Paris, Unesco:IIEP, 1972.

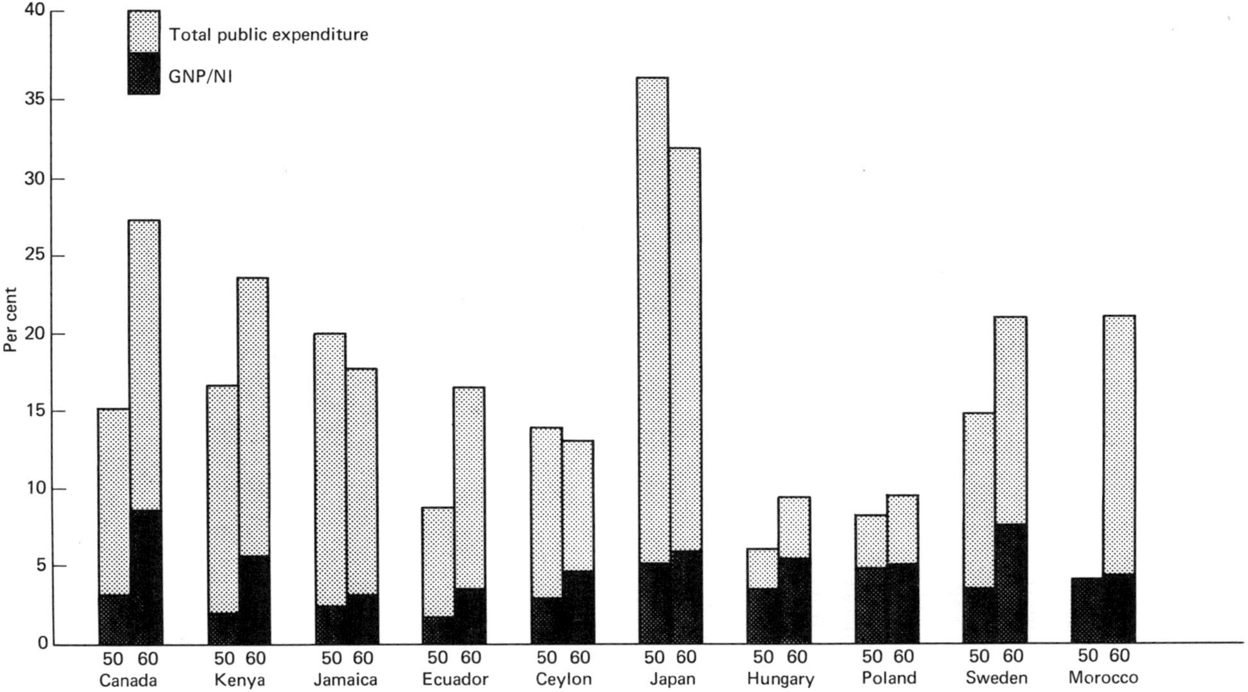

FIGURE 5.1.
Over-all public educational expenditure as percentage of GNP/NI and of total public expenditure.

five headings: (1) inflation; (2) educational demand; (3) the factor costs of education; (4) educational revenues; and (5) foreign aid.

The Impact of Inflation on Education

A substantial part of the impressive rise in educational expenditures from 1950 to 1970 was not "real"; part of it—somewhat less than half in most countries—reflected the inflation of prices and wages.

This suggests that planners and cost analysts, especially in inflation-prone countries (as in much of Latin America), should keep a sharp weather eye on inflationary tendencies, for even mild inflations can play havoc with educational systems. Their budgets and salaries almost invariably lag behind the general rise in prices and wages, thereby robbing education's real purchasing power and reducing its ability to attract and hold good teachers and administrators. Wherever inflationary forces are present, it is advisable for planners to explore the implications of alternative assumptions about the future behavior of prices and wages, and to prepare contingency plans for use in the event of a higher rate of inflation than envisaged by the official educational plan.[2]

The fact should also be faced that education is not merely a victim of inflation; it is often an important contributor to the very inflation that hurts it. Rapidly rising educational expenditures often constitute 20 to 25 per cent of the whole government budget, and when, as is typically the case, one of the main causes of inflation is a large excess of government spending over receipts, then education, knowingly or not, is one of the guilty parties. This is worth remembering the next time the Finance Ministry's popularity index plummets to a new low because the Ministry is slashing everyone's budget proposals deeply in its war against inflation.

2. We suggest also that they seek the aid of local economists to construct two educational price indexes of the sort described in Chapter 4, one for current items (including teacher costs), the other for capital items, since the two sets of costs often behave quite differently.

Educational systems have a big stake in defeating inflation and what may seem like a budgetary sacrifice in the short run may be a boon to education in the long run if it helps to halt an inflation.

The Impact of Rising Demand on the Costs of Education

Inflation aside, certainly the greatest cause of the sharp rise in over-all educational expenditures from 1950 to 1970 was the explosive increase in demand for education. Four main factors underlying this increase are worth noting for what they can tell us about the future: (1) the record-breaking increases in the youth *population* (which were inadequately allowed for in setting educational expansion targets in many developing nations); (2) a "revolution of rising *expectations*" on the part of millions of families long deprived of educational opportunities and who now regarded education as the key to individual advancement; (3) the widespread adoption of public policies aimed at *democratizing educational opportunities*—virtually all developing nations in the early 1960's adopted the goal of universal primary education by 1980 or sooner, while many industrialized nations extended compulsory school attendance into secondary education and encouraged higher participation rates in post-secondary education; and (4) the rapid expansion, upgrading, and diversification of *manpower requirements* due to technological advances in the economy, a new emphasis of public policy on economic development, and a clearer recognition of education's role in economic growth.

Educational systems everywhere, faced with a tidal wave of demand coming from these four forces, had no choice but to expand their enrolments as rapidly as possible. What followed is well known.

In most countries education was granted a favorable claim on national resources to make the expansion possible (hence the impressive rise in the percentage of public budgets going to education). Even so, resources could not keep pace with the rising need and therefore became spread thinner and thinner over more and more students. In the terms of our systems analysis, there was a watering down of inputs per student, taking the form of overcrowded classrooms, a decline in the teacher-student ratio and in the qualifications of the teaching force, and a shorter supply per student of textbooks, instructional materials, laboratory equipment, and other learning aids. Often the most serious bottleneck was not money *per se* but a physical shortage of the real resources needed by education, especially qualified personnel willing to teach and construction capacity to build new facilities.

All this had far-reaching effects on the internal costs of educational systems and on their cost effectiveness. The watering down of inputs, taken by itself, tended to reduce costs per student, but this tendency was usually more than offset by rising "factor costs" —particularly increases in teacher salaries to keep pace with rising wages and salaries elsewhere in the economy in order that education's competitive position in the tight manpower market would not deteriorate further. Thus, on balance, the real costs per student rose, even as educational effectiveness in many cases declined.

This phenomenon of rising costs and declining effectiveness is best evidenced by the sharp rise in "dropouts" and "repeaters" that occurred in many educational systems and still goes on. This is due, however, not only to the inadequacy of educational resources but also to the broadening clientele of schools, including large numbers of children from uneducated homes who present a much greater pedagogical challenge than the schools yet know how to cope with. The high rate of dropouts and repeaters results in sharply higher costs and a heavy waste of scarce educational resources. The high repetition rate means that the actual time taken by many children to complete a normal six-year primary program is seven or eight years, which has the effect of increasing by one-sixth to one-third the total cost of putting one child through primary school. Worse still, if the costs of the dropouts are figured in, the total outlay per actual "graduate" often amounts to the equivalent cost of fifteen to twenty pupil years. One must recognize, of course, so as not to exaggerate the point, that many dropouts undoubtedy carry away something useful from their unfinished school experience. Yet the great majority, who lea before gaining permanent literacy, must unfortunately be as investments of dubious value. In any event, the objecti schools is certainly not to produce dropouts; it is to produce "finishers," and by this criterion their cost-effectiveness ratio must be judged very low.

What about the future? How are the four "demand" factors mentioned above likely to affect educational costs and effectiveness in coming years?

Population. The first factor, the rising school age population, has by now subsided in most industrialized countries, but in most developing nations it continues at the galloping rate of a 2.5 to 3 per cent increase per year. This means that before the schools and universities in these countries can even begin to raise their participation rates (i.e. the percentage of each corresponding age group actually attending school), they must absorb this large annual population increment. They must, in other words, run fast just to stand still. This alone will inevitably absorb a substantial part of whatever annual budgetary increases they can get. As a result, the attainment of the cherished goal of universal primary education is receding farther into the distance for many poor countries.[3]

Educational planners in such nations will obviously do well to consult demographic experts very carefully before projecting future enrolments and costs and before advising policy-makers on what is and is not feasible.

Rising popular demand. The second and most powerful demand factor—the "revolution of rising expectations"—shows every sign of continuing and perhaps exerting an even stronger influence in the future on educational costs and budgets. From all indications the popular hunger for education seems to keep right on growing. In many developing nations the great majority of young people are still not getting a full primary schooling. Equally important

3. The IIEP has recently completed an international study of the impact of various rates of population increase on educational resource requirements and costs, which will be published shortly.

—and this applies to industrialized nations as well—those who do get some education want more and more, if not for themselves, then for their children. The demand for education feeds on itself once educational expansion gets moving, and this process is now in full swing all over the world. As more youngsters complete primary school, more will want to go to secondary school, then on to higher education. This phenomenon occurs irrespective of the economy's ability to support the rising educational demand or to absorb the increased output of educated people into jobs befitting their education and training.

Thus the real question for educational planners and policy-makers in the years ahead is not whether the social demand for education will continue to spiral, for it surely will, but how to cope with this continuously rising demand in the face of limited educational resources. Some excruciating choices will have to be faced, and whatever ones are made, they will have far-reaching consequences for educational costs.

Democratization of opportunity. The third demand-increasing factor—the spread of public policies aimed at democratizing educational opportunity—requires little comment. It would be our guess that these policies are irreversible and here to stay. Perhaps, as some argue, they were pushed too hard and too soon in the first place, without enough consideration being given to their enormous cost implications. Be that as it may, this is now water over the dam. The best that most leaders can probably do is to avoid exacerbating the problem further by making fresh promises and setting deadlines that clearly are not feasible. The democratization of educational opportunity, after all, is an eminently worthy objective. The problem, if there is one, arises not from the objective but from the timetables chosen to implement it, and these in many instances will no doubt have to be stretched out. But the very existence of these policies, for better or for worse, will surely continue to exert a strong upward pressure on educational demand, budget, and costs.

Manpower requirements. The fourth and final demand-raising factor of the 1950's and 1960's—the ravenous appetite of many economic systems for more educated manpower—had begun to reverse sharply by 1970. By then educational systems had managed to catch up with unmet manpower demands and gone on to produce "surpluses," judged at least by what the employment market was able to absorb, as distinct from what the economy theoretically "needed."

The consequent "softening" of employment markets for high-level manpower has had the effect of diminishing or eliminating teacher shortages as better qualified candidates have become available in larger numbers at prevailing salaries. Thus, in one country after another, schools and universities have become increasingly able to get better quality for their money—provided they have posts to fill and the money to fill them. This does not reduce teacher costs in financial terms, since the salary structure remains the same or rises, but it does, in effect, lower the cost of well-qualified teachers and tends to increase the cost-effectiveness ratio.

Another aspect of this shift in the manpower picture is less encouraging. If an educational system goes on producing high-cost specialists for whom there are no appropriate jobs, the benefits will decline in relation to the costs, making such education a poorer investment for all concerned. Part of the solution may be to redeploy the same educational resources in more rewarding directions, but a no less important part in many cases is to remedy the defects of the economy itself so it will generate more employment. This whole matter of employment for the educated promises to be a towering issue in the 1970's. It has a host of implications for educational costs and benefits.

Market Forces That Influence Education's Factor Costs

Turning from rising educational demand as the prime mover of rising educational expenditures, let us now look at education as a purchaser of goods and services and at how the prices education must pay for its inputs get determined.

Like any other buyer, education has to pay the going market

rates and usually gets only what it pays for. This is true even when education "sets its own price," as in establishing a teacher salary structure or a cost ceiling on a new building. For example, if education offers an identical salary for humanities teachers and science teachers, but the former are abundant and the latter very scarce, then education can hope to fill its humanities posts with well-qualified teachers (who have few, if any, better options), but most of its science posts will either go begging or become filled with poorly qualified people. Similarly, if a school system decides to set an $800,000 cost limit on a new building which would actually cost $1,000,000 to build under present market conditions, it will end up either with less of a building for $800,000 or with no building at all.

In short, education's input prices generally get determined by the interplay of forces in the market or, in the case of centrally controlled "non-market" economies, by government authorities who fix prices for the economy at large, and where necessary use allocation controls to divide scarce supplies among competing users.

There is an important qualification to be made, however, now that educational systems have become "big business" in most countries and hence major buyers of goods and services. In these circumstances their own buying practices exert a large influence on certain market prices which both they and other buyers have to pay. Thus, for example, if the educational system, as the largest buyer of books in a market economy, suddenly doubles its purchases, this could well affect the general market price of books, either up or down, depending on the capacity, cost conditions, and degree of competition in the book industry.

Similarly, a large educational construction program, launched at a time when the construction industry is already operating close to full capacity, could push up the costs of construction for education and everyone else. Obviously the best time to build is when the construction industry is partly idle and anxious for more business, but education is usually in a hurry and cannot wait for more favorable terms.

If education as a large buyer in the marketplace acts blindly, it will get a good deal less for its money. But if it is a careful and well-informed buyer, and a good negotiator, it can often use its large buying power to get better prices and quality, and thus a maximum for its money. A clever educational purchasing agent can save the system many times his salary, provided he is not too hemmed in by archaic rules and red tape that keep him from being an effective buyer.

Education systems in developing countries need to be especially sharp in buying equipment abroad which cannot be supplied locally. They need to "shop around" and get the best value they can, taking full advantage of competition among supplier nations. But when buying new equipment they need to keep in view the later problem of replacement parts and maintenance. If they get too many brands of equipment from too many sources, each brand needing its own special replacement parts, they will have to carry a large inventory of spare parts or else risk having much of their equipment idle much of the time awaiting delivery of parts; either way it is a costly affair.

As already emphasized, education is first and foremost a heavy buyer of human services. Being both a consumer and a producer of high-level manpower (unlike other industries, which are simply users), educational systems are inextricably tied to the national manpower market on both their input and output side and therefore exposed to whatever winds, fair or foul, blow across the manpower scene. We will examine the implications of this when we come to a discussion of teacher costs in Chapter 8.

Forces That Determine Educational Revenues

The ultimate determinant and limit on educational costs, from a financial point of view, is the amount of revenue an educational system has available to spend each year. What determines this?

Some educational administrators might quickly reply, "The Finance Ministry, which never gives us enough!" Perhaps it appears so, seen at short range from an institutional vantage point, but the real determinants of educational revenues run much wider and deeper. They include in particular: (1) competing public needs and priorities; (2) the economy's rate of growth; (3) the sources of education's revenues and how these respond to changes in national income; and (4) the ups and downs of foreign trade, especially in countries that depend heavily on raw-materials exports. We will look briefly at each of these.

COMPETING PUBLIC NEEDS AND PRIORITIES

Education obviously enjoyed a relatively high-priority claim on total public revenues in the 1950's and 1960's in most countries. The acid proof is that, despite many other pressing public needs, education's share of the total expanded, at the sacrifice of other things.

But this steady and substantial increase in education's percentage share cannot go on indefinitely, for the simple reason that corresponding shrinkage in the shares going to other public needs will meet increasing resistance. In point of fact, the rising curve of education's share of the public budget had already begun to taper off in a number of countries by the end of the 1960's. In some others the curve had flattened altogether or even begun to turn down. In a minority of cases where the curve had never moved up significantly there still remained a large cushion for increasing educational budgets, if and when national priorities shifted in that direction.

This slowing down in the rate of growth of educational revenues will exert a progressive squeeze on educational systems, a squeeze compounded by rising unit costs, which must also be anticipated.[4]

THE IMPORTANCE OF ECONOMIC GROWTH TO EDUCATION

Even when the percentage of total public revenues allocated to education becomes stabilized in any country, it does not follow that the educational budget will grow no more. It simply means that its future growth will have to stay in line with the growth of

4. For a fuller analysis of this point, see P. H. Coombs, *The World Educational Crisis: A Systems Analysis*, New York, Oxford University Press, 1968, Chapters II and IV.

over-all public revenues, which in turn will depend in large measure on the growth of the economy. But the annual increments to the education budget are likely to be smaller than before, leaving less latitude for new undertakings, expansion, and improvement. If in the past the education budget has been growing 10 to 15 per cent each year, let us say, against an average annual growth of 5 per cent in total public revenues (a fairly typical picture), then a reduction to a 5 per cent increase for education means a serious cutback. The difficulty is that educational demand will go right on expanding, compounded by the population explosion in many cases, and unit costs will go right on rising, quite independently of this slowdown in budget increases.

In the circumstances educational systems will have only three routes of escape from this suffocating squeeze. First, they can find new supplemental sources of income—for example, greater local government contributions, increased private fees and gifts, special education levies on industry, etc. Second, they can adopt far-reaching innovations and efficiency measures designed to hold down unit costs while still permitting quality to rise. Third, they can hope for a high rate of national economic growth.

The last of these deserves special comment. *In the last analysis it is mainly from increases in the national income that increases in educational revenues must come.* The seemingly, small difference between an economic growth rate of 4 per cent and 6 per cent a year can readily make a difference of 50 per cent in the amount of the annual increases in the education budget.

But there is a proviso here which educators need to understand very clearly. If a nation is to accelerate its economic growth, it must increase its rate of saving (that is, it must decrease its rate of consumption) in order to raise its rate of investment in additional productive facilities—in industry, agriculture, transportation, power and so forth. Such an increase in so-called "productive investment," at least for the time being, is likely to be in part at the expense of education because limited investment funds cannot be used in two places at once. Eventually, of course, the resulting growth of the economy will permit educational needs to be more fully met, but this is little comfort to the beleaguered educational administrator who has too many eager candidates knocking on the door *right now*.

It is true, of course, that education itself can lay claim to being an important contributor to economic growth and thus a legitimate petitioner for more investment funds. In order to grow, an economy must have not only ample amounts of developed human resources of the right sorts but also favorable institutional, social, and political environment. To the extent that education helps furnish these human and environmental prerequisites, which it unquestionably does, it too can be considered a "good investment in economic growth".

But this case must not be pressed too far, to the point of insisting that *all* educational activities and that *any amount* of additional educational expenditures will contribute as much or more to economic growth as some alternative uses of the same resources. This plainly is not true. Some education contributes nothing to economic growth, or to anything else for that matter, because it is the wrong kind of education for the place and time; it may even be counter-productive and deter national development. Other education contributes to economic development only indirectly and only after a long lapse of time, due to the long "production cycle" involved. But some education, such as work-oriented training programs related to real employment needs and opportunities, can have a prompt and substantial payoff in terms of early economic growth.

This is not an argument for supporting only that education which is keyed directly to economic growth in the near future. Such a policy would be shortsighted and self-defeating. It is rather to caution against overplaying the economic growth case for education to the point of making it specious. The issue is one of balance, timing, and relevance. When an educational system gets too far out of harmony with the rest of its economy and society, it is headed for serious trouble, which is just what has already happened in scores of countries.[5]

The often thankless task of national planners and decision-makers is to mediate between present and future needs, and among

5. *Ibid.*

the rival claims of economic growth, education, health, housing, national security, and so forth, trying their best through a process of compromise and trade-offs to strike a tolerable balance between, on the one hand, satisfying the most urgent immediate needs of society and, on the other, building an enlarged economic base for serving all such needs more amply in the future.

THE ELASTICITY AND DIVERSITY OF EDUCATION'S REVENUES

A further important determinant of an educational system's revenues is the nature of its sources of income—how they respond to changes in national income, how diversified and how well administered they are, and how reliable they are likely to be in the future. This is a subject on which educational planners and leaders must now become more sophisticated than they have ever had to be before.

Since the Second World War most educational systems have become far more dependent than previously upon public revenues, as governments have accepted prime responsibility for broadening educational opportunities and as private education has proved increasingly unable to shoulder the expanded burden. A similar shift of financial responsibility from local to central governments has taken place in many countries. This has given educational systems a large stake in the efficacy of government fiscal structures and placed them in more direct competition with other national needs and services sustained by central government budgets.

One critical question is how responsive the government's fiscal structure is to changes in national income. When a nation's economy grows, say, at 6 per cent a year, public revenues do not necessarily grow proportionately. They may grow faster or slower, depending on what economists call the "elasticity of revenues in relation to national income." [6]

Obviously, from education's point of view, a revenue structure

6. When this ratio is less than unity, revenues are "relatively inelastic," meaning that they change at a slower rate than national income. When the ratio is greater than unity, the revenues are "elastic," meaning that revenues over-respond to a change in national income.

with a high elasticity is highly desirable (at least when national income is rising, though not if it should fall). A progressive income tax, for example, is very helpful in this respect, because as individual and corporate incomes rise, an increasing percentage is claimed by taxes. But progressive income tax laws are still rare in developing countries and, even where they exist, are often poorly enforced. Land taxes are much more common, but these, unfortunately, are among the most inelastic; they tend to lag far behind inflation, real increases of national income, and advances in land values. Consumer sales taxes, payroll taxes, and import and export taxes, also relatively common among developing nations, fall between these extremes.

Too great a dependence on a single source of revenue, whether from the central or local government, can lead an educational system into trouble. In the United States, for example, public schools traditionally depended almost entirely on (inelastic) local real estate taxes, but in the period of rapid educational expansion after World War II, this local tax base became a critical constraint. State governments (whose revenues typically came from more elastic consumer sales taxes and income taxes) were obliged to step in and provide a growing share of local school support. Even this proved inadequate, especially in the lower-income states, and pressures built up for the federal government, with the most elastic tax base of all, to share in school finance (even though, under the U.S. Constitution, education is the exclusive responsibility of state and local governments).

Nigeria's experience is also instructive. Before independence, primary and secondary schools in Nigeria were largely supported by private fees, gifts, and local taxes. But, immediately after independence, the federal government rapidly assumed the lion's share of responsibility for school expansion, at first using for this purpose a cocoa stabilization fund which had accumulated over the years. But when the "Cocoa Fund" was exhausted, schools found their local revenue base weakened and they were forced into severe competition with other public needs, all seeking larger shares of the overstrained national budget.

Developing nations should take note that today's industrialized nations, such as France, that finance their schools largely from the central government's coffers, did not always do so. It was only as the economy and tax system grew in strength that the central government gradually absorbed more of the expanded educational burden from local communities. Even today, however, state and local taxes and private fees remain a substantial source of educational support in most industrialized nations. It is noteworthy also that in recent years the Soviet government has encouraged increasing financial contributions to education from industrial enterprises, farmer organizations, and other sources to supplement revenues coming from the central treasury. Less economically developed nations that too quickly concentrate the full financial load of education on the central government are likely to end up handicapping both education and other public services.

In brief, if educational systems, whether in rich or poor nations, are to have sufficient resources for further expansion and improvement in coming years, they will have to secure supplementary income from private sources, industry, and all levels of government. Only in this way can they broaden and diversify their financial base, improve its income elasticity, and circumvent the revenue bottlenecks that inevitably arise when education depends too heavily on a single source of financial support. This will be essential even if the nation's economy maintains a high rate of growth; it will be absolutely imperative if it does not.[7]

THE INFLUENCE OF FOREIGN TRADE ON EDUCATION REVENUES

A special word is needed about the potential vulnerability of educational systems in developing countries whose economic prosperity and public revenues depend heavily on raw-materials exports. Such exports not only sustain domestic employment and income, they earn precious "foreign exchange" to purchase capital

7. The IIEP intends to publish in the near future the initial results of its international research project on financing education which gives major attention to possible supplemental sources of educational revenues.

equipment for economic growth, to service foreign debts, and sometimes to meet food deficits. A commodity export tax has the advantage of being relatively easy to administer. But it can also be a very fickle source of revenue, especially in "one-commodity" countries that rely heavily, for example, on exports of rubber or copper or jute or rice or coffee whose world price is subject to fluctuations that create a "feast or famine" situation. Even a seemingly moderate swing in the world price can have a multiplier effect (either up or down) on public revenues, national income, and employment levels.

Beyond this, raw-materials exporting countries tend to experience a longer-term worsening of their *terms of trade*, meaning that the prices they pay for imported industrial goods gradually increase relative to the prices they receive for their exports, thereby reducing their real purchasing power in world markets. To compound their vulnerability, their particular raw material may be exposed to substitution by new synthetics made elsewhere (the case, for example, with rubber and jute).

In short, educational systems in raw-materials exporting countries that depend heavily on central government revenues are inherently in a precarious economic position (save perhaps those well endowed with rich oil deposits). Their educational planners and policy-makers will be well advised to take into account the workings of international trade, for whether their primary school children have textbooks to read five years from now, or their university science laboratories have equipment, may well depend on the price of copper or coffee in markets thousands of miles away.

The Influence of Foreign Aid

External assistance to developing nations coming through multilateral and bilateral channels can have a sizable impact on both the revenue and expenditure side of their educational equation.

The sum total of such aid in any one year constitutes but a small fraction of total educational outlays in most developing countries (a few African nations are exceptions). But, if well directed, such aid can have an importance all out of proportion to its apparent size, particularly by filling strategic gaps that the recipient nations cannot yet fill themselves, and by supplying the research and development resources to initiate needed reforms and innovations. There can be little doubt that external aid, despite various shortcomings, was an important boon to educational development in the 1950's and 1960's and will continue for a long time to be essential. Indeed in certain countries, especially in Africa, the sudden termination of such aid would virtually collapse whole sectors of the educational system, especially at higher levels where heavy reliance on expatriate teachers cannot be quickly ended.

But experience has shown that foreign aid is not always an unmixed blessing; it can in some circumstances seriously disrupt educational plans, raise costs, and place severe strains on local educational revenues. This can happen, for instance, when a recipient nation, in anticipation of major outside help, makes substantial complementary investments of its own (it might, for example, build new schools, expecting outside help on teacher training and books), but then the outside help does not come through, or it comes through too late to be of maximum use.

A more egregious and all too familiar case is where an outside gift, made with the best of intentions but with too little insight, ends up costing the recipient nation more than if it had never received the gift. This happens when the gift entails transplanting an ill-fitting educational model which does not match the recipient nation's needs or, at any rate, does not fit its pocketbook, and yet thereafter imposes a continuing heavy burden of operating costs on the local educational budget.

* * *

In this chapter we have explored the major determinants of educational costs and revenues—particularly those lying outside the system and beyond the immediate control of educational authorities—drawing upon the experiences of the 1950's and 1960's and attempting to forecast how some of these determinants may behave in the future. The clear prospect for most of the world is that the mounting pressure of educational demands, combined with a growing economic squeeze created by rising unit costs and a slowdown in the growth of educational revenues, will confront educational systems with problems of crisis proportions. If cost analysts are to make a maximum contribution to the solution of these problems, they must not only know what determines educational costs but also how such costs behave under various conditions—a subject to which we now turn our attention.

6 *Common Behavior Patterns of Educational Costs*

Educational costs vary greatly, not only from one country to another but within the same country, between formal and non-formal education, and, in formal education, among different types, levels, and geographic areas, among similar institutions and programs, and even within the same institution for different parts of the curriculum and different points in time.

Yet despite these cost differentials, the *behavior* of costs is strikingly similar in virtually all educational systems. This is due not only to the influence of certain economic principles at work everywhere but also to the fact that educational systems the world over operate on the basis of quite similar fundamental technologies, logistics, underlying pedagogical premises, and conventional wisdom. These have a profound influence on the economics of education, so much so that changing the behavior of costs is likely to require changing some fondly-held beliefs and practices.

The Dominance of Personnel Costs

The salaries of teachers, administrators, and ancillary personnel vary enormously from one country to another, yet in all countries the same general pattern holds: personnel costs, teacher costs in particular, dominate total educational costs. This stems from the fact, already mentioned, that education is a labor-intensive industry. In contrast to most modern industries, it uses a predominantly handicraft technology and therefore does not benefit from the higher labor productivity made possible elsewhere by combining growing amounts of capital and advanced technology with declining amounts of human resources.

This pattern is reaffirmed by a number of the IIEP cost studies. For example:

• In the U.S.S.R. nearly *three-quarters* of all state expenditures on primary and general secondary education in 1965 went for salaries and wages, barely *one-eighth* for all other current costs and *one-sixth* for capital costs (including repairs).

• In Ceylon, the combined personnel costs for primary and secondary education in 1968 represented 94 per cent of the current unit cost per student.

• In Morocco, an estimated 95 per cent of *total* costs (including capital costs) for a sample of secondary schools in 1967–68 were *current* costs, and of these current costs, salaries represented over 98 per cent.

The above figures for Ceylon and Morocco overstate the situation for the world at large but are not unusual for developing countries, which in general spend a higher percentage of their total school budgets on teacher costs than do richer countries. These poorer countries not only have far more stringent budgets, but the insistent pressures for more teachers and for higher teacher salaries eat away at provisions for textbooks, supplies, and other current items. The net effect is to upset the balance of inputs which most educators consider desirable. It was this imbalance, regarded as harmful to educational quality and teacher effectiveness, that prompted Asian Ministers of Education to agree that the Unesco Asian Model should aim by 1980 to reduce the proportion of recurrent costs going into teacher salaries to only 80 per cent for primary schools and 75 per cent for secondary schools.

The Inexorable Rise of Unit Costs

A second common pattern is the long-term rising trend of unit costs. Inflation aside, the real costs of education per student appear to have been on the upswing in most nations for years (with certain short-lived exceptions to be noted later), and the prospect is that they will keep rising in the future. This is borne out repeatedly by our case studies and other evidence, and the main reasons are clear enough.

First and foremost, the real incomes of teachers must follow the real income of equally qualified people in other employment if educational systems are to win their share of talent to produce new generations of talent. Industries with advancing technologies and hence rising labor productivity set the salary pace for other employers, and education must keep in step even if its own labor productivity is not rising. The result is rising costs for the same quality of teacher.

There are important exceptions to this rule, however, mainly in developing countries where scarcities of educated manpower initially produced an abnormally wide spread between the wages of common workers and the salaries of teachers and similar educated manpower. In such situations, for reasons we will examine in Chapter 8, the real salaries of teachers are likely to decline in the long run, relative to average wages and per capita income, until a more viable balance is reached. The contrast between teacher salaries in India and East Africa, which we will consider later, is instructive on this point.

Any such tendency for teacher salaries to decline in such instances, however, is likely to be more than offset by opposite cost-increasing tendencies, stemming especially from efforts to bolster quality—an objective to which these same nations are now firmly committed. A further factor, operative virtually everywhere, is the "cost creep" which is built into teacher salary structures in the form of automatic promotion based on years of service.

Thus, the long-run outlook everywhere—allowing for interim adjustments in special cases—is for a gradual upward march of unit costs per student, whether or not quality also rises. Theoretically, some drastically new educational designs and technologies could reverse this inexorable trend, but they are not yet in sight. The most that can be hoped for, by and large, from today's frontier technologies of education is simply to slow down the rate of increase in unit costs.

The Stability of Educational Cost Structures

While it is true that dynamic changes are constantly taking place in educational costs, the broad structure within which they occur shows some stability over time. Judging from the evidence available, the heavy proportion of teacher inputs relative to non-teacher recurrent inputs and capital inputs appears to have changed little, if any, over the years. For example, Blaug shows that salary costs in British universities had the same percentage relation to total costs in 1962 as in 1952 (though "rental of capital" showed a substantial percentage decline, offset by a rise in "other goods and services").[1]

The stability of educational cost structures reflects primarily the stability of educational technologies and practices and the hidden assumptions on which they are founded—such as the assumption that class size and the pupil-teacher ratio is the most critical determinant of how much is learned. Considering the great economic size and social importance of educational enterprises today, and their evident need to re-examine old premises and search for new practices, there has been remarkably little investment in research and development aimed at improving their performance. Until this neglect is corrected, there is every reason to expect educational cost structures to continue on their customary course, and for education—good or bad—to become increasingly expensive.

Higher Costs at Higher Levels

Another common pattern relates to the differential costs between different levels and types of education. As a general rule,

1. M. Blaug, "Comparative Analysis of Educational Expenditures in Member Countries Since 1950: Case Study of the United Kingdom" (OECD, DAS/EID/69.4, March 1969, mimeographed).

unit costs rise with each successive education level, and scientific and technical training at whatever level is more costly than general education. A linked characteristic is that non-teacher costs become a higher proportion of total unit costs as the total increases.

The figures from Thailand in Table 6.1 bring out this common behavior pattern (the contrasts would be even greater if capital costs were included):

TABLE 6.1.
Estimated recurrent expenditures per student in Thailand by level and type (1964) (in Thai bahts).

	(1) TOTAL RECURRENT COST	(2) PERSONNEL COST	(2) AS A PERCENTAGE OF (1)
Primary education	261	240	92
Secondary general	1005	874	87
Technical and vocational	2367	1685	71
Teacher training	3138	2206	70
Higher education	9423	5437	58
Average—all levels	383	314	82

Note: At the time of the case study, the rate of exchange was $1 = 20.8 bahts.

Source: H. W. Reiff, "Thailand: The Use of Cost Analysis in Estimating the Total Cost of an Educational Plan and Testing Its Feasibility," in *Educational Cost Analysis in Action: Case Studies for Planners*, Vol. I, Paris, Unesco:IIEP, 1972.

Several obvious factors account for the higher unit costs and higher percentage of non-teacher costs in secondary and higher education. Teachers are higher paid than in primary schools and teach fewer hours; pupil-teacher ratios are lower; more expensive equipment and larger libraries are required; and, not least important, there are often sizable board and room costs and student grants. Despite these routine explanations, however, one is still prompted by the figures showing extreme cost differentials between primary, secondary, and higher education to wonder whether they make good sense and are really necessary, or whether in fact they reflect a poor deployment and inefficient use of overall educational resources. It is an arresting fact, for example, that in Thailand (which is not an exceptional case among developing nations) the cost per year for one university student is equivalent to the cost of 9.4 secondary students or 36 elementary students. One of the important functions of cost analysis is to bring such facts to light, in order to stimulate re-examination of the causes and justification of unusually high educational costs.

Similar searching questions might well be raised regarding the unusually high costs of technical and scientific training. The easy explanation, of course, is that smaller classes and more expensive equipment, laboratories, and supplies are needed in these subjects. But is this the whole of the story, or even the bulk of it? How does one explain, for example, the paradox that science and technology have done so much to raise human productivity and to lower economic costs in so many other fields, yet have done so little along these lines within the academic home of science and technology? We do not pretend to have answers, nor is it essential to our present purpose; we cite the high costs of scientific and technological training as illustrative of the sometimes uncomfortable issues which cost analysis can usefully provoke in the interest of getting better results from available educational resources.

Economies of Scale: A Major Key to Improved Efficiency

In many kinds of educational situations, unit costs decline as the size of the activity expands, to the point where the economies of scale are exhausted (and where possibly dis-economies of size set in). This phenomenon of declining unit costs is an important basis for improving the cost effectiveness of education in a variety of circumstances. It must be remembered, however, that what may be an improvement in economic efficiency may not always be an improvement in educational efficiency; the two sets of considerations must be weighed against each other and an appropriate accommodation reached. In other words it is a matter not of maximizing educational results but of optimizing them within set cost limits.

In the case of school consolidation, educational and economic advantages largely coincide. We have seen, for example, that both Norway and the U.S.S.R. intend to consolidate their small rural schools into larger units in order to get better over-all educational results at lower costs per student (though some educators might argue that *some* educational sacrifices are made when a child is obliged to travel to a distant school rather than walking to a more intimate-sized one in his own village).

A similar consolidation movement in the United States reduced the total number of independent school districts from more than 80,000 in 1950 to fewer than 20,000 by 1970. Even then, there still remained further consolidating to do, for in 1970 four states still had more than 1000 separate school districts each, many of them too small to provide good education at a feasible cost.[2]

Ireland similarly determined in the early 1960's that its small village schools had substantially higher costs per student but were apparently producing poorer results than somewhat larger schools. These findings precipitated a school consolidation program that had had substantial results by 1970.[3]

The need to achieve efficient-sized educational units is even more imperative above the primary level where the curriculum is broader and more specialized, requiring a more diversified staff and more expensive equipment and facilities. As a general rule, the more advanced the level and the more scientific or technical the program, the larger the institution's size must be to achieve acceptable costs and a satisfactory educational program.

A secondary school, for example, or a teacher training college, requires a certain minimum complement of specialized teachers, equipment, library books, and relatively expensive supplies to support a satisfactory curriculum, in contrast to an elementary school where each teacher usually handles a variety of subjects with much

2. Statistics of the U.S. Office of Education in *American Education*, August-September 1970, p. 37.

3. *Investment in Education—Ireland*, OECD, 1966, Part III, Chapter 9.

simpler equipment. Unless there is a sufficient number of secondary students or teacher trainees enrolled in each grade level and subject (such as chemistry or physics or mathematics) to utilize fully the capacity of teachers and facilities, these subjects become too expensive to offer. This explains why the Soviet Union is building many secondary boarding schools for rural students under its program of compulsory secondary education, and why many African countries are obliged to have boarding schools. Up to a point, it is cheaper to transport day students from a wide area, but beyond a certain radius boarding facilities become essential.[4]

Technical schools present an even greater problem to operate at an optimum scale. One which offers training in several different crafts may be impossible to staff or finance unless enough students are enrolled in each skill area. Lebanon discovered through cost analysis that the best solution to this problem was to have each trade school specialize in only two or three fields, and to send students from all parts of the country to whichever school fitted their needs. Even when boarding costs were added in, this proved a cheaper way to get good quality results.[5]

The problem of "optimum size" presents the greatest difficulties at the university level, especially for small nations. Every nation is understandably anxious to have its own university, and, while this is usually feasible for some fields of study, many countries are simply too small and too poor to be able to support first-rate university programs in such expensive fields as medicine, engineering, and advanced laboratory sciences. A solution that makes excellent economic and pedagogical sense (though often is unattractive politically) is for small neighboring countries to share common facilities for advanced training and research in these specialized fields. Only in this way can they get quality results at a feasible

4. The Uganda case study by John Chesswas and Jacques Hallak, "Uganda: Behaviour of Non-Teacher Recurring Expenditures," in *Educational Cost Analysis in Action: Case Studies for Planners*, Vol. III, Paris, Unesco:IIEP, 1972, demonstrates a crude methodology for calculating the maximum transportation distance beyond which it would pay to use boarding schools.

5. Information based on an interview by one of the authors with the Director of Technical Education of Lebanon.

cost. This was the underlying rationale of the University of East Africa, whose specialized faculties were shared by Uganda, Kenya, and Tanzania.[6] The same logic underlies the cooperative university system in Central America.

The proliferation of uneconomic mini-universities of dubious quality has become a problem for a number of Latin American nations and even for more developed countries, such as Finland and Denmark. Notwithstanding the adverse economic and educational considerations, strong local aspirations and political pressures have often won out. One way in which cost analysis can help in such situations is by identifying those areas of university-level study which can be conducted with reasonable efficiency and effectiveness on a modest scale and thus might form the core of community-level institutions, leaving more costly and advanced studies to the central university.

Economies of scale are of critical importance in using mass media, especially television, for educational purposes. The key problem here is to spread the heavy costs of program production and transmission over a sufficiently large student clientele to bring the per capita costs within reach of the education budget. This problem is dealt with at length in the IIEP publication, *The New Media: Memo to Educational Planners* (Paris, Unesco:IIEP, 1967), which, like the present book, is based on an international series of case studies. It demonstrates from actual experience how television or radio instruction can be brought within the economic grasp of developing nations, but also how these powerful modern educational tools can become an economic liability if they are not well planned and if full advantage is not taken of the potential economies of scale. The Ivory Coast case study in the present IIEP series presents a good example of thoughtful planning and of exploiting the economies of scale.[7] Figure 6.1 shows the esti-

6. See Nicholas Bennett, "Uganda: The Use of Cost Evaluation in the Planning of Makerere College," in *Educational Cost Analysis in Action: Case Studies for Planners,* Vol. III, Paris, Unesco:IIEP, 1972.

7. Ta Ngoc Châu, "Ivory Coast: The Cost of Introducing a Reform in Primary Education," in *Educational Cost Analysis in Action: Case Studies for Planners,* Vol. II, Paris, Unesco:IIEP, 1972.

mated decline in unit costs of television instruction in the Ivory Coast as the number of students served by television increases.

The same economic principle applies, of course, to school construction. As the United Kingdom case study demonstrates, school building costs can be materially reduced by the mass production and bulk purchase of standardized components used in the construction of many schools, still allowing each to have its own distinctive design.

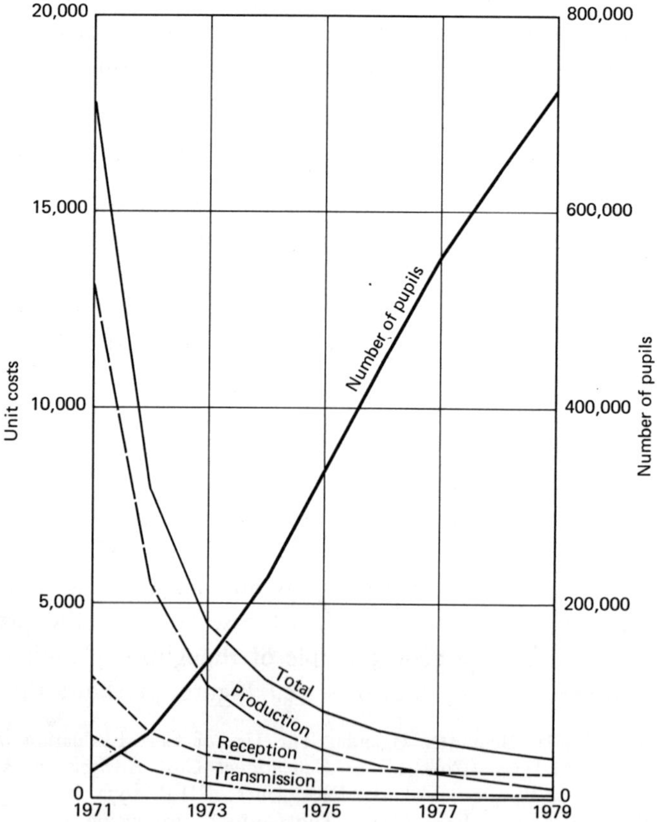

Figure 6.1.
Ivory Coast: unit operation costs and number of pupils.

The Phenomenon of Diminishing Average Costs

Where economies of scale are available, the marginal costs of adding additional students (that is, the increment to total existing costs involved in going to a larger scale) are lower than the existing *average* cost per student. This is more than economic jargon; it is a critically important fact of life for anyone who desires to raise the efficiency of any existing educational institution without eroding quality.

We can illustrate the point with a simple arithmetic example: suppose that a university with a planned capacity, including faculty members as well as facilities, of 5000 students has actual enrolments of only 2500, and an average cost per enrolled student of $4000. The cost of adding 500 more students would obviously be minor—to stretch a point, let us assume it is virtually zero. Adding the 500 would therefore bring the average cost per student down from $4000 to $3300. Even then the economies of scale would be far from exhausted since there is still an unused capacity of 2000 students.

The IIEP case study of Makerere University College in East Africa illustrates this principle of diminishing average costs resulting from low marginal costs.[8] The same principle showed up in the Barbados case study of team teaching and is illustrated by Table 6.2.

Again, in the quite different context of under-utilized secondary school capacity, diminishing average costs made it possible in Tanzania to enlarge secondary enrolments despite the failure of capital construction plans to materialize fully and at the same time to reduce average cost per student.[9] This case, incidentally, demonstrates the important lesson that, before deciding how much

8. Nicholas Bennett, "Uganda: The Use of Cost Evaluation in the Planning of Makerere College," in *Educational Cost Analysis in Action: Case Studies for Planners,* Vol. III, Paris, Unesco:IIEP, 1972.

9. Nicholas Bennett, "Tanzania: Planning for Implementation," in *Educational Cost Analysis in Action: Case Studies for Planners,* Vol. I, Paris, Unesco:IIEP, 1972.

new construction is needed, it is important for planners to find out how much unused capacity there is in existing institutions. The marginal costs of using them more fully will almost always be substantially lower than the cost of creating and staffing additional new facilities.

TABLE 6.2.
Estimated diminishing unit costs of team teaching in Barbados.

	NO. OF PUPILS TEAMED	PER PUPIL COST OF PROGRAM
1969-70	3950	$21.15
1970-71	6750	14.20
1971-72	10,000	11.70
1972-73	13,250	10.05
1973-74	16,500	9.20

Source: Richard M. Durstine and Barclay M. Hudson, "Barbados: Marginal Costs for Marginal Decisions—the Case of Team Teaching," in *Educational Cost Analysis in Action: Case Studies for Planners*, Vol. II, Paris, Unesco: IIEP, 1972.

One should not have the illusion, of course, that these "bargains at the margin" are available without limit. Once existing facilities become utilized to their potential capacity, the "cushion" for further expansion at low marginal cost is exhausted. Then the marginal cost of adding a still further batch of students suddenly leaps upward because this requires new facilities and staff.

Much depends, however, on the definition of "capacity." Most education facilities in fact have a considerably greater *potential* capacity than allowed by traditional academic schedules and customary ways of using such facilities. This point warrants special consideration.

The High Cost of Academic Calendars

The typical academic timetable results in substantial—sometimes even scandalous—under-utilization of expensive educational facilities, and often staff as well. This, of course, is a touchy subject because the life styles of many individuals are involved—not only administrators and teachers, but students and their families as well. But when, because of budgetary and other resource constraints, it comes down to a choice between sticking to accustomed practices or giving a larger number of able young people a fair chance at an education, custom cannot reasonably be allowed to stand in the way. Take, for example, the familiar case of a college which has traditionally held classes in the morning, filled the laboratories and sports fields in the afternoon and the library in the evening, not to mention shutting down for long holiday periods. A space utilization study in such a situation would reveal a shockingly low rate of utilization, on both a daily and year-round basis, which would be hard to justify under conditions of serious resource shortages and educational deprivation. And certainly it would be difficult to condone the construction of still more buildings to be under-utilized in the same fashion, hallowed traditions notwithstanding.

We know of a private college in the American midwest which discovered some years ago that by shifting its schedules (with no serious inconvenience to anyone) it could readily enroll at least 50 per cent more students simply by adding more dormitory space. It proceeded to do so, maintained its distinction for high quality, and put itself on a sounder economic footing.

One of the U.S.S.R. case studies stresses the need for utilizing Soviet schools more fully outside of normal hours—for example, to accommodate "continuation" students and as community centers.

One of the greatest wastes is the well-equipped technical school one runs across in developing countries whose doors close late in the afternoon and are not reopened until the next morning, but which could be profitably used evenings, weekends, and holiday periods to upgrade workers and supervisors in local industries.

The whole matter of space utilization, academic schedules, and out-of-hours use of educational facilities merits close scrutiny by cost analysts and educational managers in virtually all countries. Changes here often could greatly improve the behavior of costs for both formal and non-formal education.

The Behavior of Costs Under Rapid Educational Growth

Many of the points made in this and previous chapters can be knitted together and placed in perspective by looking at what happens to the costs of an educational system when it moves from a state of equilibrium and slow growth into an era of greatly accelerated growth, marked by disequilibrium and a succession of evolutionary phases. For this purpose we present below a simplified model of a more or less typical educational system in a developing country and trace it through three general stages of growth. This descriptive model does not fit precisely any actual educational system but it has familiar features and basic behavior patterns common to many. It could readily be elaborated into an internally consistent mathematical model, but we will not attempt that here.

PHASE I—INITIAL STATE OF EQUILIBRIUM AND SLOW GROWTH

We begin with a picture of this system just prior to the onset of accelerated growth; it might be described as being in a state of "normalcy."

It is small by subsequent standards, serving well below half the total primary-school-age population and far smaller proportions of secondary- and post-secondary-age young people. Its annual draft on the nation's resources is also modest, barely 1 per cent of the GNP and below 10 per cent of total public expenditures. It is a conventional, academically oriented system whose quality is regarded as generally satisfactory. The majority of its graduates enter teaching or the civil service or the practice of law and politics. A few go abroad to study medicine and other advanced specialties, but many never return. The system supplies relatively little manpower to the industrial, commercial, or agricultural sectors.

At this point the system is as close as it will ever get to a state of equilibrium, both internally and in relation to its economy and society. Its pyramidal enrolment structure and its student flows from primary to secondary to higher education are in good balance; its dropout and repeater rates at each level are considered wholesome—just high enough to accomplish the classical "weeding out" job. The supply of newly trained teachers is well matched to annual replacement requirements and to the very modest rate of enrolment expansion. The qualifications profile of the teaching force is high; only a small fraction of elementary teachers are technically unqualified, but they have been carefully chosen and are en route to being upgraded. Physical facilities are reasonably adequate; occasionally an old building needs replacement or a new one needs to be added, but for most years the main capital outlays are for maintenance and replacement. The same is true for instructional materials; the supply of textbooks is adequate but a portion needs replacing each year.

The schools and university are in good standing with the people and the government; not every one is in school who would like to be, but the political pressures to enlarge admissions are far from intolerable. The graduates at each level have little difficulty getting appropriate jobs because their limited supply is in good balance with the employment demand.

What do educational costs look like under this condition of equilibrium? The general level and structure of costs, and their relationship to one another, have been relatively stable for years, though drifting steadily upward. The over-all budget rises 6 to 8 per cent annually, reflecting mainly a gradual rise in average cost per student, which in turn reflects mainly an upward drift in average cost per teacher. The rest of the increase is largely accounted for by a slow expansion of enrolments. The division of total expenditures between primary, secondary, and higher education has remained fairly stable. So has the ratio of unit costs per student between levels, though university unit costs have been creeping up faster than other levels. Capital costs are a minor item compared to recurrent costs, except for years when a new building is put underway.

PHASE II—RAPID GROWTH SETS IN

For familiar reasons—a rise in the youth population, the gaining of national independence, the unleashing of human aspirations, a new emphasis on national development—the system rather suddenly finds itself hit by a sharp rise in educational demand and the necessity to embark on a major expansion which in ten years will more than double its size. The new tidal wave of students first hits the elementary schools, but soon washes into secondary and higher education.

Shortages quickly become the order of the day—shortages of classrooms, teachers, textbooks, laboratories, equipment, and supplies, shortages of everything but students. The first response of the system to these new conditions is to expand class size, to find provisional classroom space, and to hire large numbers of "temporary," unqualified teachers. Only later does a major expansion program get underway to build more classrooms, and even later to train more teachers. The pressures grow for teacher salary increases as an expedient way to improve teacher supply, but despite such increases the qualifications profile of the over-all teacher corps continues to decline. Meanwhile, concern mounts over the "erosion of quality" and over the sharp upswing of dropout and repeater rates. For some years, however, there is a vigorous employment market for graduates from each level, though it soon softens with respect to primary-school-leavers.

What is now happening to educational costs? The first noteworthy fact is that over-all recurrent costs for the system have moved up at roughly the same rate as enrolments, about 10 to 15 per cent per year, but after a time they rise faster than enrolments. Meanwhile, capital outlays become a much higher proportion of the budget than ever before.

Behind these aggregate cost movements some very interesting developments are taking place. At the elementary level, unit costs per student actually declined somewhat at first, thanks to the increase in pupil-teacher ratios and the hiring of many young, unqualified teachers. But eventually the unit costs start moving upward again, reflecting salary increases, the "aging" of these younger teachers, the upgrading of many to a higher qualification level, and the stabilizing of class sizes (at a high figure). In other words, the initial cost-reducing potentialities (mainly through enlarged class size and the heavy use of unqualified teachers) have now been exhausted and the cost-increasing forces have taken over. Paradoxically, even as unit cost per *enrolled* student was declining, the cost per *completed* student was rising rapidly, due to the upswing of dropout and repeater rates.

So long as primary education is expanding substantially faster than secondary and higher education, the comparatively lower cost of primary schooling holds down the system's over-all average cost per student. But as the accelerated expansion of enrolments shifts toward the higher levels, the over-all average cost per student rises disproportionately.

By the end of ten years of rapid expansion, over-all enrolments have somewhat more than doubled and over-all expenditures have trebled, becoming a much increased percentage of the GNP and total public expenditures. The equilibrium the system started with has been shattered in all directions, and things are still very much on the move, propelling the system now into a third phase.

PHASE III—TEACHER SHORTAGES EASE BUT COSTS KEEP RISING

This new phase is marked especially by a relatively rapid shift in the national manpower balance, from widespread shortages earlier to incipient surpluses now. The many positions that were hard to fill just after independence, especially in government and education, have now been largely filled, albeit often with underqualified people. Meanwhile, the greatly enlarged output of the education system and the return of many degree-holding students who studied at foreign universities has greatly improved the supply situation. Early worries about manpower shortages are now turning into worries about the mounting "educated unemployed."

The one bright spot for educational administrators is that the back of the teacher shortage has finally been broken (save in a few lingering shortage fields such as the sciences and technical subjects). More and more of the ablest graduates, unable to get jobs of their first choice, are turning to teaching. Thus, at the same price, the schools are able to get better quality. Teacher training capacity has finally caught up with the earlier demand; the new question is whether there will soon be an overproduction of teachers.

The schools certainly could use more teachers, both to reduce the still inflated pupil-teacher ratio and to handle further expansion of enrolments. But now a grave new problem looms; it is getting increasingly difficult to expand the education budget each year. Earlier it was not too difficult to win a 15 per cent increment annually, but now even 5 per cent has to be fought for hard. To make matters worse, unit costs are by now rising even faster as the teacher corps regains a more normal age distribution and its qualifications improve. And any progress toward reducing oversized classes simply makes unit costs per student rise even faster.

Thus we find a new cost configuration. Average cost per teacher and average cost per pupil are both rising steadily, even though many classes are still oversized and textbooks remain scarce. The earlier extreme spread between cost per primary teacher and per university teacher is narrowing somewhat as primary teachers move up on the qualifications scale. Capital costs continue to run high as new facilities are created, but each new building imposes high recurrent costs on the future, and by now the cumulative effect of previous new construction has become enormous.

In some respects the system is finding a new equilibrium; teacher supply and demand are back in better balance; primary, secondary, and higher education are in better proportion; and there is a better fit for the moment between educational output and national manpower needs. But this new equilibrium will not last. The pressure to expand enrolments is greater than ever and will soon push educational output well beyond the economy's absorptive capacity. At the same time unit costs are rising inexorably and pressing harder and harder against budget ceilings which rise less and less each year. The outlook, to put it mildly, is disconcerting. A new sort of disequilibrium is evolving that threatens to become a way of life for years to come.

This is the condition in which the great majority of educational systems find themselves as this book is written—a ubiquitous condition which can be called a world educational crisis.

III *Doing Your Own Cost Analysis*

By this point most readers are no doubt anxious, having read enough about the nature and behavior of costs and about how others are using cost analysis, to get to their own question: How can I apply cost analysis to my problem?

The next four chapters are addressed to this question. Three deal respectively with recurrent costs, especially teacher costs (Chapter 8), capital costs (Chapter 9), and checking consistency and feasibility (Chapter 10). First, however, Chapter 7 presents a number of practical suggestions on how to get started on cost analysis, the minimum facts needed, where to look for them, some important analytical and accounting distinctions to bear in mind, and some common pitfalls to avoid.

Obviously, we cannot consider each type of use in detail, much less each local variant. Thus we have chosen the compromise of offering selected suggestions, caveats, methodologies, and illustrations that will be relevant to a wide range of uses and circumstances, leaving it to the reader's ingenuity to adapt them to his own situation.

Space limitations also preclude us from demonstrating the arithmetic of each methodology discussed. Readers who want help on this score are urged to explore the useful two-volume manual by John D. Chesswas, Methodologies of Educational Planning for Developing Countries (Paris, Unesco:IIEP, 1969).

7 *Some Down-to-Earth Suggestions and Cautions*

Effective educational cost analysis involves much more than simply knowing the right analytical methods. It also involves choosing appropriate tactics and maintaining good human relations; knowing where and how to get the necessary basic data and how to judge the reliability of different sources; allocating your time judiciously; avoiding certain conceptual and accounting pitfalls; and skillfully arranging trade-offs between economic, pedagogical, and other considerations.

This chapter offers a potpourri of practical suggestions and cautions about such matters, drawn from a wide range of experience and stated in down-to-earth terms. If you are already an experienced hand in these affairs, then we suggest that you scan these pages and move on quickly to the next chapter.

Getting Off to a Good Start

Your first serious cost analysis assignment may well be a crash operation. Perhaps the deadline will be close at hand for submitting the new draft educational plan, but it must first be costed and its feasibility tested; or a project proposal must be quickly readied for a mission from the World Bank scheduled to arrive soon; or a major decision on salary policy is impending but its economic implications must first be determined. If you are lucky, you will previously have had a chance to make a more general exploration of costs in your educational system, but this would make you an exception to the general rule.

In all events, getting started right is half the battle. By honoring the following simple rules you may save much time, avoid many difficulties later, and increase the ultimate impact of your efforts.

Clarify your objectives at the outset. Before getting too committed to a particular approach or too buried in a mass of statistics, we suggest that you take time to define clearly the objectives of your exercise, the key questions you will seek to answer, and what you hope to accomplish, being certain that all of these have a direct bearing on real and important issues requiring decisions.

You may find it useful to ask yourself such questions as these: What are the most critical emergent problems confronting this educational system which cost analysis might help to solve? What experts on the scene could contribute to an analysis aimed at solving these problems? Who in particular might be interested in the results of such cost analysis and could put them to effective use? How and when can the results best get injected into the decision-making process in order to have a maximum impact on what is decided? In what form should the final results be presented to be of greatest effect?

Consult your main clients at the outset. The best way to answer these questions and to guarantee that your efforts will count most is to bring the potential users of your analytical results in at the takeoff. They include especially the managers and decision-makers who need the help of cost analysis and who alone can put the results into action. Ask them what *they* see as the main problems and questions needing attention. You may not agree entirely with their initial answers and perhaps you can gently persuade them that there are even more important questions to start with. But in all events it is wise to give heavy weight to their views and to meet them more than half way, not only because they may have valuable experience beyond your own, but because without their interest and cooperation you may not get very far.

You may, of course, run up against some clients who are so skeptical of cost analysis, or who feel so threatened by it, that they are not prepared to take your questions seriously. If so, the burden of proof will be on you. The best tactic in such circumstances is not to write such people off as "the enemy," but to do your diplomatic best to persuade them to reserve judgment until you have had a chance to demonstrate how cost analysis might help them. There is no more ardent apostle, after all, than a "doubting Thomas" who finally sees the light. It is up to you to furnish the light.

Find some able collaborators. It is well to identify as early as possible some technical collaborators who have skills and access to sources of information that supplement your own. They may include, for example, an able educational statistician and an experienced budget officer in the education ministry, a general economist at the planning commission interested in human resource development, a manpower expert at the ministry of labor, an imaginative demographer at the university or the census bureau, a fiscal expert at the ministry of finance, and a construction cost estimator in the ministry of works.

Things usually move faster and more smoothly, especially in the early stages, if this sort of collaboration is kept as informal and unstructured as possible. To try right at the outset to set up a formal inter-ministerial committee to deal with technical and informational matters often wastes time, creates irrelevant bureaucratic problems, and, worst of all, jeopardizes the essential climate of informal give-and-take among professional colleagues.

Needless to say, in these matters of tactics you must be the judge of your own particular situation. But the main point holds in all circumstances: to be a successful cost analyst one must be not only technically competent but able to work well with others in an atmosphere of professional objectivity and mutual respect, regardless of traditional bureaucratic obstacles to easy communication.

Use a systems approach from the outset. To identify all the key questions that should be answered by your inquiry, whatever its objective, we suggest that you view the matter in its full context, using the broad perspective which systems approach affords.

To illustrate, let us suppose that your first assignment is to cost a proposed new teacher training project whose aim is to increase the supply of fully qualified teachers and thus upgrade the qualifications profile of the teaching corps. Since an international capital loan is being considered, you will naturally want to give careful attention to the capital costs involved. But it would be a grave mistake to stop there. The most important issue is not whether your government can qualify for the loan, but whether, if it gets the loan, it can afford the subsequent annual cost consequences. The questions thus posed go beyond capital cost analysis. For example: What would be the effects of this project on the future teacher salary bill and other recurrent costs? Can we afford it without seriously penalizing other educational activities? Is this the best way to upgrade the teacher corps, or are there alternative ways to achieve the same result more quickly, cheaply, and effectively? Finally, taking a longer view, do we run the risk of overexpanding teacher training capacity—once the immediate backlog of demand for trained teachers is met, will the annual demand settle down at a lower level?

The guiding rule suggested by this illustration is that there is no such thing as a narrowly circumscribed, isolated problem for cost analysis. Any such problem is part of the seamless web of interconnecting and interacting elements which can only be seen in proper perspective through the wide-angle lens of systems analysis.

The Minimum Necessary Facts

Once you have identified your objectives and key questions and mapped out your study plans, you will begin in earnest the search for pertinent facts. At first you may be dismayed by how few pertinent facts are readily available. The stockpiles and flows of information are often shockingly deficient even in the most sophisticated educational systems. If you have just joined the educational management team from some other field, you may be astonished at how little hard data is available for assessing the system's performance and for planning its future.

But do not be easily discouraged; even in the poorest circumstances, cost analysis can be helpful. As we noted earlier, however, the less adequate and less sophisticated the data you have to work with, the more ingenious and sophisticated you will have to be in using them. Also, the more frequently you will have to substitute judgments and "guesstimates" for hard facts.

There can be no single magic list of the "minimum essential facts" needed for cost analysis in all places and for all purposes.[1] But cost analysts in any situation will find themselves severely handicapped if they do not have at least the following statistics to go on:

- Total enrolments broken down by levels and types of institutions, geographic areas, and, if possible, by individual grade levels.
- Annual number of graduates from each category of institutions.
- Annual number of dropouts and repeaters (shown separately) by type of institution, geographic area, and, if possible, by individual grades.
- Total teachers, distributed by types of institutions and levels, and divided, if possible, by qualification and salary categories.
- Total annual expenditures on each level and type of institution, broken down by recurrent and capital costs and by major sub-categories within each of these (particularly separating teacher costs from other recurrent costs, and new construction and equipment from repairs, maintenance, and replacements).
- A breakdown of annual revenues by source of finance (e.g. central and local government, private grants and fees, etc.) for each main educational sector.

In addition to these more or less standard educational statistics,

1. For a fuller discussion of this subject, see J. D. Chesswas, *Methodologies of Educational Planning for Developing Countries*, Paris, Unesco:IIEP, 1969 (two volumes), and *Methods and Statistical Needs for Educational Planning*, Paris, OECD, 1967 (designed mainly for more developed countries but nevertheless useful for less developed ones).

cost analysis and planning require much information on economic and social trends of a sort that educational administrators have not been so accustomed to using. This includes data on the growth and distribution of national income and public revenues; population growth, migration, and distribution; manpower needs and employment trends; general price, wage, and construction cost trends and changes in the structure of the economy. Such data are usually available in some form in various government bureaus.

Inevitably the facts and estimates contained in your presentations will vary greatly in precision and reliability. We therefore make three suggestions. First, you should not be apologetic or embarrassed about making "crude" and approximate estimates if that is the best the situation allows. But you should always be very candid about it. Policy-makers must be made aware of the possible margin of error in any set of estimates you give them so that they will not treat them as scientifically revealed truth if in fact they are only rough approximations. Second, even where more refined estimates might be possible, rough and ready ones are often sufficient for answering broad questions; to embellish them further would go beyond the point of diminishing returns and be a poor use of your time. Finally, to cover the above situations, we suggest that you adopt a scale of accuracy ratings and attach to each set of figures you circulate an "estimate of accuracy." This will help those who use your findings to make due allowance for whatever margin of possible error they may contain.

Strengthening the Information System

At the same time that you are struggling to extract the best possible immediate answers from the partial evidence at hand, you should also try to strengthen your information system for the future. But here a word of caution is in order. Beware the statistician who considers that all statistics are of equal importance. In fact, some are absolutely essential, some are useful but not essential, and still others have too little value to justify the cost of collecting them. Thus, a cost-benefit mentality is important when selecting the statistics that should be given priority in improving an educational system's information system. The first question to be asked is: What are the most critical questions to which educational managers need answers, and what specific kinds of facts are essential to providing these answers? Unless the matter is approached in this fashion, great effort may be wasted on the indiscriminate collection of facts that are of secondary importance and may go unused, while certain really essential facts remain uncollected.

Once the different categories of statistics have been sorted out according to their relative importance for decision-making and management, two other questions should be asked: With what frequency and regularity will each particular set of facts be needed? Must they be collected from all educational units or will it suffice to use a sample? [2]

Too often limited data-gathering resources are dissipated on a full census approach to every type of information instead of relying for some purposes on well-chosen samples. Obviously, to get reliable annual totals of enrolments, teachers, classrooms, graduates, and the like, data must be collected regularly from every educational unit. But, on the other hand, if you want to monitor the trend of dropouts and repeaters, for example, or to check the comparative unit costs of different levels and categories of educational institutions, this can be done better and at less cost by using a sample.

The sampling method, however, must be used with sophistication or the results can be very misleading. It is especially important to select a truly representative sample that gives proper weight to each of the categories being studied, and to design any questionnaires or interview forms carefully to ensure that the resulting data are comparable and unambiguous. If, for example, you want to study the comparative costs of different types of

2. For a fuller discussion, see J. Hallak, *The Analysis of Educational Costs and Expenditure*, Paris, Unesco:IIEP, 1969 (Fundamentals of Educational Planning, 10).

secondary schools, you should not take the easy course of loading your sample with prestige schools near the capital city just because they are convenient to visit and keep better records. A true picture requires a cross-section sample appropriately weighted to represent different types of schools—e.g. different sizes, day and boarding schools, rural and urban, academic and comprehensive, private and public, boys, girls, and coeducational schools, and whatever other classifications may be relevant.

The case studies from Morocco,[3] Uganda [4] and Thailand [5] demonstrate the value of sample studies. In all three instances, an examination of a sample of individual school accounts provided important insights into significant cost variations among different categories of institutions that could not have been revealed by full census studies.

Critical Ratios and Norms

Beyond the basic statistics listed above, there are a number of crucial relationships, indicators, and patterns that are invaluable to the cost analyst for a variety of purposes. Some of these can be derived from combinations of aggregate statistics while others require sample studies of institutional accounts. Among the most important are:

- The ratio of educational expenditures to the GNP and to total public expenditures.
- The ratio of teacher costs to other recurrent costs.
- The comparative level and composition of unit costs per student in rural vs. urban schools.

3. J. Proust, "Morocco: Costs of Public Secondary Education—Analysis of the Results of a Governmental Survey," in *Educational Cost Analysis in Action: Case Studies for Planners,* Vol. III, Paris, Unesco:IIEP, 1972.

4. John Chesswas and Jacques Hallak, "Uganda: Behaviour of Non-Teacher Recurring Expenditures," in *Educational Cost Analysis in Action: Case Studies for Planners,* Vol. III, Paris, Unesco:IIEP, 1972.

5. H. W. Reiff, "Thailand: Educational Cost Analysis," in *Educational Cost Analysis in Action: Case Studies for Planners,* Vol. I, Paris, Unesco: IIEP, 1972.

• The comparative cost per student in primary, secondary, and post-secondary education.

• Comparative costs per student (teaching and non-teaching, recurrent and capital) of day schools and boarding schools.

• Comparative costs of full-time and part-time instruction, or of formal technical schools vs. on-the-job training schemes.

• The theoretical cost of a primary school graduate (cost per year × normal number of grades) as against the *actual* cost per graduate (allowing for dropouts and grade-repeating).

• The comparative costs and composition of undergraduate and postgraduate university students, broken down by major fields of study.

• The relative size of classes in different types of institutions and in various subject areas.

• Indicators of space and equipment utilization.

Unit cost figures and ratios such as these do for the educational diagnostician what x-ray photos do for the medical diagnostician; they reveal what is going on internally, how the patient is faring, and what remedial actions may be needed.

It may be useful, when studying the foregoing indicators, to compare them with certain critical norms that have been established on pedagogical or other grounds to see if there are any substantial deviations. We saw, for example, how class sizes in rural primary schools in the Soviet Union were found to be far below the pedagogically acceptable norm, thereby revealing possibilities for achieving economies by raising class size.[6] Similarly, the case study of Makerere University College showed how major economies were achieved by enforcing norms previously recommended by a group of international experts pertaining to staff-student ratio, staff-student contact hours, and the ratio of senior to junior staff. A survey of staff utilization in this instance revealed that, instead of an official staffing establishment of 208, there were 300 professional staff members—many supplied from abroad and

6. V. I. Basov, "U.S.S.R.: Estimating the Annual Budget Requirements of the Educational System," in *Educational Cost Analysis in Action: Case Studies for Planners*, Vol. I, Paris, Unesco:IIEP, 1972.

not shown in the official budget or staff establishment, yet teaching and doing research.[7]

We saw also how Hungarian and Soviet planners make extensive use of norms for planning and costing, and, in the case of the Soviet Union, for monitoring and controlling costs in individual institutions.[8]

Limitations of Central Budgets and Records

The first data source that a cost analyst naturally turns to is the central education budget. If he is dealing with a centralized educational system, as in France or Tanzania, he merely has to go to the national Ministry of Education to examine the public budgetary records and other central records on teachers, enrolments, facilities, and so forth. But if he is working in a decentralized system, as in India, Brazil, Nigeria, the U.S.A., Germany, or the United Kingdom, he may have to travel further and add pieces together from a combination of national, state, district, and local public accounts.

These central accounts and records (at whatever government level) are a rich and convenient source of data, but they have serious limitations and pitfalls which must constantly be borne in mind. Typically they conceal as much as they reveal because they deal in broad aggregates and averages which hide cost and expenditure differentials of great importance to cost analysts. Thus, for example, they may yield the necessary data for tracing broad trends, but not sufficient data to compute many of the criti-

7. Nicholas Bennett, "Uganda: The Use of Cost Evaluation in the Planning of Makerere College," in *Educational Cost Analysis in Action: Case Studies for Planners,* Vol. III, Paris, Unesco:IIEP, 1972.

8. L. Falugévi, "Hungary: Programming Annual Current and Capital Expenditure During the Planning Period," in *Educational Cost Analysis in Action; Case Studies for Planners,* Vol. III, Paris, Unesco:IIEP, 1972, and D. Chuprunov and L. Tul'chinskii, "U.S.S.R.: Economic Planning and the Financing of Higher Education," in *Educational Cost Analysis in Action: Case Studies for Planners,* Vol. I, Paris, Unesco:IIEP, 1972.

cal ratios and differentials listed above. Moreover, the public education budget does not usually include all of the public costs of education, but at the same time it may include certain non-educational items (such as museums, libraries, etc.).

A further limitation is that public (and for that matter, private) education accounts are usually broken down into expenditure classifications which are not very meaningful for most cost-analysis purposes. Most often they show expenditures by object (e.g. salaries, utilities, supplies, equipment, etc.) but not by function or program objective. One can usually piece together the aggregate costs of teachers or supplies, but it is impossible to tell, for example, how much was spent for first graders as against second graders, or for learning to read and write as against learning arithmetic, or for what goes on inside the classrooms as against other school costs.

These shortcomings reflect the fact that education budgets were originally designed to serve the purpose of appropriations bodies and auditors, not the needs of educational planning and management. Members of a legislative committee, for example, can tell from the budget how much more of the taxpayers' money the schools and universities are spending this year than last, but they cannot tell for what specific educational purposes the money is being spent, what results are being attained, or what society is getting for its money. Similarly, a government auditor may be able to catch a thief by examining the budget accounts, but he is not likely to catch inherent inefficiencies in the educational system.

What it all comes down to, as we said earlier, is that cost analysis of the sort discussed in this book has not until recently been of great concern to most educational administrators. Now that it has become essential, budgetary accounts will have to be modified and amplified to serve these new purposes as well as the old ones. It is interesting, therefore, that some educational systems have already begun remodeling their budgets and adding new classifications in order to tell a fuller story and to be more useful for planning and management. The case study on Hungary, for example, shows how the annual budget has been made into a tool for implementing each annual slice of the Five-Year Plan.[9] A few other educational systems are moving toward "program budgeting." We will discuss new types of budgeting further in the final chapter.

Apart from budgetary accounts there are other types of central records of great value to the cost analysis, if they happen to be well kept. They include data on enrolments and completions by year, summary information on teachers, and detailed records on facilities. Educational systems vary greatly, however, in the extent and detail of such central records and in how well they are maintained. This, too, was demonstrated by the various IIEP case studies. Relatively few systems, for example, have the detailed central records on teachers that made it possible to project elementary teacher costs in Tanzania by a more sophisticated and accurate method.[10] We saw in the case of Chile that the absence of up-to-date central records on the disposition of technical teachers concealed a major opportunity for improving efficiency by redeploying teachers.[11] The Moroccan case study revealed a great disparity between what the central files showed about the condition and utilization of individual secondary school facilities and equipment and the actual conditions found in a field survey.[12]

In summary, central educational records on expenditures, enrolments, teachers, and facilities are usually the richest single source of data for the cost analyst, but they do not suffice for all purposes and they contain major pitfalls that must be carefully guarded against. Some of these pitfalls are noted below.

9. L. Faluvégi, "Hungary: Programming Annual Current and Capital Expenditure During the Planning Period," in *Educational Cost Analysis in Action: Case Studies for Planners,* Vol. III, Paris, Unesco:IIEP, 1972.

10. John D. Chesswas, "Tanzania: Factors Influencing Change in Teachers' Basic Salaries," in *Educational Cost Analysis in Action: Case Studies for Planners,* Vol. I, Paris, Unesco:IIEP, 1972.

11. Lucila Arrigazzi and José de Simone, "Chile: Improving Efficiency in the Use of Teachers in Technical Education," in *Educational Cost Analysis in Action: Case Studies for Planners,* Vol. III, Paris, Unesco:IIEP, 1972.

12. J. Proust, "Morocco: Costs of Public Secondary Education—Analysis of the Results of a Governmental Survey," in *Educational Cost Analysis in Action: Case Studies for Planners,* Vol. III, Paris, Unesco:IIEP, 1972.

Pitfalls To Avoid

In measuring today's costs or projecting tomorrow's, you can easily get into trouble unless you are clear at all times *what* costs and *whose* costs you are trying to measure and unless you are careful to include *all* the appropriate costs for the purpose you have in mind. Here are a few tips to help avoid such trouble.

Full costs vs. partial costs. Education budgets, whether public or private, never reveal the full financial costs of education to the economy at large.

The national education budget omits (1) all private costs; (2) the costs of educational activities conducted or supported by other governmental agencies; and (3) the costs of education to lower echelons of government. It may also omit (4) certain costs of formal education within the jurisdiction of the education ministry that are actually carried on the budgets of other governmental agencies, such as contributions to teacher retirement, teacher housing costs, student dormitories, or utility costs.

Thus, if you are trying to measure the full budgetary costs of education supported by *public* funds, you will have to search beyond the national education budget and extract appropriate items from other public budgets as well. If, on the other hand, you are trying to measure the full budgetary costs of education to the nation at large, you will in addition have to collect data (or make estimates) on the budgets of private educational institutions (being careful not to double-count government subsidies to private education).

Even after adding together all the public and private budgetary costs of education, however, you will still not have the full picture of total financial costs of education to the economy. The main item missing will be the financial outlays of students and their families for such items as transportation, meals, school uniforms, books, and so forth, which are not reflected in educational budgets.

For many purposes, of course, you will not need to include all of these financial costs of education, and even when you do, you can use rough estimating methods for some of the smaller elements (such as financial costs to families). What is important, however, is that you know when you are leaving something out and that you make your clients aware of the fact.

Financial costs vs. opportunity costs. In a strictly economic sense, the financial costs of education usually understate the real economic costs to the whole economy. As noted earlier, the real costs to the economy are measured by the *opportunity costs* of education, that is, by the value which the resources used in education would have in the best alternative uses. This, in effect, is what the economy foregoes or sacrifices in terms of other goods and services in order to have education.

To illustrate, if a certain technical school had not been built, the same capital might have gone instead into a new factory. Likewise, the teachers and students might instead have been employed in producing goods or services of some sort which sold in the market. The factory would presumably have earned interest on the capital. The teachers and students would have earned incomes. The Gross National Product would have been that much larger. The production thus lost (measured by the interest and earnings foregone) represents the real economic costs of the technical school to the economy.

If it were possible to get a precise measure of the opportunity costs of education (which ordinarily it is not), there is no reason to suppose that they would coincide exactly with the financial costs discussed above. In most circumstances they would be higher, especially because financial costs make no allowance for "income foregone" by working-age students attending school. Much depends, however, on the conditions of employment in the economy. If there is high unemployment, then possibly the income foregone by students is zero because their real alternative to going to school might be unemployment. It is conceivable that in such conditions the teachers themselves would be earning much less outside of school, in which case their teaching salaries exceed the opportunity costs to the economy.

For most purposes it is sufficient for educational cost analysts to work with financial costs, and more particularly with institutional budgetary costs. But the opportunity cost notion is important to bear in mind, particularly when one is considering the true costs of education to the economy. This would be the case, for example, in doing a broad cost-benefit study which seeks to differentiate the social benefits accruing respectively from primary, secondary, and university education. It would also be the case when economic planners and top authorities are trying to achieve a more or less optimum allocation of scarce resources between education and other sectors.

Costs to whom? It should be clear from what has just been said that the cost analyst should always ask himself: *Whose* costs are being dealt with in this particular analysis? Is it concerned only with financial costs to the central government, or to all levels of government combined, or with private financial costs as well? Is it concerned only with financial costs, or with the full, real costs to the economy? Is it concerned only with costs to the domestic economy, or to foreign economies too? The latter distinction becomes important where foreign aid is a big factor. For example, in examining the over-all educational expenditures of certain African countries whose educational systems are heavily dependent at the moment on external assistance, it is important to know to what extent the figures include or exclude such assistance; otherwise the true burden on the local economy and taxpayers cannot be properly assessed.

On this point we should also mention the distinction between the cost of foreign aid to a donor nation and its economic value to the recipient country; the two are seldom the same. The cost to the donor country is measured in terms of its own prices, wages, and salaries and usually includes substantial transport and other special costs. The value of the particular item of aid to the receiving country, on the other hand, should be measured in terms of its own prevailing costs and what it would cost to do the same thing on its own.

Take the case of a Peace Corps teacher who is sent to an African country. Let us suppose (hypothetically): (1) that the total cost of this teacher to the United States, including training, transportation, and salary, etc., averages out to $12,000 per year; (2) that the host government pays $500 per year toward the teacher's local maintenance; and (3) that the total cost of an equivalent local teacher (if available) would be $2000 per year. From the point of view of the host country, the value of the aid received in the form of this teacher is $1500 ($2000 minus $500), despite the fact that the cost to the sending government was much higher.

This same proposition holds with respect to capital assistance. A new technical school, fully equipped, might cost a donor nation $2,500,000 (using its own equipment and high-level manpower), but the recipient government might have built and equipped an equivalent facility for only $1,500,000 (using entirely domestic personnel and materials at local prices and shopping in the world market for the best buys on equipment).

The practical point is that you should always try to segregate foreign costs from domestic costs, and in assessing the real value of foreign aid, you should cost it in terms of local equivalent value rather than the actual costs to the donor.

Hidden costs. Whether one is dealing with the public or private costs of education, or with domestic or foreign costs, it is important to keep an eye out for hidden costs which do not get reflected in the budget. Certain of the unbudgeted private costs mentioned earlier, such as family outlays for books, school meals, and transportation, are hidden costs. The salaries of the foreign professors at the University of East Africa who were rendering teaching services but were not included in the university budget or the official staff establishment were important hidden costs. A very common hidden cost these days is the "free" broadcast time received by schools from private or public television stations for instructional programs. The service may be free so far as the school budget is concerned, but it is a real cost to someone else, and the day may come when it will be a real cost to the school budget itself.

Thus, one important reason to keep these various hidden costs in view is because later on they may no longer be hidden. When the "inexpensive" foreign teachers are replaced by indigenous teachers, or when the experiment in television instruction succeeds so well that the schools need their own broadcast station, these real costs suddenly show up on the educational budget. A good rule to remember is that nothing an educational system uses is truly free if it would have a real economic value in some alternative use.

Transfer payments. The opposite of leaving out an important cost is to count the same expenditure twice. This happens if one is not careful in dealing with so-called transfer payments. Broadly speaking, a transfer payment is simply a conveyance of purchasing power from one institutional or individual pocket to another without any real expenditure taking place which would generate additional national production and income. The educational cost analyst needs to be especially alert with respect to two particular possibilities. The first is where the national government makes educational subsidy payments, usually from the Ministry of Education's budget, to local governments or to private schools, which in turn spend the money on school buildings, teacher salaries, and other educational purposes. The payment from the ministry's budget is merely a cash transfer; it does not actually buy anything. It only becomes a real expenditure when spent by the local government or the schools themselves. Care should be taken not to count the same money twice when combining public and private or national and local educational expenditures.

The second possibility is the granting of student scholarships, fellowships, and bursaries which are then spent by the students for tuition fees, dormitory charges, and the like. When payment is made to the students, it is merely a transfer; the real expenditure occurs only when the students buy something with the money. Often, however, university budgets show both the transfer payment (under "student assistance" or some such label) and the costs of the educational services which the students partially pay for with the grants (e.g. room and board, staff salaries, etc.). This is a perfectly legitimate (even if sometimes an illogical) accounting procedure for universities to use, but it can trap the unwary cost analyst into double-counting. He should eliminate such transfer payments in computing the real costs of education.

Unit cost of what unit? The term "unit cost" can also be a trap if one is not careful. It is used most often to mean the annual cost per enrolled student. But there are a variety of other types of unit cost measures that come in handy for certain purposes and it is important to keep them straight. They include, for example:

- The total cost per graduate
- The capital cost per student place
- The capital cost per occupied student place
- The average cost per teacher
- Cost per classroom
- Cost per school
- Cost per course
- Cost per square or cubic foot

It all depends what the most appropriate unit is for costing the particular item with which you are concerned. If you are costing the number of pencils and textbooks needed, or the food bill, then the individual student is the most appropriate unit because in these cases cost varies in direct proportion to the number of students. But if you are estimating requirements for teachers, or for desks, maps, globes, and various other items of classroom equipment, then the classroom is usually the best unit, since the staffing and equipment requirements vary with the number of classrooms rather than the number of students. In estimating heating and lighting costs, square or cubic footage may be the best unit.

As we saw in the case of the Soviet Union, several different norms are used for estimating educational costs and for making educational budgets, based on a variety of costing "units," each selected to fit best the particular item being costed.

To avoid confusion it is a good idea when using the term "unit cost" to be explicit about what kind of unit cost is in question, unless this is already clear from the context.

Joint costs. As the name implies, joint costs are common costs shared by a number of different educational units or activities.

The teacher is a joint cost for all the students in a class; the principal and his secretary are joint costs for all the students in the school; maintenance of the building is a joint cost for the regular daytime classes and evening adult classes using it; and the Ministry of Education is a joint cost for all the schools in the system.

Difficulties often arise when it becomes necessary to allocate joint costs to different users of the same service in order to calculate their respective total or unit costs. There is no standard solution for all cases; the cost analyst simply has to devise the most reasonable basis he can in each instance, taking care not to use a more elaborate and time-consuming method than the circumstances warrant, and being sure to apply consistently whatever formula he adopts.

The simplest method in many situations is simply to divide up the joint cost according to the number of students in each category affected, or by the number of classrooms or teachers or schools, as the case may be. We suggest that in disposing of joint cost problems, you content yourself with a pragmatic solution that seems reasonable and not get bogged down in metaphysical debates with your colleagues over, for example, how to divide school inspector costs between older teachers and younger teachers, or between first-grade and second-grade students.

When do costs occur? Another tricky problem you will encounter is how to allocate costs by time periods. This problem arises mainly when dealing with capital costs, but it also applies to research and development costs.

For illustration, take the case of a new university science building, built with a loan, which required three years to construct. While under construction it tied up considerable capital that was yielding no return. Two questions immediately arise: First, to what year or years should this capital outlay and the interest charges be assigned for purposes of making a time series of capital expenditures? Second, in computing annual capital costs in subsequent years, how should this building be treated?

The best way to handle the first problem is to apportion the three-year capital outlay and interest charges among the three years on the basis of actual cash disbursements in each year (if this information is available), since this gives the most accurate picture of what really happened. If you use this preferred method, however, it should also be followed for all other capital outlays in your time series; otherwise the series will not be consistent and comparable from year to year. Alternative methods would be to assign the full amount of a new capital project either to the year of authorization, or to the year when construction was started, or to the year of completion. These solutions give a deceptive picture of actual capital outlays, but an accurate one of capital authorizations, construction starts, or completions. Decide which it is you want to show and be sure to state clearly what method you have used or your readers may be misled.

The more important question is how to charge this new capital outlay against educational costs in the future. If you are computing the total cost per student (capital plus recurrent), it would obviously make no sense to charge the full capital costs to the first crop of students. The right approach for this purpose would be to amortize the cost (including interest) over the building's useful lifetime and apportion it annually to all the students who use it over time. We will return to the subject of amortization when we discuss capital costs in Chapter 9.

We should also mention in this connection that it is always preferable when using budgetary accounts to take year-end figures of actual expenditures rather than beginning-of-the-year authorizations, again to get a more accurate picture of the reality. A budget, after all, is only a forecast of things to come, and until they have actually come and gone, the figures shown are purely hypothetical.

Research and development costs. These are the special costs involved in undertaking a new departure—such as a major experiment or innovation—which will hopefully succeed and become generally applied. Such costs behave in special ways and present special timing problems, similar to but more complicated than a new building.

It is important to distinguish between the "starting-up" costs of such undertakings, which are "one-time-only" costs, and the longer-term "normal" costs that will be reached at a later stage. As we saw in the Barbados team-teaching case, for example, the five-year experimental phase involved relatively high costs for outside advisors, special teacher training, and other items associated with the experiment itself. Moreover, the experiment applied to only a small fraction of the pupils in the system, hence cost per pupil ran high. But the projected cost per pupil after the experimental phase dropped sharply, first, because the initial research and development costs would then be eliminated and, second, because team teaching would be extended to all schools and its overhead costs would be spread over a much larger number of students.

It is generally true that the cost per student during the starting phase of a major educational experiment or innovation is abnormally high. If these costs are mistakenly regarded as an indicator of future costs, the experiment might be thrown out on grounds of not being economically feasible. It is essential, therefore, to develop two sets of cost projections, the first applying to the developmental period and the second showing the anticipated "normal" costs beyond this period.

This serves two important purposes: it prevents initial prejudice against the innovation; but it also guards against wishful thinking, for the fact may be that the longer-range normal costs, though lower than the initial costs, may still be too high to be afforded. To take an extreme example, there is little doubt that African children could learn a great deal in computerized classrooms, but there are the gravest doubts whether this new technology could be afforded once the experimental period was over, regardless of how impressive the pedagogical results might be.

The IIEP publication on new educational media which we mentioned earlier demonstrates in detail the principle of high costs per student during the developmental phase of television instructional programs, followed by substantially lower unit costs later.[13] Undoubtedly the Ivory Coast television project described

13. W. Schramm, P. H. Coombs, F. Kahnert, and J. Lyle, *The New Media: Memo to Educational Planners*, Paris, Unesco:IIEP, 1967.

in Chapter 2 of the present book will, if successful, experience this same phenomenon.[14]

So much for the various pitfalls and accounting puzzles you are likely to encounter. We will conclude this chapter with some comments on the important matter of "trade-offs" in which you will inevitably find yourself heavily engaged.

The Nature of Trade-offs

If educational systems did not live in a world of limited resources (including time, the most fixed resource of all), there would be little need for cost analysis. But they always have and always will, even in the most affluent nations. Therefore the managers of educational systems are constantly having to make choices between alternative ways of allocating and combining the resources available to get the best results.

What makes these choices so difficult is that several sets of variables, measured on quite different scales, must all be weighed simultaneously. It is not the simple matter, for example, of minimizing costs regardless of the educational consequences. Nor is it the simple matter of getting the best conceivable pedagogical results regardless of the cost. Rather it is the much more complicated matter of striking a good balance between the pedagogical considerations on the one hand and the costs and other feasibility considerations on the other. This means that educational planners and decision-makers are constantly having to make trade-offs, and to do this well they must examine each situation through the lens of a systems analysis.

To bring the subject down to practical terms, let us take a few homely examples:

- A financial limit is imposed on a draft educational plan which had envisaged a large expansion of both primary and secondary education. Cost analysis shows that with the limited additional

14. Ta Ngoc Châu, "Ivory Coast: The Cost of Introducing a Reform in Primary Education," in *Educational Cost Analysis in Action: Case Studies for Planners*, Vol. II, Paris, Unesco:IIEP, 1972.

funds available 1000 university students could be added, *or* 3000 secondary students, *or* 15,000 elementary students, or some combination of all three within these limits. In this case there must obviously be a trade-off among students at different levels, requiring a Solomon-like judgment. The cost analysis does not provide the answer, but it defines the parameters within which the answer must fall.

- A classroom teacher devotes an hour each to reading, writing, and arithmetic every day, and the rest of the time to other subjects, recreation, and rest periods. She is pleased with the progress her class has been making on reading and writing but perturbed by their slower progress in arithmetic. Should she reallocate time, reducing the amount spent on reading and writing in order to improve arithmetic? Or should she steal extra time for arithmetic from the other subjects, recreation, or rest periods? The costs here are in terms of time, not money, and the outputs are in terms of student learning results, health, and educational diversity. This is the sort of trade-off situation teachers are confronted by all the time.
- A primary school, handicapped by resource scarcities and poor quality results, would like to add another teacher in order to reduce class size, and also have a substantially enlarged supply of books and other self-instructional materials. But it does not have enough money to do both and so is forced into a trade-off between adding the teacher or adding instructional materials. The question, of course, is which will improve learning results the most. Again cost analysis *per se* cannot decide the answer. It can only define the parameters of the choice so the decision can be made on pedagogical grounds.

Our case studies offer a variety of other illustrations of trade-offs between pedagogical, economic, and other factors. The school consolidation option in the rural areas of Norway and the Soviet Union involved trade-offs between lower unit costs and improved pedagogical results in larger school units as against the social and psychological advantages of having children attend school in their own village. The Barbados cost analysis identified a series of op-

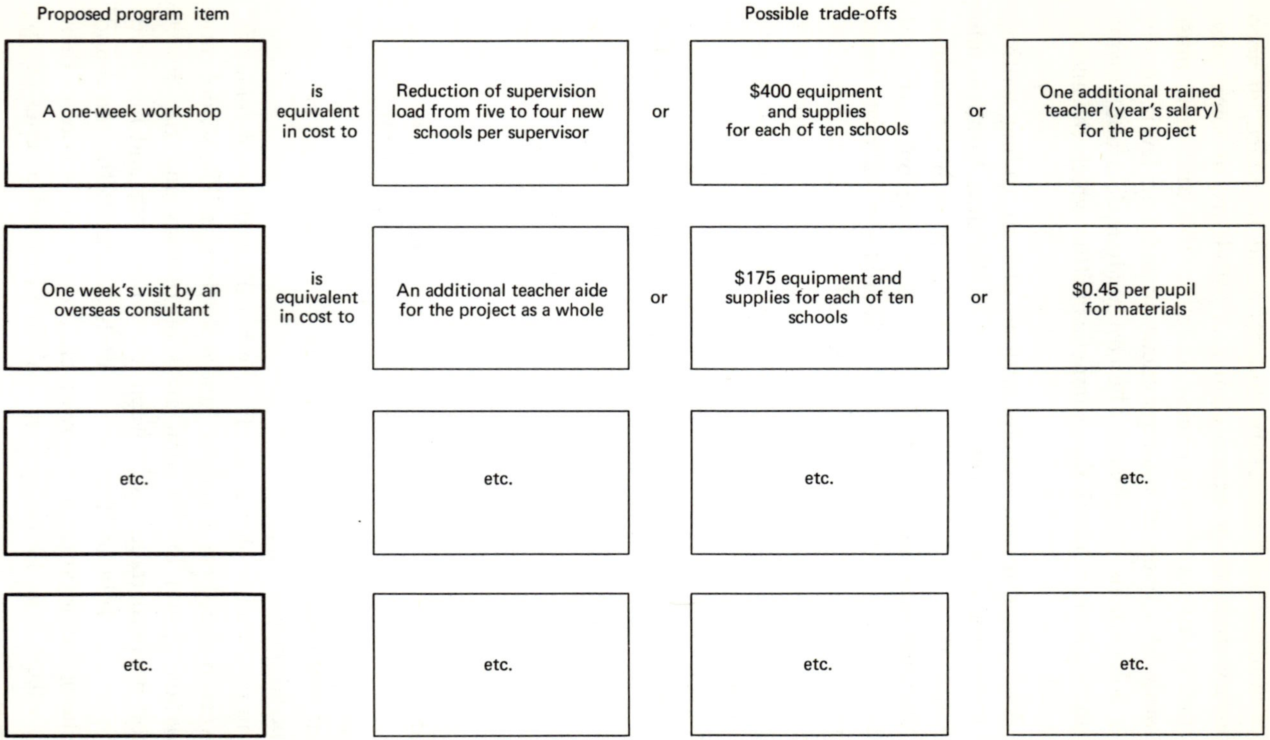

FIGURE 7.1.
Possible trade-offs in the Barbados team-teaching project.

tions to school authorities on how to spend a given amount of money, leaving them to decide which were the best ones pedagogically (see Figure 7.1). It is interesting that in Poland, where the choice was between alternative approaches to teacher training, and in the Ivory Coast, where the choice was between using two different grades of teachers in conjunction with television instruction, the authorities in both instances knowingly elected the higher-cost option. In short, they traded what they thought would be significant pedagogical advantages for economic resources, thus in all probability imposing a future sacrifice on some other parts of the educational system.

Most of the suggestions and caveats presented in this chapter apply whether you are dealing with recurrent costs or capital costs, and to any purpose your cost analysis is meant to serve. With these in mind, we will move on now to an examination of problems and methods relating particularly to recurrent costs, and from there to the treatment of capital costs.

8 *Treating Teacher Costs and Other Recurrent Costs*

Recurrent costs apply to human services and physical supplies that are consumed in the educational process within a single budget year. Since these typically account for 60 to 90 per cent of total educational costs, they merit major attention in any cost analysis, whatever its particular purpose. In any such analysis, non-teacher recurrent costs should be viewed separately from teacher costs because the two often behave quite differently. Following are a few basic guidelines that apply to all types of recurrent costs.

Some General Guidelines

The impact of old and new decisions. In economic theory, capital costs are "fixed costs" and recurrent costs are "variable costs" because, in principle, capital costs do not fluctuate with output whereas recurrent costs do.

As a practical matter, however, recurrent costs are largely fixed in the short run and only acquire substantial variability as time goes on. In other words, educational managers with a new budget that is 10 per cent higher than the previous year actually have relatively little room for maneuver in deploying these new funds. Most of the money is already committed as the result of previous decisions and practices, some running back twenty years or more (such as old decisions on teacher salary structures and qualifications, staffing norms, and architectural designs). These inherited commitments and the needs of on-going operations must first be satisfied before any new departures can be considered. If by then the educational managers still have as much as 5 per cent of the new budget left for fresh expansion, improvements, and innovations, they can consider themselves lucky.

But if they take a longer view, five to ten years ahead, their margin for maneuver is much greater. And if they have clear objectives and priorities, and a well-conceived strategy, this cumulative margin can be used to achieve many important changes. But this can only happen if every decision is examined with care before it becomes cast in concrete. For in the same way that past decisions have imposed fixed commitments and constraints on the present, new decisions will have a binding effect on the future.

Projecting future costs. In forecasting future recurrent costs, you should devote at the outset a good share of your total effort to examining present costs and recent trends, for these are the handwriting on the wall. But future costs cannot be accurately estimated simply by extrapolating past trends; allowance must be made for the influence of new policies and plans, prospective economic conditions, and a variety of internal and external cost-influencing forces that will make the future different from the past.

Serious errors can result from assuming simplistically that some major element of recurrent costs will remain static. The real issue is how fast and how far each of these elements is likely to travel in a given period, under various sets of dynamic assumptions.

If recent history is any guide, the chances are strong that your recurrent costs per student will rise in future years, and your main problem will be how to slow the rate of increase. The unit cost experiences of India and France from the early 1950's to the mid-1960's, depicted in Tables 8.1 and 8.2, are instructive in this respect.

The main components of recurrent costs. Many different inputs enter into recurrent costs, some very large (particularly teacher costs) and others relatively small (such as office supplies). A good

TABLE 8.1.
India: recurrent unit cost per student.

LEVEL OF EDUCATION	1950-51	1965-66
	IN RUPEES, AT CURRENT PRICES	
Pre-primary	55	55
Primary (part 1)	20	30
Primary (part 2)	37	45
Secondary	73	107
Vocational and technical	197	417
Special	109	135
Higher (colleges)	231	328

Note: At the time of the case study, the rate of exchange was \$1 = 7.50 rupees.

Source: Government of India, Ministry of Education, *Report of the Education Commission, 1964–1966, Education and National Development,* tables 19-10A and 19-10B, New Delhi, 1966.

general rule is to allocate your energies according to the relative quantitative importance of each item, and to avoid being a perfectionist down to the last detail.

Another general rule is this: the further you break down broad categories into meaningful subdivisions, the more versatile, useful, and accurate your analysis will be. Thus, for example, separate unit cost figures for primary, secondary, and higher education obviously tell a much larger story than a composite figure for all levels combined. Separate unit cost figures for rural and urban primary education, or for secondary boarding and day schools, or for different

TABLE 8.2.
*France: recurrent unit costs in public education.**

LEVEL OF EDUCATION	1952	1959	1964
	IN 1963 CONSTANT FRANCS		
Primary	305	374	578
Secondary	1578	1726	2588
Technical	1735	2144	2707
Universities	1375	2324	3062

* Based on National Education Budget.

Source: Raymond Poignant, *Education and Economic and Social Planning in France,* Paris, Unesco:IIEP (in preparation).

TABLE 8.3.
Recurrent costs per pupil by faculty, Makerere University College (1964-65) (in shillings per annum).

FACULTY	DEPARTMENT EXPENDITURES	FACULTY ADMINISTRATION	LIBRARY	CENTRAL ADMINISTRATION	AMENITIES	MISC. GRANTS	RESID. HALLS	TOTAL
Arts and Social Science	5202	180	1056	3518	658	124	2634	13,372
Agriculture	25,722	820	1056	3518	658	124	2634	34,532
Education	4550	706	1056	3518	658	124	2634	13,246
Science	17,018	532	1056	3518	658	124	2634	25,540
Fine Art	10,486	18	1056	3518	658	124	2634	18,656
Medicine	19,144	966	778	3518	658	124	2634	27,822

Note: Evidently the cost analysts in this case allocated departmental expenditures and faculty administrative costs on the basis of actual budget accounts, but they allocated joint costs (library, central administration, etc.) arbitrarily in equal amounts to each faculty. An alternative (and perhaps better) method would have been to allocate joint costs according to relative enrolments in each faculty.

Source: Nicholas Bennett, "Uganda: The Use of Cost Analysis in the Planning of Makerere College," in *Educational Cost Analysis in Action: Case Studies for Planners,* Vol. III, Paris, Unesco:IIEP, 1972.

programs of the university, will serve many more useful purposes, and all purposes more accurately, than broader averages for mixed categories.

The case study of Makerere University College illustrates the value of differentiating recurrent costs per student in different faculties or departments of higher educational institutions. Table 8.3 shows the spread in unit costs by fields, ranging from 13,372 shillings in Arts and Social Sciences to 34,532 per student in Agriculture. While this wide spread was not in itself conclusive evidence that unit costs were too high in some areas and possibly not high enough in others, it prompted a deeper investigation into the causes. This led to some important changes and economies in *all* departments and faculties.

TABLE 8.4.
Classification of recurrent costs by object and purpose.

TYPE	PURPOSE					
	INSTRUCTION	ADMIN.	FOOD AND DORMS	TRANSP.	HEALTH	GEN. MAINT.
1. *Personnel costs*						
a. Teachers						
b. Administrative staff						
c. Other staff						
2. *Non-personnel costs*						
a. Materials and supplies						
b. Utilities						
c. Miscellaneous						

Recurrent costs should also be broken down by "object" of expenditure (e.g. teacher costs, other staff costs, and various non-personnel costs) and by "purpose" (e.g. instruction, administration, student welfare services, transportation, etc.). The results of such breakdowns can usefully be summarized on a cross-classification form similar to that in Table 8.4 (using such categories and labels, of course, as fit your particular needs and conventions).

Whatever categories and estimating techniques you may choose for any of the above purposes, be sure to apply them consistently so that your figures will be comparable among different institutions and from one year to the next. Be sure also to include *all* relevant costs, even if you must estimate some of them crudely. Finally, it is especially important to separate teacher costs from other staff costs, and instructional costs from non-instructional costs.

What costs to include and exclude. Before you start compiling statistics of recurrent costs, be very clear what it is you are trying to measure. For many purposes you will simply be measuring the *financial* costs of education to the *public* budget (including public subventions to private institutions). Bear in mind when you do so that this is an understatement of total educational costs to the economy; it excludes private costs and various hidden costs. It also excludes, arbitrarily, all of the costs of non-formal education, which may be quite substantial and may have a critical importance for the nation's social and economic development. The caveats noted in Chapter 7 with respect to the foregoing matters should be constantly kept in view. Remember, too, that it is not enough for you, as the planner or cost analyst, to know what your final figures include and exclude; they should be clearly labeled so that others can also know.

Comments on Non-Teacher Recurrent Costs

This is a rather cumbersome label for what remains after teacher costs are subtracted from total recurrent costs. The main items included are "other staff costs" (including administrative and service personnel), instructional materials and supplies, other types of supplies and materials, transportation, maintenance, board and room, and other student welfare costs.

It is common practice in costing educational targets to lump these non-teacher recurrent costs together and project them as a fixed percentage of teacher costs, using the present ratio of one to the other. This avoids having to make separate projections for each item of non-teacher recurrent costs. This "quick and dirty" method can be justified if you are simply making a fast and preliminary check, for example, on the feasibility of alternative expansion targets. But for more serious planning and decision-making it can get you into serious trouble. First, this crude method puts the entire burden for accuracy on your estimate of teacher costs and any error here, in either direction, becomes compounded. Second, the prices of non-teacher components often move differently from teacher costs (they tend on the whole to rise more slowly); hence, to tie them rigidly together can lead to substantial error. Third, if expenditures on teachers and on non-teacher items are seriously out of balance in the base period (as they frequently are in developing countries), this method tends to perpetuate the imbalance. Finally, as one moves upward from the primary school level, the ratio of non-teacher costs to teacher costs rises sharply (often moving from about 1 to 10 at primary to 1 to 1 at the university level); thus, substantial errors made in estimating non-teacher costs above the primary level can result in large errors in the final estimate of total costs.

To go beyond this crude method, however, requires substantial additional work. Whether this is worthwhile must be judged case by case. It clearly was worthwhile in the study of Uganda's secondary school non-teacher recurrent costs. This study revealed important differences in the cost patterns of secondary day schools and boarding schools, some of which are shown in Table 8.5. It showed, for instance, that non-teaching staff costs have twice the weight in day schools as in boarding schools; that the costs of instructional materials differ even more; and that administration and transportation are relatively minor cost items in both types of schools, and can therefore be estimated by cruder methods without serious risk.

The Woodhall-Blaug study of secondary school costs in the United Kingdom demonstrates the danger of assuming that non-teacher recurrent costs and teacher costs will march together from year to year in fixed relationship. It showed, for example, that between 1950–51 and 1963–64 per-student administrative staff and maintenance costs rose 46 per cent while per-student teacher costs rose only 27 per cent (all measured in constant prices). Per-student capital costs also rose more than teacher costs (equipment and furniture, 39 per cent, and buildings, 35 per cent).[1]

When separate projections are made for each major item of non-teacher cost, it is necessary to tie each estimate to an appropriate variable—such as the number of students or teachers or classrooms—but the same variable will not do for all purposes. Requirements for textbooks, food, or student grants, for example, will vary mainly with the number of students, whereas utility and maintenance requirements vary with the size and type of buildings; other items may vary with the number of teachers or classrooms or administrative units.

TABLE 8.5.
Uganda: average non-teacher recurrent expenditures per student in eleven specimen day and boarding schools.

	DAY		BOARDING	
	% OF TOTAL	UNIT COST IN SHILLINGS	% OF TOTAL	UNIT COST IN SHILLINGS
Non-teaching staff	30.0	70.40	15.0	161.70
Instructional supplies	14.7	97.90	15.9	170.40
Maintenance	18.9	44.40	13.0	139.20
Administration	8.1	19.00	5.6	60.20
Transport	1.3	2.90	4.8	51.70
Boarding	—	—	45.7	490.30
Total		234.60		1073.50

Note: For technical reasons, the percentage columns do not add up to 100 per cent.
Source: John Chesswas and Jacques Hallak, "Uganda: Behaviour of Non-Teacher Recurring Expenditures," in *Educational Cost Analysis in Action: Case Studies for Planners*, Vol. III, Paris, Unesco:IIEP, 1972.

Particular care needs to be taken with student welfare costs, such as transportation, boarding, and scholarships. Although these costs are basically tied to the number of students, they do not necessarily change uniformly with the number of students. For example, the proportion of secondary boarding students may de-

1. M. Blaug and M. Woodhall, "Productivity Trends in British Secondary Education, 1950–63" in J. Hallak (ed.), *Educational Costs and Productivity*, Paris, Unesco:IIEP, 1967 (mimeographed).

cline over the years, thus reducing the relative size of boarding costs for secondary education as a whole. Or an elementary school system that has achieved high participation rates in urban areas and is now concentrating on raising rural school attendance is likely to find its transportation and school lunch costs rising disproportionately. A large expansion of enrolments in higher education that raises the proportion of students from indigent families may cause a disproportionate increase in scholarship aid.

The costs of student welfare services (sometimes called "intervention costs") vary greatly in importance from country to country, as shown by the figures in Table 8.6. They can also vary greatly among regions and institutions within the same country.

TABLE 8.6.
Student welfare costs in relation to total recurrent costs (sample of seven developing nations).

COUNTRY	TOTAL UNIT COSTS (U.S. $)	STUDENT WELFARE COSTS (U.S. $)
Cameroon	18.23	0.32
Central African Republic	26.11	1.11
Chad	22.53	2.94
Dahomey	66.05	12.36
Gabon	42.71	0.48
Mauritania	76.14	12.19
Upper Volta	51.94	3.42

Source: Nguyen Huu Chau, *Les depenses d'enseignement dans quatorze pays africains d'expression française*, IIEP, 1965 (mimeographed).

Differences in student welfare costs help to explain the wide spread in average recurrent costs per student between primary education and higher levels. In the Ivory Coast in 1964, for example, student welfare services represented less than 1 per cent of recurrent costs in primary education but 46.4 per cent in higher education.[2]

So much for non-teacher costs. On the whole they are less com-

2. J. Hallak and R. Poignant, *Les aspects financiers de l'éducation en Côte-d'Ivoire*, Paris, Unesco:IIEP, 1966 (Monographies africaines, 8).

plicated to deal with and require somewhat less precise treatment than teacher costs. The largest ones should be separately estimated if time permits, but simpler and cruder methods will usually suffice for the minor items.

Key Factors in Estimating Teacher Costs

The figures in Table 8.7 are a reminder of the dominant role played by teacher costs, and of how they vary from one education level to another. They are drawn from fifteen widely scattered countries, and are not strictly comparable (for example, some cover all personnel costs and others only teacher costs), but the impression they convey is valid enough for our purposes.

Another important reminder is that teacher costs are constantly under the influence of dynamic forces operating both inside and outside the educational system. Virtually any change of educational policy affecting size, program, methods, or staffing is likely to have an impact on teacher costs. Similarly, changes in supply-demand conditions for high-level manpower, in the general structure of wages and salaries, or in the general movement of prices, are likely to have repercussions on teacher costs and on the size and quality of teacher supply. These realities warn against making the simplistic assumption that teacher costs per student, the average cost per teacher, will remain constant in coming years.

To construct a trustworthy projection of future teacher costs, you must start with the following building blocks:

- The present teacher force—its size, structure and costs
- Future teacher requirements
- Prospective teacher supply
- Prospective teacher structure
- Prospective trends in teacher salaries

Each of these elements is examined below, but a few words must first be said about two crucial factors that strongly influence over-all teacher costs: the teacher salary structure and the composition of the teaching force.

Official teacher salary structures differ in detail and terminology, but in most nations they share the following four characteristics.

First, each education level has its own teacher classifications and salary schedules; the median salary is lowest for elementary teachers and highest for university professors, with secondary salaries in between.

TABLE 8.7.
Teacher costs in fifteen sample countries (as a percentage of total recurrent costs).

COUNTRY	LEVEL	YEAR	SALARY COSTS AS % OF CURRENT COST	COMMENTS
Argentina	Higher	1964	52	National universities. Teachers
Brazil	Middle level	1967	96	State of Rio Grande do Sul. Budget. Personnel.
Burma	All levels	1965	22	Teacher rough estimate. Public.
Ceylon	Levels I + II	1969	81	Teachers. Budget.
Chile	Technical	1968	77	Sample basis. Teachers.
Ecuador	All levels	1965	60.5	Teacher rough estimate.
France	Higher	1967	53	Personnel.
Iran	All levels	1965	81	Teacher rough estimate. Public.
Ivory Coast	Primary	1967	89.5	Staff.
Madagascar	Primary	1966	84	Teachers.
Morocco	Secondary	1968	98	School accounts. Staff.
Netherlands	Compulsory	1964	67	Staff cost.
Thailand	Vocational	1964	65	Teachers.
Turkey	All levels	1967	73	Staff. Government accounts.
Uganda	Secondary	1967	72	Teachers' salaries in one school (Kitante).

Source: Unpublished IIEP analysis.

Second, within any one education level there are also different teacher classifications and salary schedules, according to professional qualifications (e.g. Grade A, B, and C elementary teachers in Tanzania, or "monitors," assistant teachers, and teachers in

Ivory Coast). There may also be different pay schedules for men and women teachers, and for local and expatriate teachers.[3]

Third, within each salary schedule there are "incremental steps" which each teacher climbs automatically according to years of service until he or she reaches the ceiling.

Fourth, teachers with lower qualifications can shift to a higher-paying schedule by improving their professional qualifications through in-service training.

The salary scales for primary and secondary teachers in Uganda, shown in Table 8.8, illustrate the foregoing features. It will be seen that there are wide differentials according to length and type of professional preparation and years of teaching service, ranging from a starting salary of only 132 pounds per annum for the least qualified primary teachers to a maximum of 1752 for the most qualified secondary teachers. The cost of direct-hire expatriate teachers in Uganda runs about 40 per cent above these local scales.

The salary differentials and increments described above endow teacher costs with an internal dynamic of their own. Even if the general level of teacher salaries remains stable, changes in the distribution and composition of the teacher corps can considerably alter the average cost per teacher, for the system as a whole, and at each education level. Thus, for example:

- In a period when primary education is expanding much more rapidly than secondary and higher education, average cost per teacher for the system as a whole will decline; but the reverse happens later on when expansion quickens at the secondary and higher level.
- If large numbers of young and poorly qualified teachers are hired during the first wave of an elementary school expansion, average cost per teacher at the elementary level declines; but later, as these young teachers grow older, and as some become up-

3. Some industrialized countries, such as the United States, have gradually abolished some of these distinctions and adopted a "single salary schedule" for elementary and secondary teachers and for men and women; but they still retain different pay scales according to professional qualifications and years of teaching service.

TABLE 8.8.
Teacher salary schedules in Uganda (1966), by qualifications and years of service.

CLASSIFICATION	FORMAL EDUCATION COMPLETED		SALARY (£ PER ANNUM)			
	LEVEL	YEARS	MINIMUM	MAXIMUM	MID-POINT	INCREMENTS
Secondary teachers						
	Honors Degree	17	798	1752	1272	22
	Degree	17	738	1572	1155	21
Primary teachers						
Grade 5	HSC + T2	16	612	1080	846	16
Grades 3, 4	CSC + T2	14	300	828	564	24
Grade 2	JSC + T4	12	189	354	272	13
Grade 2	JSC + T2	10	180	354	267	14
Grade 1	P6 + T2	8	132	276	204	17

Notes: Years of formal education are assumed to include years spent at teacher training colleges. The number of years thus spent is shown after the letter T in the previous column.

Source: *Estimates of Expenditure*, 1965-66; *Report of the Uganda Civil Service Salaries Commission*, 1962.

graded through in-service training, the average cost per teacher will rise rapidly.

- As local teacher supplies improve, the substitution of indigenous teachers for foreign teachers raises the average cost per teacher if the foreign teachers were low-cost volunteers, but it lowers the average cost if the expatriates were high-cost, contract teachers.

In short, quite apart from what is happening to the over-all size of the teacher corps or to pupil-teacher ratios (both of which obviously affect *total* teacher *costs*), changes in the *composition* of the teacher force have a strong influence on the average cost per teacher at each education level, thanks to the salary differentials and automatic increases embodied in the teacher salary structure. In projecting teacher costs, therefore, cost analysts must pay close attention to prospective changes in composition.

Present Teacher Costs and Recent Trends

The first requirement for making good projections of future teacher costs is to obtain a clear cross-sectional picture of the present teacher force and costs, and a longitudinal picture of what has been happening to these in recent years. These pictures should reveal:

- Total teacher costs, broken down by major sub-systems
- The relationship of teacher costs to total recurrent costs
- Average cost per teacher at each level
- The sources of finance for teacher costs
- Recent changes in the size and composition of the teacher force.

Outlined below are five simple exercises you can do to become acquainted with the techniques and problems involved in sketching the above pictures. You can probably obtain most of the data needed for these exercises from budgetary and teacher records in the national ministry of education if your educational system is centralized, but if it is decentralized you will have to consult records at the state, district, or local level.

To keep these exercises simple, we have confined them to *formal* education and to teacher costs financed mainly by public funds. For the moment, we have also left out any reference to expatriate teachers, but you may wish to include them as a separate category if they are important to your situation. Finally, if your system includes a number of part-time teachers, we suggest you convert them to "full-time equivalent teachers" for purposes of this analysis.

EXERCISE NO. 1
—DETERMINING TOTAL TEACHER COSTS

The aim of this first exercise is to compile an over-all figure of (publicly financed) teacher costs, broken down by educational levels, for the most recent year for which complete data are available. Remember that teacher costs include more than salaries; ordinarily they include the following four components:

• *Salary payments to teachers.* These should be measured *before* income tax payments and should be segregated from over-all personnel or staff costs (thereby excluding salaries and wages of administrators, clerks, custodial personnel, bus drivers, etc.).

• *Supplementary payments and allowances.*[4] These include payments for overtime work, extra responsibilities, hardship posts, cost-of-living allowances, family allowances, etc., which for all practical purposes are part of the teacher's "take-home pay."

• *Special benefits.* These include retirement fund contributions, medical coverage, free housing, free tuition for children of teach-

4. In some countries these supplementary payments add up to substantial amounts. In Iran, allowances paid to teachers in isolated areas and cold regions range from 40 to 100 per cent of the basic salary. (Source: *Status of Teachers in Asia.*) In British Guiana in 1965, teachers serving also as headmasters in Grade A schools (enrolments of 750 or above) were paid responsibility allowances of (West Indian) $129 per month on top of their basic salaries, which ranged from $420 to $520. (Source: *Survey of the Status of the Teaching Profession in the Americas,* by Margarita Davies, WCTOP, Washington, 1964.) A number of educational systems pay extra premiums for science or math teachers, or other types of teachers in particularly scarce supply.

ers, holiday travel, and other "fringe benefits" of direct value to the teacher but not part of take-home pay.

• *Indirect teacher costs.* These include necessary costs of teacher recruitment or improvement that do not involve direct payments or benefits to teachers, such as costs of recruiting trips and interviews, family moving costs, in-service professional improvement programs, etc. These are usually only marginal in size and therefore can be estimated roughly.

TABLE 8.9.
*Publicly financed teacher costs (1970), by education level and type of cost.**

EDUCATION LEVEL	TYPE OF COST				
	SALARIES	SUPPLEMENTARY PAYMENTS	BENEFITS	INDIRECT COSTS	SUBSYSTEM TOTALS
Primary					
Secondary					
Post-secondary					
System totals					

* Includes teachers in government and government-aided schools whose salaries and benefits are financed by public funds.

The chances are that your public education budget accounts are not broken down into precisely these categories, and it may also be that certain of the costs (such as fringe benefits) are carried partly on the budget of some agency other than the education ministry or department. All you can do in such cases is to use your best detective instincts and statistical ingenuity. Whatever solutions you arrive at for treating particular accounting problems, be sure to stick with them consistently and to leave clear tracks behind so that later others will know exactly what you did. Finally, when you have summarized your findings on a tabular form similar to that in Table 8.9, be sure to give it an accurate descriptive heading and to include such qualifying footnotes as may be necessary to define the exact meaning of the figures.

EXERCISE NO. 2—RATIO OF TEACHER COSTS TO TOTAL RECURRENT COSTS

With little additional effort, you can determine the relationship of teacher costs to total recurrent costs *for the same year* covered by Exercise No. 1, using the same budgetary sources of information. In arriving at the figures for total recurrent costs, be sure to *exclude* any items in the education budget that are not for formal education (such as museums, libraries, public recreation, special youth programs, and so forth). Your new findings can be summarized in a form similar to that in Table 8.10.

TABLE 8.10.
*Ratio of teacher costs to total recurrent costs (1970).**

	(1) TEACHER COSTS	(2) TOTAL RECURRENT COSTS	RATIO OF (1) TO (2)
Primary			
Secondary			
Post-secondary			
System total			

* Covers only publicly financed costs, in formal educational institutions.

EXERCISE NO. 3—AVERAGE COST PER TEACHER

One further simple step will complete your thumbnail sketch of present teacher costs, namely, the calculation of average recurrent cost per teacher. For this you will need to collect data on the number of teachers (full-time equivalent) at each education level, for the same year as in the previous exercises, including only teachers financed by public funds. By dividing the number of teachers at each level into the corresponding total recurrent costs, you will arrive at a simple "average cost per teacher" for each level. This is only a crude average which, like most such averages, conceals important differentials; but when combined with similar figures for other years, it is a significant indicator of the general direction in which teacher costs are moving. At times it can be a crucial early warning signal of trouble ahead.

The results of Exercise No. 3 can be entered on a simple summary table similar to that in Table 8.11.

TABLE 8.11.
*Average recurrent cost per teacher, by education levels (1970).**

LEVEL	(1) TOTAL RECURRENT COSTS	(2) TOTAL TEACHERS (FULL-TIME EQUIV.)	(3) AVERAGE COST PER TEACHER
Primary			
Secondary			
Post-secondary			
System total			

* Includes only formal education financed by public funds.

EXERCISE NO. 4—RECENT TRENDS IN TEACHER COSTS

If you are still game, we recommend that you now repeat the three previous exercises for each of the five preceding years (though if you are hard-pressed for time, you might limit yourself to only one earlier year, say, five years back). It will be a worthwhile investment of your time because only in this way can you detect and measure the dynamic forces that have been altering your educational costs in the recent past and are likely to influence them in the future.

The resulting time profile, presented in summary form as in Table 8.12, may produce some surprises, even for education officials who have been closest to the situation. Hopefully it will also provoke some searching questions as to why teacher costs have behaved in the manner shown.

EXERCISE NO. 5—SOURCES OF FINANCE FOR TEACHER COSTS

From the same basic data you assembled for the previous exercises, you can now put together an outline picture of where the funds came from to finance teacher costs in the same years. This will come in handy later when you are trying to determine what income is likely to be available to defray future teacher costs.

Remember to include *all* levels of government and to show their respective contributions separately. If such contributions were not specifically earmarked for teacher costs but were presumably available for recurrent costs generally, you can reasonably assume that a proportionate share went for teacher costs (unless you have reason to believe otherwise).

Your findings, summarized on a form similar to Table 8.13, will

TABLE 8.12.
*Summary of recent trends in teacher costs (1966–70).**

EDUCATION LEVEL	YEAR				
	1966	1967	1968	1969	1970
Primary					
Total recurrent costs					
Total teacher costs					
Ratio of teacher costs to recurrent costs (%)					
Average cost per teacher					
Secondary					
Total recurrent costs					
Total teacher costs					
Ratio of teacher costs to recurrent costs (%)					
Average cost per teacher					
Post-secondary					
Total recurrent costs					
Total teacher costs					
Ratio of teacher costs to recurrent costs (%)					
Average cost per teacher					
System total					
Total recurrent costs					
Total teacher costs					
Ratio of teacher costs to recurrent costs (%)					
Average cost per teacher					

* Includes only formal education, financed directly or indirectly by public funds.

TABLE 8.13.
Sources of public funds for teacher costs (1966–70).

	1966	1967	1968	1969	1970
Primary teachers					
National government					
State government					
Local government					
Total					
Secondary teachers					
National government					
State government					
Local government					
Total					
Post-secondary teachers					
National government					
State government					
Local government					
Total					
System total					
National government					
State government					
Local government					
Total					

provide a view of teacher costs seen from the revenue side, as distinct from the expenditure side used in the earlier exercises. The totals should coincide, unless some statistical quirks have crept in.

The five exercises above will have given you both a snapshot picture and a moving-picture of teacher costs in your educational system in recent years. This is the necessary foundation for projecting future costs and sources of finance. But the statistics alone are not enough. To benefit fully from the lessons of the recent past, you must disclose *why* the statistics behaved as they did.

Determining the Causes of Changes in Teacher Costs

Discovering the causes of recent changes in teacher costs requires statistical ingenuity and some additional information. In all probability, several different factors in combination have caused a change in teacher costs. Your problem is to sort them out and measure their relative importance. The following exercise illustrates how you might go about it.

Let us assume for the sake of argument that your Exercise No. 4 above (Table 8.12) showed an increase of 55 per cent in over-all costs of secondary school teachers between 1966 and 1970. Theoretically this could have been caused either by an increase in the number of teachers, or by an increase in the average cost per teacher, or some combination of the two. It is easy to find the answer

The data from which you constructed Table 8.12 reveal, let us say, that the total number of secondary teachers increased from 5000 in 1966 to 6300 in 1970—or roughly 26 per cent. Obviously this is a good part of the explanation, but not all of it. Table 8.12 also tells you that the average cost per secondary teacher rose about 15 per cent in the same period. On the face of it, this would seem to be the rest of the answer. But we still need an explanation of why the average cost per teacher rose by this amount.

A good part of the explanation, common knowledge tells you, was an 11 per cent across-the-board salary increase granted to all teachers in this period. What about the remaining 4 per cent? Logically, this can only be explained by a change in the *composition* of the teacher force. A quick check confirms this. Going behind your teacher totals you find that the number of Grade A teachers (with higher salaries) increased from 2000 to 3000, while Grade B teachers increased only from 3000 to 3300. Thus, the qualifications profile of the teacher force improved, and this seems to account for the missing 4 per cent.

But wait. The answer is not that simple. By examining the composition of the teacher force more closely, you discover that important changes have taken place in the distribution of teachers by points on the promotional steps of the salary scale. To see this clearly we need another table—Table 8.14.[5] This table shows a

5. The salaries shown on Table 8.14 were those prevailing in 1966, prior to the across-the-board increase of 11 per cent. Since this increase applied uniformly to all points on all salary scales, we can ignore it for present purposes.

salary range for Grade A teachers from a minimum of $1000 to a maximum of $2200, and for Grade B teachers from $500 to $1400. But the table also seems to present a paradox.

We know that the number of higher-paid Grade A teachers (average salary of $1530 in 1966) increased 50 per cent from 1966 to 1970, whereas the number of lower-paid Grade B teachers (average salary of $860 in 1966) increased by only 10 per cent. Then should not the over-all average cost per teacher have increased much more than 4 per cent? Yes, indeed, it should have. There must have been a strong cost-reducing force at work that we have not yet accounted for.

TABLE 8.14.
Illustration: changes in the distribution of teachers on the automatic salary promotion scale.

	NUMBER OF TEACHERS AT EACH STEP			
	1966		1970	
STEPS ON SALARY SCALE	GRADE A	GRADE B	GRADE A	GRADE B
$2200	300		300	
2000	200		200	
1800	200		300	
1600	250		400	
1400	300	450	500	700
1200	350	250	600	600
1000	400	300	700	500
900		300		500
800		350		400
700		400		300
600		450		300
500		500		
Average salary	$1530	$860	$1453	$1018

The mystery is quickly solved. As can be seen from the figures in Table 8.14, the average salary for Grade A teachers *declined* by 5 per cent over the five years (from $1530 to $1453), whereas the average for Grade B teachers rose by about 18 per cent (from $860 to $1018). This was because of the redistribution of teachers by salary steps; many new Grade A teachers came in at the bottom of the Grade A salary scale, while the number at the bottom of the Grade B scale declined and the number at the top increased. In other words, the Grade A teacher group grew younger, while the Grade B group grew older.

In summary, then, the 55 per cent increase in total teacher costs resulted from:

- A 40 per cent increase in the number of teachers
- An 11 per cent salary increase for all teachers
- A 4 per cent *net* increase in the average cost per teacher, resulting from a combination of (a) an increase in the proportion of Grade A teachers and (b) a redistribution of teachers by salary steps

The first two cost-increasing factors (a rise in the number of teachers and in the general level of teacher salaries) were fairly easy to identify and measure. But the third factor (changes in composition of the teaching force) was more subtle and required more effort to detect and measure. This example demonstrates why it is important when you are projecting future teacher costs to look carefully at any likely changes in composition of the teacher force, as well as at changes in its size and in the general level of teacher salaries. Otherwise you may be tricked into a serious error. For example, looking back for a moment at the columns of figures in Table 8.14, we can see that by 1975 the large number of new teachers at the low end of the Grade A scale in 1970 will have moved up the automatic promotion scale, causing the average salary of Grade A teachers to turn upward (unless they are offset by a larger number of new teachers coming in at the bottom).[6]

Projecting Future Teacher Costs

With all of the foregoing knowledge about how teacher costs have behaved in the recent past, you are now much better equipped to forecast their future behavior. But your work is only half done. Remembering what was said in Chapters 5 and 6 re-

6. A concrete example of this technique of analysis as applied to Uganda will be found in J. Hallak, *The Analysis of Educational Costs and Expenditure*, Paris, Unesco:IIEP, 1969 (Fundamentals of Educational Planning, 10).

garding the many internal and external factors that influence teacher costs, you must now consider carefully how each of them may influence teacher costs in the future. The balance of this chapter discusses the following items to which you will need to give special attention: (1) teacher requirements; (2) teacher supply prospects; (3) changes in the composition of the teacher force; (4) changes in the general level of teacher salaries; (5) price inflation; (6) changes in the general structure of salary and wage relationships in the economy; (7) teacher training costs; and (8) expatriate teachers.

PROJECTING TEACHER REQUIREMENTS

We cannot take time here to examine methodologies for projecting student enrolments and teacher requirements, but it should be emphasized that unless these foundations are solidly prepared, you cannot make trustworthy projections of teacher costs.[7]

The most commonly used method of calculating teacher requirements is simply to apply the present pupil teacher ratio (or any desired modification of it) to the projected number of students at each education level for the final year of the plan period. The resulting figure shows the size of teacher stock needed to serve the projected number of students, and how much the present stock must be enlarged. The total cost of teachers in the final plan year can then be calculated by applying an appropriate figure of average cost per teacher at each education level (either the present average cost, or some modification of it).

This simple method is handy for making a quick, rough check of feasibility, but its deficiencies are too great to make it a reliable method for careful planning. First, it tells you nothing about the other years in the plan period, or about the number of new teachers that will be needed to replace those in the present stock who will retire, die, or resign; it only tells you the *net* addition to stock

7. These matters are covered by other IIEP publications, particularly J. D. Chesswas, *Methodologies of Educational Planning for Developing Countries*, Paris, Unesco:IIEP, 1969 (two volumes).

required, and this is not an adequate guide for planning teacher supply. Second, a single pupil-teacher ratio applying, for example, to all of primary education in the nation obscures important differentials which may considerably affect the real demand for teachers in the next five years—such as the differential in pupil-teacher ratio and class size as between urban and rural schools. In reality, many existing classes may be undersized and capable of absorbing increased enrolments with no corresponding increase of teachers; whereas in other situations, over-sized classes need to be reduced, whether or not enrolments expand. You will get a much more reliable estimate of teacher requirements, therefore, by basing it on an estimate of the number of *classes* that need to be staffed, not on the number of students *per se*. And in estimating the additional number of classes needed, you should differentiate between (1) urban classes (that may need to be increased in number *both* to reduce present oversized classes and to handle a net increase in students); (2) rural classes in *existing* schools that can probably absorb more students; and (3) classes in *new* rural schools, built to serve new areas, that will clearly need new teachers.

The practical importance of these rural-urban distinctions showed up clearly in the case studies from Norway, the U.S.S.R., and Madagascar. In a quite different context, the case study of secondary education in Chile showed that a sizable increase in enrolments could be satisfactorily handled (in the particular circumstances) simply by redeploying the existing stock of teachers rather than by adding to it. And the Makerere University College case emphasized the possibility of handling more university students with virtually no increase in the number of teachers, if present class sizes and pupil-teacher ratios are well below the accepted norm.

For all these reasons, we would urge you to look skeptically at any teacher requirement figures before accepting them as a sound basis on which to calculate future teacher costs.

PROJECTING TEACHER SUPPLIES

Regardless of how carefully teacher requirements are calculated, they can turn out to be wide of the mark if they are not tested for feasibility in a confrontation with teacher supply prospects. An educational system may theoretically *need* a given increase in teacher stock in order to accommodate more students, but if there is clear evidence that a physical shortage of new teachers will make it impossible to recruit this number, then it is more realistic and responsible to adjust the projected requirements to fit the likely supply. Otherwise, you will end up costing teachers who will not be there. At the same time, you may fail to allow sufficient financing to expand teacher training capacity and output in order to reduce the teacher shortage.

PROJECTING THE COMPOSITION OF THE TEACHER FORCE

The approaches suggested above for estimating future teacher requirements, adjusted to fit the realistic supply prospects, will give you a more accurate estimate of the *number* of teachers to be financed, but there still remains the problem of projecting the *composition* of the teacher stock.

To add to what has been said about this matter in earlier pages, we can here suggest a practical method to use if you do not have good data on the present distribution of teachers by years of service and steps on the promotional scale, but you do have data on past teacher training output and on the present distribution of teachers by professional categories. In this situation (which is quite common), you can use a trial and error method of arriving at an estimated distribution of teachers by points on the salary scale. It consists of breaking down the present stock of teachers on the basis of annual graduating classes from teacher training institutions who entered teaching the following year; then calculating how far up the automatic promotion ladder each group of graduates should be in the present year (allowing arbitrarily for some assumed rate of attrition).[8] This same exercise is done for each professional category of teachers coming from different training programs. The result gives you a theoretical distribution of teachers in the present stock by years of service and position on the promotion scale. To test it out, you can then cost the present teacher force, assuming this distribution, on the basis of the existing salary schedule. If the resulting total teacher bill differs substantially from the actual bill, you can then make successive adjustments in the theoretical distribution pattern until its total cost coincides with the actual total shown in the budget accounts. This adjusted theoretical pattern can then be used to project future changes in the composition of the teacher force.

Perhaps it will clarify matters if you look at Table 8.15 which shows the distribution of primary teachers in Tanzania as of 1967, and their corresponding year of graduation from teacher training. To illustrate, there were 88 Grade A teachers who graduated before 1954 and who, by 1967, had progressed to the top of the salary scale (£610 per year). At the other extreme, there were 476 graduates of the 1966 graduating class at the bottom of the Grade A scale (£330). Looking ahead, we can predict that the latter group (minus any who leave the service) will be found eight notches higher on the salary scale by 1975. How much this will raise the average cost of a Grade A teacher will depend on how many new teachers enter at the bottom of the scale in the intervening years.

PROJECTING TEACHER SALARIES

Having projected the size and composition of the future teacher force, it remains to put a price on the package. One way is simply to cost it at existing teacher salary rates. But if it seems likely, judging from local knowledge, that one or more general teacher salary increases are in store over the next few years, this must be

8. This rate varies considerably from country to country, and in each country according to the status, conditions of service, and structure of the teaching force; 2 per cent would be a low attrition rate, 4 per cent a high one.

taken into account. Since you cannot be sure, the best practice is to make two or three alternative assumptions and cost each one out.

A distinction should be made between two types of possibilities:

TABLE 8.15.
Distribution of primary teachers in Tanzania (1967), by qualifications and years of service.

	GRADE A		GRADE B		GRADE C	
YEAR OF GRADUATION OF ORIGINAL GROUP	NUMBERS IN SERVICE	POINT ON SCALE £ P.A.	NUMBERS IN SERVICE	POINT ON SCALE £ P.A.	NUMBERS IN SERVICE	POINT ON SCALE £ P.A.
1954 and prior	81	av. 610	147	av. 492	5128 (1)	M 348 F 330
1955	15	540	29	402	836	285
1956	21	516	43	384	690	273
1957	22	492	44	366	558	261
1958	24	468	44	348	481	249
1959	43	444	89	330	272	237
1960	45	423	93	315	306	228
1961	44	402	166	300	412	219
1962	84	384			665	210
1963	81	366	209 (2)	285	694	201
1964	175	348	256 (2)	273	678	189
1965	279	330	368 (2)	261	835	180
1966	476	330	75 (2)	249	619	180
Totals	1390	av. 370	1563	av. 313	12174	av. 276

(1) 4335 male, 793 female.
(2) Year of upgrading following the one year of pre-service training.
Note: At the time of the case study, the rate of exchange was \$1 = £0.305.

first, where general price inflation is taking place and teacher salaries may be changing in relation to the cost of living, and, second, where changes are taking place in the relationship between teacher salaries and the general structure of wages and per capita income in the economy. Either phenomenon can affect not only teacher costs but the ability of education to attract and hold an adequate supply of manpower.

ALLOWING FOR INFLATION

The exercises suggested earlier in this chapter dealt with teacher costs in terms of current prices and salaries prevailing in each particular year. But current prices can be quite deceptive if the economy is undergoing substantial price inflation. If, for example, teachers are granted a 10 per cent across-the-board salary increase in a given year, but the cost-of-living index proceeds to rise 20 per cent in the next twelve months, the teachers clearly end up worse off than before their salary increase. Their *real* income, measured in constant prices and real purchasing power, has declined.

This has been a common phenomenon in a number of Latin American countries. In Argentina, for example, teacher salaries seemed always to be running a losing race against consumer prices. In an effort to put a stop to this race, a new Teachers' Charter in 1958 granted a sizable salary increase, designed to catch up with past inflation, and went on to provide for automatic future cost-of-living adjustments.[9]

It is interesting to see what happened under this new arrangement. As Figure 8.1 and Table 8.16 show, the "catching up" salary adjustment in 1958 was more than wiped out by further inflation in the next two years, before sufficient adjustments could be made in teacher salaries. By 1960, the cost-of-living index had climbed 140 per cent over 1958, while the teacher-salary index rose only 10 per cent. This was tantamount to more than a 50 per cent cut in the real income of teachers. Thereafter, however, the new cost-of-living adjustment system took hold and up to 1964 (where our data leave off) teachers managed to keep fairly well in line with further inflation. But they never fully regained the ground lost from 1958 to 1960.

9. This is an understandable protective measure for any employee group to demand whose incomes tend to lag behind inflation. But if widely adopted throughout the economy, it may simply add fuel to an already spiraling inflation, unless it finally forces the government to pursue much more stringent anti-inflationary fiscal and monetary policies, probably including heavier taxes on wages and salaries.

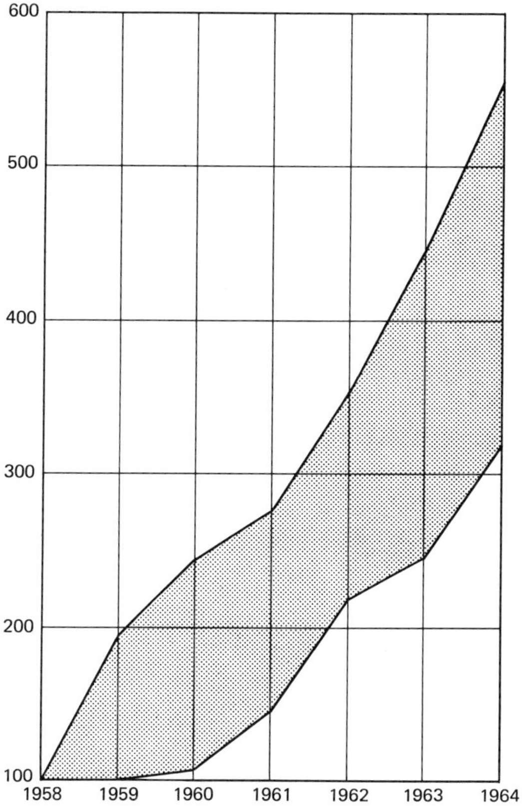

FIGURE 8.1.
Argentina: comparative trend of cost-of-living index and teacher-salary index (1958 = 100).

This is a rather extreme case, but teachers and educational systems in a great many nations have been the serious victims of inflation. If you live in an inflation-prone country, we suggest that you establish, with the help of a local economist, a weighted index of teacher remuneration, similar to that in Argentina. This can be regularly compared to the cost-of-living index. It will be useful both for projecting teacher costs and for weighing alternative salary policies.

We also repeat our earlier suggestion that you make alternative assumptions about the future rate of inflation. In all probability your government will not consider it prudent to publish those assumptions that anticipate further inflation, lest they become self-fulfilling prophecies and political liabilities. Therefore your contingency projections should remain "unofficial" and be kept under lock and key. But the truth is that where rampant inflation has been going on for some years, the greatest victory the government can hope for is to slow it down substantially, not to stop it altogether. Therefore it could mislead decision-makers seriously if you were simply to assume that prices and salaries would suddenly become stabilized. Less ideal prospects must be frankly contemplated if educational planning is to be part of the real world.

TABLE 8.16.
Argentina: comparative trend of the cost-of-living index and the index of teacher salaries (1958–64).
1958 = 100

YEAR	COST-OF-LIVING INDEX 1	INDEX OF REMUNERATION OF TEACHING STAFF 2	RATIO 1:2
1958	100	100	1
1959	198.1	100	2
1960	240.4	110	2.2
1961	276	146	1.9
1962	353.6	216.9	1.6
1963	446.4	245	1.8
1964	556.7	320.6	1.7

Source: Cost of living: CONADE, National Accounting Section. Remuneration of teaching staff: Teachers' Charter.

FORESHADOWING CHANGES IN WAGE RELATIONSHIPS

Even in the absence of price infiation, the real income of teachers and the cost of teachers to the educational system may rise or fall, or remain steady, depending on how teacher salaries behave relative to average per capita income and to other wages and salaries in the economy. There are a number of possibilities and your problem is to choose some assumptions that best fit the conditions and prospects of your particular economy.

One commonly used assumption is that the real incomes of teachers will move up in line with incomes generally in the country. Thus, for example, if real income *per capita* for the nation at large is expected to rise by 2 per cent each year, thanks to economic growth and rising productivity in the economy as a whole, then the projection of teacher costs would allow for an average rise of 2 per cent each year in the real salaries of teachers (whether or not the productivity of teachers rose by this amount). Professor Edding points out that real teacher incomes must keep pace with rising real incomes elsewhere in the economy if education is to maintain its competitive position in the national manpower market. This, he notes, is what happened between 1951 and 1962 in the Federal Republic of Germany; Gross Domestic Product per employed person rose by an average of 8.9 per cent per year in this period, while teacher salaries rose by 8.7 per cent.[10]

An alternative assumption, commonly used, is that the real salaries of teachers will remain constant. This is tantamount to saying either (a) that per capita incomes as a whole will remain constant (possibly because population is growing at the same rate as the economy), and teacher salaries will retain a constant relationship to average per capita income and to other wages and salaries, or (b) that teachers as a group will not participate in the productivity gains of the economy—in other words, their real earnings will stand still even though the earnings of other groups rise.

The third logical possibility, of course, is that the real earnings of teachers will rise faster than the incomes of others, placing teachers in the favored position of getting a disproportionate share of the economy's gains. This would be the case, for example, if teacher salaries (after adjusting for any changes in consumer prices) rose 5 per cent annually while average per capita national income, or earnings of employed persons, rose an average of only 2 per cent annually.

Actually, one can find examples of all three of the above pat-

10. Frederick Edding, *Methods of Analyzing Educational Outlays*, Paris, Unesco, 1966.

terns in different countries, varying with their economic circumstances, and even the same nation may move from one pattern to another in the course of time.

By and large, Edding's proposition (that the real income of teachers tends to move in step with average real income per capita for the nation at large) is a good assumption to make in the case of industrialized countries with relatively full employment and a reasonably good supply-demand balance for educated manpower. But it would be a precarious assumption to make in the case of many developing nations. We can illustrate the point by contrasting the experiences of India and East Africa during the 1960's.[11]

When independence came to the middle African countries, there quickly developed severe shortages of educated manpower, particularly for government services and teaching. One result was that large numbers of expatriate experts, administrators, and teachers were retained or recruited to fill the gap. Another result, fostered by the first, was that the high expatriate salary scales from the colonial period quickly came to be applied to East African personnel who assumed comparable posts. In short, the new governments, as the dominant employers of educated manpower, adopted a policy of non-discriminatory salaries as between Africans and expatriates, but the salaries chosen were based on economic conditions in highly developed metropolitan countries, not on African economic conditions. These salaries, therefore, were a much higher multiple of the average per capita income in African countries than in the metropolitan countries on which they were based. In the mid-1960's, for example, the average Ugandan secondary school graduate was earning twenty times the average per capita income, and the average university graduate was earning

11. The data and interpretations used in this comparison are drawn largely from: J. B. Knight, "Earnings, Employment, Education and Income Redistribution in Uganda," Bulletin of the Oxford University Institute of Statistics, 1968; R. Jolly, *Costs and Confusions in African Education: Some Future Implications of Recent Trends*, University of Sussex, Institute of Development Studies, 5 November 1968 (Mimeo No. 18); and M. Blaug, P. R. G. Layard, and M. Woodhall, *The Causes of Graduate Unemployment in India*, London, Allen Lane, Penguin Press, 1969.

nearly fifty times. This meant that the cost of adding one more qualified primary school teacher was equivalent to the annual incomes of twenty or more Ugandans. By contrast, the cost of a similarly qualified elementary teacher in more industrialized countries would be only five to ten times the average per capita income.

So long as the number of educated persons thus employed was relatively small, the African economies could support such salaries, but as government establishments and educational systems expanded, and as public budgets became increasingly strained, these unusually high salaries (relative to other wages in the economy) became a major roadblock to further expansion. Meanwhile, to make matters worse, these high salaries had grown even higher.[12] What happens in such circumstances when the supply of educated people finally becomes more abundant, and when at the same time demand for them falls off because the initial vacancies have become filled (even in some cases with less qualified people)? One of two things has to happen. One possibility is that the abnormally wide spread between the wages of uneducated workers and the high salaries of educated people continues, in which case further expansion of education finally becomes financially prohibitive, and many of the newly educated either find themselves unemployed or take jobs beneath their qualifications. The alternative possibility is a general readjustment of the national wage structure which brings the bottom and the top closer together, thereby reducing the relative cost of educated people and opening up more jobs for them within the prevailing fiscal limitations. This was the hard choice that faced most newly independent African nations by the late 1960's.

Obviously the second alternative would best serve the nation's

12. Jolly concluded that in Uganda during the 1960's, "the rise in teachers' salaries is almost as important a factor as the increase in enrolments for explaining the more than three-fold increase in educational expenditure. Only a small part of the increase in average teachers' salary (less than one third) can be accounted for by upgrading of teachers' qualifications." *Costs and Confusions in African Education: Some Future Implications of Recent Trends*, University of Sussex, Institute of Development Studies, 5 November 1968 (Mimeo No. 18).

development, but bringing about such fundamental salary readjustments posed excruciating difficulties, both political and economic. To their credit, some African governments began to grasp the nettle. "Indeed, already the Ugandan Second Five-Year Plan has spelt out guidelines for changes in incomes over the years ahead. Incomes over £600 per annum are not to rise at all, incomes between £210 and £600 by 1.0 per cent per year, incomes between £90 and £210 by 2.5 per cent and incomes under £90 by 3.5 per cent. Such ideas are in the air, and when it comes to it, larger changes may emerge." [13]

India, by contrast, did not begin its independence by localizing colonial salary rates. Moreover, it had a large head start on educational expansion and was reaching the point of employment market "saturation" in many occupations by the late 1950's. Accordingly, in the 1960's India had a drastically different set of wage and salary conditions for educated people, including teachers. Table 8.17, drawn from Professor Jolly's article, contrasts the relative earnings of people with different amounts of education in India and Uganda. The statistics are only approximate and not precisely comparable, but the general story they tell is true. The two countries had roughly equal per capita incomes, but the typical secondary graduate in Uganda was earning more than two and one-half times as much as an Indian graduate (measured by per capita income in each country). Unfortunately, no figure was available for Indian university graduates, but from other evidence it is clear that they were far less well off than Ugandan graduates.

The extreme wage and salary spreads in African countries such as Uganda are clearly not economically viable in the long run. As the supply of well-educated local people improves, thereby reducing and finally eliminating the earlier need to fill many jobs with expatriates, the major prop will be removed from under the artificial salary structure and it will be forced into a new shape by local economic and political realities.

There is a lesson here for all. As any nation's supply of educated manpower becomes more abundant, both the quantity and quality

13. *Ibid.*

of teacher supply are likely to improve and the cost of teachers to become stabilized or to fall—not absolutely, but relative to lower-paying jobs in the economy and to the average per capita income.

The history of today's industrialized countries reinforces this proposition. As their economies developed and per capita income rose, the spread between lower and higher salaries and wages gradually diminished, mainly because the wages at the bottom moved

TABLE 8.17.
Average salaries by level of education in Uganda and India.

	ANNUAL EARNINGS	
EDUCATIONAL LEVEL	UGANDA 1965 (£'S PER YEAR)	INDIA 1960–61 (£'S PER YEAR)
Junior secondary/middle	209	131
School certificate/secondary	556	185
Higher certificate/graduate	852	311
Ugandan graduate	1373	n.a.
Per capita income	28	25
SALARIES AS MULTIPLES OF PER CAPITA INCOME		
Junior secondary/middle	7.3	5.4
School certificate/secondary	20.0	7.7
Ugandan graduate	49.0	

Notes: a. Data refer to average earnings over all age groups.
b. Uganda data refers to civil service earnings; India data to average urban earnings.
c. Indian earnings are converted from rupees to pounds at the 1961 exchange rate.
d. Educational level shows first the Ugandan level, then the roughly comparable Indian level.

Source: Uganda: J. Knight, *Earning, Employment, Education and Income Redistribution in Uganda,* Bulletin of the Oxford University Institute of Statistics, 1968, p. 255.
India: M. Blaug, P. R. G. Layard, and M. Woodhall, *The Causes of Graduate Unemployment in India, London, Allen Lane, Penguin Press,* 1969, calculated from Table 7-5, urban Indian data.

up faster than those at the top. The encouraging thing about this long-term adjustment process is that most people gain by it (except perhaps the extremely high-income people), but those who began near the bottom gain the most. The process itself can only take place, however, if the economy grows, and the danger is that distorted wage structures may inhibit its growth, along with the development of education.

As a nation moves across the spectrum ranging from the special African conditions of the early 1960's at the one extreme to the most industrialized nations at the other, the scarcity value of educated manpower declines, the over-all spread of incomes narrows, and so does the spread of salaries between lower and higher echelons of the educational system and between more qualified and less qualified teachers. Thus, for example, in Portugal, between 1955 and 1965, the Gross Domestic Product per capita rose an average of 7 per cent annually (in current prices), while the average salaries of qualified teachers rose at 4.5 per cent and those of unqualified teachers rose twice as fast, by 9.5 per cent.[14] In Israel, elementary and secondary school teachers with equal qualifications get equal pay (the former, however, teach thirty hours per week and the latter only twenty-four).

The central point that emerges from the foregoing discussion is that educational planners and cost analysts, in any country, in close consultation with knowledgeable local economists, must carefully assess at what point on the spectrum of development that particular country stands at the moment, in order to choose a reasonable set of assumptions as to what is likely to happen to teacher salaries in the coming plan period. There is no common assumption appropriate for all countries, or even for the same country from one decade to the next. Teacher costs, as we said before, live in a highly dynamic world, and to project them with reasonable accuracy the cost analyst's assumptions must be just as dynamic.

14. Computed by IIEP on the basis of salary data given by J. Sheehan, "Inter-Country Comparisons," in M. Ferreira Leite, P. Lynch, J. Sheehan, and J. Vaizey, *The Economics of Educational Costing: Inter-Country and Inter-Regional Comparisons*, Vol. I, Lisbon, Instituto Gulbenkian de Ciência, 1968.

THE COSTS OF TEACHER TRAINING

In the earlier exercises in this chapter we omitted the costs of teacher training in the interest of simplicity, but now we must return to them for they have a substantial direct and indirect bearing on teacher costs.

Logically, teacher training costs are in the category of capital costs, insofar as they involve expenditures in one time period that are intended to result in useful services in later periods. It is not customary accounting practice, however, to treat them as capital costs, except insofar as physical facilities for teacher training are concerned. We strongly recommend, however, against blending teacher training costs in with recurrent costs for present classroom services; they should be treated in a separate category so that they can be clearly related to *future* teacher supplies and costs. This applies to both pre-service and in-service training.[15]

In any one year, teacher training costs are likely to be a very modest fraction of total education costs, but do not be deceived by this. During a period of rapid expansion they can add up to a substantial total over a few years. Even more important, they can have a large multiplier effect on future teacher costs, not only by adding to the number of trained teachers, but by raising the level of teacher qualifications to higher salary categories.

One of the strategic uses of cost analysis is in choosing among alternative approaches to teacher training, and to upgrading the quality and effectiveness of existing teacher force. The Polish cost analysts, it will be recalled, helped the decision-makers by costing several alternative approaches, so that they could compare relative costs of different schemes of teacher training against their relative pedagogical merits and against other feasibility factors.[16]

Policy-makers are often obliged to decide how best to allocate scarce resources between pre-service and in-service teacher training.

15. See also John Vaizey's articles in M. Ferreira Leite, P. Lynch, J. Sheehan, and J. Vaizey, *The Economics of Educational Costing: Inter-Country and Inter-Regional Comparisons*, Lisbon, Instituto Gulbenkian de Ciência, 1968.

16. K. Podoski, "Poland: The Role of Cost Analysis in Planning a Teacher-Training Program," in *Educational Cost Analysis in Action: Case Studies for Planners*, Vol. II, Paris, Unesco:IIEP, 1972.

Both the relative costs and relative time factors play a major role in such decisions. If all the effort is put into pre-service training, it will take many years to make a sizable impact on the quality of the whole teacher force, but if the reverse course is followed, of putting all the resources into in-service training, the vicious circle of poor quality teacher supply may never be broken. Thus the problem is to strike the best balance, and the relative costs and future cost implications of the two types of training are a crucial factor to consider in reaching the best balance.

Analysis of teacher training costs also becomes an important element in planning and assessing a long-range educational reform. This happened in Madagascar, where, in order to create a large number of four-year primary schools in rural areas, a major new teacher training effort had to be undertaken (and the failure of this effort to keep on schedule in the early years became a major bottleneck to the whole reform and expansion plan).

One important question to ask about any program of pre-service teacher training is: How much does it cost to put a newly trained teacher in a classroom? Often it costs very much more than meets the eye. Heavy wastage of student-teacher trainees during the training period, plus heavy attrition among successful graduates who finally choose employment other than teaching, can put the cost of each graduate who *does* enter teaching at a very high multiple of the average annual cost per student enrolled in teacher training institutions. The cost jumps even higher if many of the newly trained teachers fail to remain in teaching very long. If a teacher remains in teaching for thirty years, his original training cost, amortized over the whole period, is obviously much smaller than if he remained in teaching only two or three years. It is therefore important when dealing with teacher training costs to get the best data you can on three different rates of attrition: (1) student dropouts from teacher training; (2) teacher training graduates who fail to enter teaching; and (3) graduates who enter teaching, but depart prematurely.

The most important question of all to ask about teacher training costs is this: What impact will a given program or strategy of teacher training (either pre-service or in-service) have on future recurrent costs of teachers through altering the qualifications structure of the teaching force? To demonstrate the importance of this question we will cite two examples, from Tanzania and Uganda.

For the Tanzanian example we must ask you to refer back to Table 8.15, which shows the distribution of elementary teachers in 1967 by Grades A, B, and C and by points on the promotion scale. Let us assume, hypothetically, that a policy decision is made to halt the training of new Grade C teachers (the least qualified and lowest paid), and to upgrade existing Grade C teachers as rapidly as possible to Grade B through intensive in-service training. Our problem is to examine the cost implications.

You will note on Table 8.15 that the Grade C teachers who entered service in 1958 or earlier are already getting salaries at least as high as the bottom of the Grade B scale. Presumably, therefore, no extra cost would result from reclassifying them to Grade B after appropriate training. The remaining Grade C teachers, however, who entered service after 1958, would get a salary increase when they were shifted from their present position on the Grade C scale to the bottom of the Grade B scale, after additional training. The extra salary cost (exclusive of the in-service training costs) can be easily calculated. The 4481 post-1958 teachers presently earn total salaries of 893,466 pounds (before the reform). By moving to the starting salary of the Grade B scale (£249) they would earn 1,115,769 pounds, or an increase of 264,303 pounds. This represents a 30 per cent increase over their present cost, or an 8 per cent increase over the initial total for *all* Grade C teachers (including the pre-1958 ones). To this would have to be added the costs of in-service training.

In subsequent years, of course, all the former Grade C teachers would be moving up the Grade B scale; thus the eventual costs of the reform would substantially exceed the increases shown above. All this is not to suggest, of course, that the policy of eliminating the lowest-quality category of teachers should be rejected out of hand. It is simply to emphasize the importance of weighing the financial consequences carefully before embracing such a policy.

The second case, from Uganda, is not hypothetical; it actually happened—or to be more precise, it *almost* happened.[17] Uganda had, in the early 1960's, some two dozen small, teacher training colleges which, it was generally agreed, were economically inefficient and pedagogically weak. Plans were therefore considered for consolidating them by enlarging several of the best and most conveniently located ones and closing the others. Along came a foreign aid agency, however, with a more attractive proposition. It offered to replace them all with four brand new, much larger, modern training colleges, similar to those in the donor country. These new colleges would train only the highest classification of primary teachers (then a minority in Uganda) and thus accelerate the upgrading of the whole teacher force. The existing less-qualified teachers would be phased out as rapidly as possible. This was a very attractive proposition, pedagogically, and presumably it would also have economic advantages by reducing the unit costs of training through economies of scale. The proposal was accepted in principle by the government of Uganda, but the matter took on a different face when the educational planners probed more deeply into the cost implications. Briefly, here is what they found.

First, the new facilities would, in fact, cost half as much again to build and equip as had been initially estimated. This, however, was a problem for the donor agency, not Uganda.

Second, the unit cost per graduate would not be lower but, in fact, about two and one-half times as high as in the inefficient smaller institutions. This was because the program would be greatly enriched, reflecting practices in the donor nation.

Third, and most important, the introduction of nothing but top-grade teachers into the system, and the elimination of low-grade teachers, would soon multiply the annual teacher salary

17. Nicholas Bennett, "Uganda: Educational Cost Evaluation," in *Educational Cost Analysis in Action: Case Studies for Planners*, Vol. III, Paris, Unesco:IIEP, 1972.

bill beyond Uganda's ability to pay. This came as a shock because, up to then, the main focus of attention had been on what it would cost to construct these new facilities.

With this new information in hand, the Uganda education authorities, in cooperation with the foreign aid agency, proceeded to do some cutting and reorienting of the project, and some stretching out of its time schedule. In the end, Uganda would upgrade its teachers, but to try to do it too quickly would result in an economic disaster.

A NOTE ON EXPATRIATE TEACHERS

We have left this matter to the end because it affects only a limited number of nations, mostly in Africa, but for them it is exceedingly important and has many cost ramifications.

Two basic points are vital to keep in mind. First, the cost of expatriate teachers usually differs greatly from the cost of equivalent local teachers. It is usually much higher, by at least 40 to 60 per cent, when they are foreign "contract teachers" who receive all their salary and allowances, as well as transportation, from the host nation. But even when a substantial foreign subsidy is involved, the local costs may be higher than for an indigenous teacher. In the Ivory Coast in 1965, for example, the allowances to expatriate teachers for housing alone cost more to the budget than the total salary of local teachers with equivalent qualifications.[18] Volunteer teachers, on the other hand, such as Peace Corps volunteers, may cost considerably less to the host system than equivalent local teachers. The point here is that in projecting future teacher costs careful estimates must be made of the number and types of expatriate teachers, for this can make a large difference to the total costs.

The second point is that expatriate teachers are a highly volatile component of the total teaching corps. Not only do they remain for relatively short periods—typically one to two years—but their percentage representation in the whole teaching staff

18. See J. Hallak, *The Analysis of Educational Costs and Expenditure*, Paris, Unesco:IIEP, 1969 (Fundamentals of Educational Planning, 10).

keeps shifting. Understandably, African countries are eager to Africanize their teaching staffs as rapidly as possible, but the rate at which they can achieve this depends, first, on how fast they can build up their own teacher supply, and, second, on how rapidly they are attempting to expand their educational systems (particularly in secondary and higher education where foreign teachers are most needed). A relatively small marginal increase in the rate of expansion can result in a relatively large proportionate increase in the number of expatriate teachers needed. This was demonstrated dramatically in one of the Uganda case studies. A decision by the government, it will be recalled, to increase the expansion targets in secondary and higher education beyond those recommended by the planning group meant that instead of reducing the proportion of expatriate teachers, there would have to be a substantial increase. This, in turn, meant a substantial upswing in the marginal costs of the additional students.

From this lengthy and diversified discussion of teacher costs, we turn now to a somewhat briefer consideration of how to treat capital costs.

9 *Treating Capital Costs*

When capital costs are spread over a period of years, they typically account for only a modest fraction of total unit cost per student. Nevertheless, they deserve the careful attention of planners and cost analysts for several reasons:

- Capital outlays usually involve large lump-sum expenditures, raising special financing problems. Borrowed capital funds must later be paid back with interest, thus mortgaging future revenues for years to come.
- Apart from debt service, the creation of additional facilities increases future operating revenues; the cost of using and maintaining a new educational facility often equals its initial capital cost every three to five years.
- The layout and location of new facilities can impose severe constraints on educational technologies and logistical patterns in years ahead, thereby inhibiting needed changes and innovations and perpetuating old inefficiencies.
- The planning of new facilities provides a strategic occasion for maximizing the utilization of both existing and future facilities, which is a major key to improving over-all educational efficiency and holding down costs.
- The creation of new facilities for new programs in any one sector of the educational system has major repercussions, including cost impacts, on other sectors. Unless these are identified, assessed, and provided for in advance, the new program may later create severe difficulties elsewhere and encounter setbacks.

For all these reasons, educational planners and managers need sharp eyes and sharper pencils when dealing with capital costs.

Identifying and Measuring Capital Costs

Practical accounting problems arise in distinguishing between capital costs and recurrent costs. Conceptually, the distinction is clear enough. Capital costs are associated with durable educational inputs—particularly land and site utilities, buildings, furniture, and equipment—which give service for more than a single fiscal year; recurrent costs involve services and supplies that can be consumed within a single accounting year. But the practical line of demarcation must often be drawn arbitrarily and can create confusion in accounting systems.

By the above definition, for example, books are capital items because they usually last for several years before needing replacement. Thus it is common practice to treat the initial bulk purchase of textbooks and library books for a new school or university as a capital outlay; but it is equally common practice to treat the purchase of additional books and replacements thereafter as a current expense. The latter violates a theoretical nicety, but in this case no harm is done so long as the same accounting method is used consistently, every one understands what is going on, and the books actually get bought.

However, the treatment of major repairs and replacements which prolong the life of existing capital items is another matter. If these irregular and frequently sizable expenditures are not adequately provided for on schedule (which is what often happens when they are treated incorrectly as current costs and thrown into direct competition with teacher costs), the result can be serious physical deterioration of capital, disruption of educational programs, increased inefficiency and costs, and lowered productivity. To avert this risk, educational systems should set up a special capital reserve account for major repairs and replacements that can be added to annually and drawn upon as needed, independently of the recurrent budget.

Educational systems in developing nations will be well advised to keep a special foreign currency reserve earmarked for the prompt purchase of replacement parts for imported equipment, as well as a minimal inventory of critical spare parts. Each time a machine breaks down, the educational process may remain disrupted for many weeks, due to the time-consuming process of obtaining an official allocation of foreign exchange, and of ordering and awaiting delivery of the needed parts.

The following basic concepts will help you unravel confusing accounting records and avoid errors in measuring capital costs.

Capital stocks vs. capital flows. The stock of capital is the inventory of buildings, equipment, and other capital items existing *at a given point in time.* It is like a reservoir that can be drawn down (by depreciation) or replenished and enlarged by new inflows. The value of an educational system's capital stock can be measured by depreciating the *original cost* of each item in the inventory at an appropriate rate (adjusted for major repairs, additions, and replacements made in the interim). Alternatively, it can be measured by estimating the *replacement value* (what it would cost today to replace the facilities), *minus* depreciation. Or it can be measured by its estimated *market value,* if appropriate evidence is available for making such an estimate.

These distinct concepts and measurements—of capital stock at a particular time, of capital inflows over past years, and of new inflows needed in future years—are basic tools for a variety of practical purposes. You will need them especially for estimating total unit costs per student in different parts of the educational system, for measuring the full costs of education to the economy, for comparing the relative merits of alternative courses of action, for costing individual projects, for projecting future capital fund requirements, and for applying cost-benefit tests.

Depreciation and amortization. In addition to the stock and flow concepts just mentioned, there is the important concept of spreading the costs of capital items over their useful lifetime in order to allocate a proper share of these costs to each time period and to each group served. This method is essential to determining the total unit cost per student (recurrent cost *plus* capital cost) and to making cost-benefit assessments.

Capital costs can be spread over time by applying an appropriate *depreciation* charge to each year, the rate of depreciation varying with the expected useful life of each item. But this is not the whole of the story; for most purposes interest costs should be added to depreciation costs, resulting in a figure of *amortization* cost. Even when there is no interest cost shown in the budget, it is important in estimating full capital costs to include an imputed interest charge (reflecting what the capital would earn in some alternative use in the economy). In this manner you can arrive at an *imputed rent* for all capital facilities which can be used for estimating total education costs (or unit cost per student) in any one year or over a period of years.[1]

Budgetary costs vs. full costs. The caveats in Chapter 7 regarding public and private costs, as well as budgetary costs versus costs to the economy, apply with special force to capital costs. Remember always to ask the operative questions: What kind of costs do I want to measure? And costs *to whom?* If, for example, you are only concerned at the moment with estimating capital requirements to be met through government budgets (which will often be the case), it is legitimate to ignore private capital outlays and the full costs to the economy, so long as you are aware of these omissions. On the other hand, if your aim is to measure the nation's *total* capital outlays on education, you must include an estimate for private outlays. Or, if you are attempting to assess the full costs to the economy, you must estimate the opportunity costs of *all* capital used by education, including both the existing stock and any new inflows.

Domestic vs. foreign costs. When you are projecting future capital requirements, it is vital to distinguish between those to be met from domestic resources and those that hopefully will be financed by foreign resources. Often it is also desirable to set a

1. Of course, in the rare cases where schools actually occupy rented premises, the actual rent will be included in your estimation instead of an imputed rent.

value on foreign-supplied facilities in terms of their equivalent *domestic* costs (by shadow pricing) instead of using the actual cost to the foreign donor or lender. This is important, for example, if you are assessing the value of the present capital stock, or if you are estimating what it would cost to replicate, with domestic resources, a pilot facility supplied from abroad.

The several distinctions made above can help you untangle budget forms and accounting records which, from the cost analyst's point of view, frequently "mix apples and bananas." It often happens, for example, that the official education budget includes both debt service on facilities built in the past and capital funds needed to build new facilities. If you include both these figures in an annual time series of capital expenditures, you will be guilty of double-counting. Choose whichever best serves your purpose, but never add them together. There are many similar accounting pitfalls that the above concepts can help you avoid.

Constructing a Time Series of Capital Expenditures

One of your first exercises should be to construct an annual time series of capital outlays, running back several years. This will put the past in perspective and shed useful light on the future. It can be done fairly easily. Capital outlays from public funds can usually be extracted without great difficulty from public budget accounts. But to get a full national picture you will have to add in private outlays as well. These private figures are generally hard to obtain and you may have to estimate them. You can do this quite simply if you have annual figures on the number of new classrooms or the amount of new space added to various types of private education. Apply to these physical quantities the cost factors derived from public construction experience with similar types of facilities. The resulting estimate will be rough, but it will usually suffice. (Again, remember not to double-count public subsidies for the construction of private education facilities.)

We suggest the following guidelines for constructing a time

series of capital outlays: (1) Use *actual expenditures* where possible rather than budgetary allotment figures; they are a much more accurate measure of what actually happened; (2) separate expenditures on new facilities and equipment from expenditures on major repairs and replacements that simply maintain old facilities; (3) break down the capital total at least by education levels and, if possible, by categories of institutions (e.g. general secondary schools vs. technical schools; rural vs. urban schools, etc.); (4) in addition, make an annual breakdown by *sources* of capital funds, separating especially funds from domestic and foreign sources, from public vs. private domestic sources, and from different levels of government;[2] (5) once having put the whole picture together in terms of *current* prices, translate the series into *constant* prices, using an educational construction cost index as a price deflator.

These breakdowns will provide a picture not only of the overall trend of capital outlays but, equally important, of any changes in the pattern of allocation within the educational system (which has important implications for the future pattern of recurrent costs), and changes in the pattern of sources of capital funds (which may provide important clues to future financing possibilities).

Do not be surprised if the resulting time series of capital flows shows a very erratic movement of outlays from year to year (in contrast to the much smoother curve of recurrent expenditures that you obtained in the exercise in Chapter 8). A variety of factors cause sharp annual fluctuations in capital outlays: discontinuities in the flow of foreign aid, spasmodic decisions to launch

2. Local contributions are often substantial, even in centralized systems. For example, the case study by Nicholas Bennett on Tanzania, "Tanzania: Planning for Implementation," in *Educational Cost Analysis in Action: Case Studies for Planners*, Vol. I, Paris, Unesco:IIEP, 1972, states that during the plan period the central government would "supply local authorities with prefabricated primary classroom kits at a cost of about £250 per classroom. The local authority would then supply the labor and some materials, to the value of £250–350, and a good permanent classroom would be constructed." In this instance at least half the capital for new elementary schools was supplied locally.

major new educational programs, ups and downs in the economy and in the flow of public revenues.

The figures from a diversified sample of countries given in Table 9.1 demonstrate the unevenness of capital outlays. The first column shows the percentage of total (public) educational expenditures in 1965 that was represented by capital expenditures. The second column shows the highest percentage for capital expenditures in any year between 1960 and 1965. It is evident that 1965 was the highest capital outlay year for seven of the countries whose figures are identical in the two columns. But for some of the others there is a marked difference between 1965 and the year of highest capital outlay. The extreme case is Mali, whose capital expenditures ranged from 4.2 per cent in 1965 to 38.6 per cent in the highest year. Niger ranged from 5.1 per cent to 17.2 per cent.

Caution should be exercised in making inter-country compari-

TABLE 9.1.
Capital expenditures as a percentage of total public expenditures on education (16 sample countries).

	CAPITAL PERCENTAGE IN 1965	HIGHEST PERCENTAGE OVER 1960–65
Ethiopia	16.1	22.8
Kenya	8.1	8.1
Mali	4.2	38.6
Niger	5.1	17.2
Argentina	7.2	7.2
Ecuador	13.7	13.7
Guyana	13.6	13.6
Uruguay	9.2	9.2
China	14.4	14.4
Japan	24.0	25.6
Pakistan	42.0	46.0
Malaysia (Sarawak)	22.0	25.7
Austria	20.9	20.9
Czechoslovakia	9.5	24.8
Denmark	24.3	25.4
Finland	18.7	22.0

Source: Data compiled on the basis of the Unesco Statistical Yearbook, 1967, Table 2.16.

sons from the evidence in Table 9.1; the figures are not strictly comparable because of differences in national accounting practices. It may be, for example, that some of the developing nations reported capital outlays from both domestic and foreign sources, while others included only domestic; some countries may have included repairs, replacements, and debt service charges along with expansion of facilities, while others did not. It is a fair deduction from Table 9.1, however, that most of these countries were undergoing rapid educational expansion between 1960 and 1965, for if they were merely maintaining existing capacity, their capital outlays would undoubtedly have been a much smaller percentage of their total educational outlays. It is also a foregone conclusion that these high capital outlays would create higher recurrent costs in subsequent years.

Determining Physical Capital Needs

In order to project the capital funds required for a new planning period (say, five years), you must begin with an estimate of physical needs. These include: (1) necessary repairs and replacements to maintain existing facilities in good condition; (2) modifications and additions to existing facilities and equipment to support qualitative changes in educational processes and programs (such as the introduction of instructional television, team teaching, more ample laboratory facilities, etc.) and (3) net additions to present capacity in order to accommodate more students (either by enlarging existing institutions on the same site, or by building separate new facilities).

The first component (repairs and maintenance) is best estimated on the basis of a full physical survey of all existing facilities, resulting in a schedule of needed repairs and replacements for each institution. Where this is not feasible, the second-best method is to survey a representative sample of institutions, classified by age, size, function, type of construction and equipment, and climatic conditions; then apply the repair and replacement needs derived from this sample to the whole establishment. If this sampling approach is not feasible, then you will be forced to use a much cruder method, based on recent past expenditures for repairs and replacements (adjusted upward if there is reason to believe that there has been considerable deferred maintenance in the past). Even for this crude method, it is important to secure, if possible, a full list of existing facilities (perhaps from central records of the ministry), classified according to the same characteristics as those suggested above for a sample survey. With the help of an experienced building engineer, you can work out a set of repair and replacement norms to apply to each category. Obviously the older institutions, those made of materials that deteriorate more rapidly, and those with more complex equipment (such as a technical school), will have the high repair and replacement requirements. Your total estimate may seem small relative to capital requirements for new construction (if your educational system is expanding rapidly), but the matter nonetheless deserves careful attention because skimping on maintenance can eventually result in eroding existing capital assets and can prove to be an extremely expensive way to "save" a little money in the short run.

The second type of capital requirement (involving qualitative modifications of existing facilities) has to be estimated on an *ad hoc* basis, program by program. If, for example, a new science program for secondary schools calls for new types of laboratory equipment, the requirements will have to be worked out and costed in terms of a list of needed equipment, the number of schools involved, and a time schedule for procurement and installation. Estimating the capital requirements for installing instructional television is somewhat more complicated, but the basic method is essentially the same. It is more complicated because a greater variety and complexity of equipment is involved (at both the broadcasting and receiving end); because it may be necessary to provide electric power sources to some schools and to modify classroom space for efficient reception; and because repair facilities may also have to be created.[3]

The third type of capital requirement (to expand existing facilities and create new ones for handling an increased number of students) is quantitatively the most important when an educational system is expanding rapidly, and therefore deserves your greatest attention.

The greatest mistake usually made in projecting the capital requirements for an expansion program is to assume (tacitly) that existing facilities are already being utilized to the hilt, and therefore that the stock of facilities must be expanded by the same percentage as the expected number of students. This, in fact, is rarely the case. Even in systems where some classrooms are grossly overcrowded, many others may have undersized classes. Moreover, it is often possible, as we have seen, to accommodate more students in existing facilities by modifying the academic time schedule. Hence we would strongly recommend that a space utilization survey be conducted before an attempt is made to calculate the need for new facilities and equipment. In short, before scarce resources are committed to building new facilities, every effort should be made to ensure that the best use is being made of the old ones.

A survey of secondary schools in some African countries by Unesco's Regional Educational Building Institute illustrates what a space utilization survey may reveal. The study in Morocco showed that "in almost all the schools surveyed, the available number of spaces is more than that required by a considerable margin . . . in the general classroom category by an average of 17.45 per cent, in the science laboratory category by an average of 33.33 per cent, and in the special classroom category by an average of 15 per cent."[4]

A similar survey in Ghana concluded that "in all space cate-

3. For a fuller discussion of television capital requirements, see W. Schramm, P. H. Coombs, F. Kahnert, and J. Lyle, *The New Media: Memo to Educational Planners*, Paris, Unesco:IIEP, 1967.

4. See *Space Utilization Survey of Secondary Schools—Morocco*, Report and Recommendations, REBIA, Khartoum, May 1969.

gories dealt with, it is apparent that provision has been made for more spaces than what is actually required to meet the needs." The average excess capacity in general classrooms was 28.69 per cent, in special purpose classrooms 42.69 per cent, and in science laboratories 33.33 per cent.[5]

Such figures, however, must be interpreted cautiously, for it is never possible to achieve 100 per cent utilization, even in the best-managed educational system. There are a number of reasons: schools in one area may be losing students to another area; new schools are en route to becoming filled up but are not as yet full; daily absentees leave desks unfilled; the academic time schedule itself imposes substantial idle time on all facilities.[6] Even after allowing for such factors, however, there is usually a sizable cushion for improving the use of expensive, scarce facilities. By bringing the facts of under-utilization to light, cost analysts can encourage decisions in favor of greater efficiency.

There are limits, of course, to what can be achieved without impairing educational effectiveness. Where these limits are must be determined case by case in each locality. But, in making such determinations, it is important that they be based on rational evidence developed by practical experimentation and observation, not simply on traditional practice and educational mythology.

Once plans have been made for the full and efficient use of *existing* facilities and the need for a net increase in facilities has been established, the next problem is to choose the best size and location for the new structures; to decide when to add to existing facilities (which is usually cheaper) and when to create new ones; to strike the right balance between different types of facilities (e.g. day schools vs. boarding schools); and to plan the opti-

5. See *Space Utilization Survey of Secondary Schools—Ghana,* Report and Recommendations, REBIA, Khartoum, June 1969.

6. A useful indicator for diagnostic and planning purposes would be an index of "occupied student places," which has been introduced by the Irish planners. Taken alongside the index of "student places," this indicator would provide a running measure of space utilization. Used for planning, it would make allowance for absentees and other factors that cause a normal under-utilization of available student places.

mum use of new facilities, for example, by adopting efficient time schedules, by using technical schools in off-hours for adult training, and other schools for general community purposes. By exploring and costing all such alternatives, cost analysts can help blaze a trail toward more and better education for more people.

Estimating the Costs of Capital Expansion

Once the *physical* needs for new facilities have been established, the next step is to estimate what it will cost to meet them. Here again the best methods to use will depend on the particular purpose and circumstances. If you are costing a specific project, such as a new teacher training institution, for which specifications have already been drawn, the costing should be much more refined and tailored to the specifications than if you are making an over-all estimate of capital fund requirements for a whole five-year national educational plan.

THE ROLE OF PHYSICAL NORMS AND PROTOTYPES

Even over-all capital requirements estimates, however, must be tied to some sort of physical specifications; otherwise, they are meaningless. Such physical specifications in turn must be related to what will go on in and around the new buildings, what educational aims and functions are to be served, what educational process is to be used, and what types of learners are to be served, including how many and for what periods of time. Thus, for example, projecting costs for primary schools obviously involves a very different set of physical norms than costing secondary technical schools or an agricultural college. In short, capital cost estimates must be based either on specific architectural plans or, for more general estimating, on a series of models or prototypes that fit the variety of physical requirements foreseen in the forthcoming plan period.

The more varied these prototypes are to fit varying categories of circumstances, and the further the over-all enrolment projections can be broken down into these categories, the more accurate the capital cost projections will be. In a typical developing country, it would be desirable to have standard cost estimates for at least the number of prototypes shown in Table 9.2.

The classifications shown in Table 9.2 obviously must be adapted to the educational structure and practices of each country. A British-type system, for example, might classify secondary schools by the number of "streams." Where appropriate, various prototypes of post-secondary institutions (such as teacher training colleges, advanced rural institutes, etc.) could be added to the list. Universities or other major institutions, however, are likely to require separate, tailor-made estimates, since each one is so individual.

TABLE 9.2.
Illustration of standard cost prototypes.

	COST PER PUPIL PLACE	SINGLE-SHIFT ENROLMENT CAPACITY	CAPITAL TOTAL COST
Primary			
Single-room school (rural)			
2 classrooms (rural)			
3 to 6 classrooms (rural, semi-rural)			
6 to 12 classrooms (urban)			
Over 12 classrooms (urban)			
Secondary (day)			
6 or less classrooms			
7 to 12 classrooms			
Over 12 classrooms			
Technical schools			
Secondary (residential)			
12 or less classrooms			
Over 12 classrooms			

Before discussing how to cost these prototypes, a brief word is in order about new trends in setting physical standards for schools.

Traditionally, physical standards for school construction have either been extremely haphazard or excessively rigid. The rigid ones have typically been defined in such terms as the minimum or maximum floor space required per student; the ratio of window space to square feet of working area; minimum-maximum ceiling heights; required number of doors per room; the proportions of classroom space, corridor space, and other types of space; number of toilet stalls and playground area per 100 students, etc. In the extreme, a single school design has been imposed by the central ministry on every community, whether it fitted local conditions or not.

Times are changing rapidly in these respects, however, toward a golden mean between the extremes of full laissez-faire and total rigidity. In a number of countries (the United Kingdom is a good example), teams of imaginative architects, educators, engineers, and cost analysts have been fashioning new approaches to the more efficient design, construction, and utilization of educational structures, and to enhancing their aesthetic and psychological features as well. One of the outcomes has been the creation of *performance* or *functional* standards as distinct from the old-fashioned, rigid *physical* specifications that leave little room for local ingenuity and adaptation. For example, instead of specifying a fixed ratio of window space to floor space, the new norms simply indicate the minimum strength of light required in all working areas, leaving it to the ingenuity of architects and lighting engineers to determine how this functional norm can best be met in a given situation. Similarly, local educators and architects are given latitude (within a prescribed cost ceiling) to make trade-offs between classroom space and other space (e.g. administrative offices, corridors, cafeteria, auditorium) that will provide maximum flexibility and educational advantage.

We strongly recommend that educational planners and cost analysts try to keep informed about new ideas on school building, through the publications and advice of such organizations as the Unesco regional school buildings centers, the Educational Facilities Laboratory in New York, and ministries of education in such countries as France, Spain, and the United Kingdom that have been fostering new approaches to school construction.

COSTING PROJECT DESIGNS AND PROTOTYPES

Once an achitectural plan has been sketched for a particular facility, it is usually the task of professional cost engineers to develop a detailed cost estimate for the project. But prior to that stage, rougher cost estimates must be worked out by general educational cost analysts (with whatever help they can get from construction experts). For the most part this means arriving at the best possible "standard costs" for the various prototypes referred to above, along with certain "adjustment factors" that can be applied to these nationwide standard costs to allow for regional cost variations, interim price changes, or any other important differentials. For some purposes, however, such as costing innovations and qualitative changes in existing facilities, other methods must be used.

By and large, the best unit to use for expressing the costs of different prototypes is the *capital cost per student place*. Once this figure is determined, it can be applied to the number of additional students that must be provided for in each category (e.g. rural primary students, secondary boarding students, etc.) to determine the over-all capital funding required for each category.

The advantage of using the cost per student place (as against the cost per classroom) is that it averages out differences in the sizes of classes and classrooms in different schools, as well as variations in the ratio of classroom space to other space. For the same reason, cost per student place makes the best costing unit for setting cost limits and enforcing them, without tying the hands of architects and local school authorities. The case study on school construction in the United Kingdom is highly informative on this point.

When it comes to costing the installation of a television system, however, the number of classrooms and the cost per classroom (rather than the number of student places) is a better unit to use for costing the television sets, whereas the number of school broadcast hours required to cover desired portions of the curriculum is the best unit for determining the size and cost of the broadcasting facilities needed.

The costing of furniture and equipment, whether for prototypes or specific projects, calls for an appropriate list of items to fit the requirements of a given size and type of facility. Appended to this chapter is a typical list for a secondary school. The bill of equipment and furniture should be costed at the best prices available on items meeting minimum standards.

The best way to establish standard costs for prototypes is on the basis of recent actual costs for a sample of projects as representative as possible of those to be built in the future. (If future structures are to differ drastically from previous ones, a different method of costing may be required.) If possible, the sample for each prototype should include no fewer than a half dozen cases in order to average out wide variations, particularly in land, site preparation, and site utility costs (which usually vary much more from project to project than construction and equipment costs). The sample cases should be analyzed uniformly, with the following minimum cost breakdown:

- Land acquisition (total area and per square foot)
- Site clearance and improvement
- Installation of site utilities and services
- Construction of structures
- Equipment and furnishing
- Architectural and other fees

The cost data from the sample cases for each prototype can then be analyzed, aggregated, and expressed in various useful ways, as illustrated in Table 9.3. Take note that the projects in the sample will probably have been built at different times; hence an educational construction price index will be needed to translate them into comparable prices before they are averaged and entered on a summary table.

Analysis of the various samples should also provide a standard set of geographic differentials in land and construction costs that can be used in calculating deviations from the nationwide standard costs when costing regional components of over-all national construction plans. The construction price index can be used to adjust for cost increases occurring since the base date for the standard costs, and for projecting future increases.

The standard costs and price adjustment factors described above can be used not only for costing an over-all national school expansion plan, region by region and level by level, but also for making initial rough cost estimates for more limited sub-systems, including even individual projects. A worksheet for calculating the costs of a sub-system is shown in Table 9.4.

TABLE 9.3.
Examples of standard characteristics and costs of a prototype urban primary school.

1. Typical number of student places	________	
2. Cost per student place	$ ________	
3. Land area (mean average)	________	sq. ft.
4. Total building area (mean average)	________	sq. ft.
5. Costs (actual)		
a. Land and site survey	$ ________	
b. Site improvement and utilities	$ ________	
c. Construction materials	$ ________	
d. Construction labor	$ ________	
e. Construction cost per square foot	$ ________	
f. Equipment, furniture, etc.	$ ________	
g. Architects' and other fees	$ ________	
h. Total	$ ________	
6. Costs (percentage breakdown)		
a. Construction	________	%
b. Architects' and other fees: ________ % of (a)	________	%
c. Equipment and furniture	________	%
d. Land and site survey	________	%
e. Site improvement and utilities	________	%
f. Total	100	%

Methods similar to those outlined above were used in Thailand in 1965 to estimate the costs of building three similar vocational schools (each to accommodate 450 students) in three different locations. The results are shown in Table 9.5. It will be seen that the construction and equipment costs, based on standard costs, are very similar for all three schools, except that the construction costs of School 2 run 10 per cent higher than the other two because of regional cost differences. The land, site improvement, and utilities costs, however, vary widely. The latter three items should always be looked at in combination. Often a "bargain" on the land cost can be much more than offset by high site improvement and utility costs. In the Thai case, School 3 had land costs of only 700,000 bahts compared to 2,000,000 bahts for School 2, yet their *combined* land, site improvement, and utility costs were roughly equal (2,540,000 bahts vs. 2,600,000 bahts).

INTERNATIONAL NORMS AND COMPARISONS

Unfortunately, we can offer no tidy international norms for educational capital costs, or any standard ratios between the major components of such costs, which an individual nation can use to assess its own past performance and future costs. As we have seen, there are often substantial variations in cost conditions even with-

TABLE 9.4.
Summary worksheet for calculating capital costs of expanding an educational sub-system.

A. Category of facility ________	
B. Typical enrolment capacity ________	
C. Breakdown of costs:	
1. Standard cost of structure	________
2. Site improvement and utility services ________ % of (1)	________
3. Total (1 + 2)	________
4. Adjustment of (3) for interim cost increases ________ %	________
* 5. Adjustment of (4) for regional cost differences ________ %	________
* 6. Architects' and site supervision fees ________ % of (5)	________
* 7. Cost of land and site survey ________ % of (5)	________
8. Standard cost of furniture and equipment	________
9. Adjustment of (8) for interim price increases ________ %	________
* 10. Adjustment of (9) for regional price differences ________ %	________
11. Total cost per institution (5 + 6 + 7 + 10)	________
12. Total cost of projected program ________ institutions × (11)	________

* Components of total cost (11).

in the same nation. The variations are much greater between nations. In a poor nation, for example, construction labor may be relatively cheap compared to the costs of materials and equipment (especially if much of the latter must be imported), whereas in a rich country quite the reverse may be true. Similarly, the costs of land and materials may be much cheaper relative to labor in one developing country than another, because it has a lower population-land ratio and a more abundant supply of trees, clay, and other raw materials to use for construction. Thus, each country must establish its own appropriate costing norms.

This is not to say, however, that countries cannot profit greatly from one another's experience in educational construction and costing. Quite the contrary is true, as our international collection of case studies has shown.

Some Parables About Capital Costs

We will conclude this chapter on capital costs with a few parables which have had many counterparts in reality and sum up many of the basic points made earlier.

PARABLE ONE: A TALE OF FALSE ECONOMY

School authorities in a certain community decided to substitute lower-cost roofing, siding, and flooring materials in their new school in order to cut costs. The savings released funds for a much-needed playing field and everyone was pleased—until it turned out that the savings were false. Within a few years after the new school was opened, the *extra* costs of janitorial services, frequent repainting and repairs, not to mention replacing the storm-torn roof of the new school, added up to five times the "savings."

The moral of this particular parable is that a penny saved in building a school is not always a penny earned; it is sometimes the cause of losing many more pennies later.

Table 9.5.
Three estimates of capital costs of similar vocational schools in Thailand (1965) (costs in Thai bahts).

	SCHOOL 1	%	SCHOOL 2 (SAME AS 1 PLUS 10 PER CENT INCREASE DUE TO GEO-GRAPHIC LOCATION)	%	SCHOOL 3	%
Construction costs						
1. Space for administration, classrooms, and library	1,710,000	17.1	1,881,000	14.8	1,710,000	15.2
2. Workshop	2,760,000	27.6	3,036,000	23.9	2,280,000	20.7
3. Cafeteria	550,000	5.5	605,000	4.8	550,000	4.9
4. Dormitories	1,704,000	17.0	1,874,000	14.8	1,704,000	15.1
5. Staff housing	700,000	7.0	770,000	6.1	700,000	6.2
6. Sanitation services	1,305,000	13.0	1,435,000	11.3	1,305,000	11.6
Total	8,729,000	87.3 *	9,601,000	75.5	8,249,000	73.0

Construction cost per place	19,398		21,337		18,331	
Other costs						
1. Site improvements	400,000	4.0	400,000	3.1	1,240,000	11.0
2. Utilities	400,000	4.0	200,000	1.6	600,000	5.3
3. Equipment	500,000	5.0	500,000	3.9	500,000	4.4
4. Land	—		2,000,000	15.7	700,000	6.2
Total	1,300,000	13.0	3,100,000	24.4	3,040,000	27.0
Grand total	10,029,000	100.0 *	12,702,000	100.0	11,289,000	100.0
Total cost per place	22,287		28,226		25,088	

* Totals do not add up correctly, due to rounding.

PARABLE TWO: THE SCHOOL THAT WAS TOO WELL BUILT

Having learned their lesson, the same school authorities built their next school of the best materials, rugged enough to outlast their grandchildren. Its floors and walls were thick, solid, and soundproof; all surfaces cleaned easily and never needed repainting or repair; the roof could laugh at any storm. It was more expensive, of course, but the extra costs were expected to be recouped manyfold by later savings on custodial and maintenance costs. And indeed they were, to the great relief of each year's operating budget. Once more everyone was pleased—until one day the unexpected happened.

Research studies based on a wide range of experiments in other school systems convinced the school authorities that their pupils would learn much more at little or no extra cost if certain innovations were adopted, including team teaching and instructional television combined with self-instructional "programmed" materials. An exciting new world of learning opened before their eyes, until they suddenly realized that their solid new school stood in the way. Its traditional, cell-like classrooms, built to accommodate thirty students and a teacher using nineteenth-century pedagogical methods, prevented the flexible redeployment of space and people that was required throughout the school day to take full advantage of these promising innovations.

A compromise solution was reluctantly adopted. It meant that the new technologies would have to be adapted to the building, not the building to the new technologies, and this reduced their effectiveness considerably. And since they did cost something extra, it was doubtful that, on balance, the school's cost effectiveness had been improved.

The moral is that old-style buildings can prevent progress; new educational facilities should be planned to accommodate whatever new and better teaching technologies may come along, perhaps even before the new school is finished.

PARABLE THREE: THE RIGHT SCHOOL IN THE WRONG PLACE

School authorities in a newly independent nation concluded that their colonial-type academic secondary school was obsolete and irrelevant to local needs; hence they launched an experiment involving a new type of multi-purpose school that combined prevocational training and university preparation. Careful pedagogical planning went into the project and enthusiasm ran high; if the new model succeeded, it would light a new way for the whole system.

Unfortunately, it did not succeed; quite frankly it failed miserably and set educational progress back several years in the process. It was not because the pedagogical planning was unsound or the resources inadequate. Basically it was because this "lighthouse" school, for quite accidental political reasons, was located in a remote site where students could not get to it easily and where its light could not be seen by other school people. For some years its enrolments ran well below capacity, causing its operating costs per student to be inordinately high. To remedy this situation, expensive boarding facilities were added to accommodate distant students. This remedy worked, the school became filled, but now its costs per student ran even higher because of the board and room costs. By now, unfortunately, disenchantment with the whole idea of multi-purpose secondary schools had spread throughout the land—mostly for the wrong reasons—and the classical academic high school continued to be the national model, despite the generally acknowledged fact that it was a misfit.

The obvious moral is that new schools should be located for the convenience of students, not politicians. Educational planners can help in this matter by demonstrating clearly the comparative costs, convenience, and pedagogical advantages of alternative locations—so clearly that political leaders will appreciate the risks they run by insisting that a costly school be put in an irrational location.

PARABLE FOUR:
THE STRANGE CASE OF TOO MANY SCHOOLS

A poor nation with a dispersed rural population finally achieved its cherished goal of universal primary education, only to be disappointed. The costs were high and kept mounting, yet the educational results were notoriously poor. Close analysis showed why: paradoxically, the nation had built too many schools.

It had continued the ancient custom of a school for each village, but meanwhile many villagers had been moving to cities and there were too few students to fill the classrooms of the rural schools. The result was a low pupil-teacher ratio and abnormally high costs per student compared to urban schools, but, unhappily, poorer learning results because the best teachers preferred the cities where they could work with better equipment, a richer curriculum, and other teachers without being professionally isolated.

In due course, the government adopted a plan to abolish the small traditional schools over a period of years (as older teachers and school buildings reached retirement age), replacing them with new medium-sized schools serving a combination of neighboring villages. This added some new transportation costs, but they were offset by lower instructional costs per student in normal-sized classes. More important, the teachers preferred these somewhat larger schools; so did the students, and they learned more. Naturally there was at first considerable local opposition to the school consolidation scheme—no village likes to lose its school. But soon the satisfaction of parents and children with the superior performance of the new schools lessened the opposition, and taxpayers generally were pleased by the lower unit costs. The government took these lessons into account as it planned a new campaign for expanding secondary education.

The moral of this story is that the romance and nostalgia which adults often feel for the one-room village school can impose heavy penalties on their children's education and on the public purse. A prerequisite for being able to afford good schools (and universities) is that they be of at least the minimum size that is economically and pedagogically viable.

PARABLE FIVE:
AN EDUCATIONAL WHITE ELEPHANT

A handsome new technical school in a developing country was dedicated jointly by the prime minister and the foreign ambassador with great hope and enthusiasm. But, sad to say, it soon became an embarrassment to both. The reasons, in retrospect, were plain to see.

The ambassador's nation, in all good faith, had met its promise to deliver a fine new technical school, as modernly equipped as the best at home. To be sure, it had cost more than expected because the policy of "tied aid," which the ambassador's country insisted upon, had required importing many of the materials, virtually all of the equipment, and much of the expert manpower from back home, at much greater cost than if the recipient country had been given the money outright and allowed to build the school in its own way. But all this was now past and paid for. The real problem and the cause of the embarrassment was the high running cost, which the recipient nation had to shoulder and could ill afford.

No one had looked into these very seriously; they had been too preoccupied with the initial capital costs. Also, too little attention had been paid to the practical problems of recruiting, training, and paying local technical teachers, of which there were virtually none. Not surprisingly, much new equipment still stood around in crates, unused, while other equipment soon broke down for lack of proper care and maintenance—all because of a lack of trained personnel. Most troublesome of all, local employers complained that the graduates of this new technical school did not fit their needs; they were over-trained or mistrained for local types of work; and they came on the job with inflated expectations of becoming shop supervisors overnight.

The moral of this sad parable is that educational gifts sometimes turn into white elephants that can eat poor educational systems out of house and home. The best way to avoid a white elephant is to discover his costly feeding habits in ample time to avoid getting stuck with him. With a modicum of tact and diplomacy, it is usually possible to obtain instead a hard-working elephant with a good disposition and more moderate appetite, who fits into the local scene more comfortably.

PARABLE SIX: THE ACCORDION SCHOOLS THAT SAVED MONEY

The educational planners in a developing country, with the help of demographers and manpower economists, plotted the changes likely to occur in the student population over the next decade, by age and geographic distribution, as well as changes in the employment patterns of the economy. Their analysis showed that certain currently pressing educational and manpower demands could be expected to subside after a few years, while other types could be expected to increase.

Once the large backload of demand for primary education in various urban neighborhoods was worked off, for example, demand would stabilize at a lower level. Meanwhile, population transfers from particular rural areas would diminish their educational demand but correspondingly raise the demand in certain urban areas. Similar ups and downs could be foreseen in the demand for various types of technical and professional training—not least of all in teacher training itself.

Thus, it became evident that if educational capacity were planned simply to fit today's pattern of demand, it would be out of joint with tomorrow's pattern. The result would be unused capacity in some places, and not enough in others. To avert such costly maladjustments and mis-investments, the country adopted a new and imaginative strategy of educational expansion. It was based on a distinction between "permanent demand" and "temporary demand," and a corresponding distinction between permanent capacity and temporary capacity. To illustrate: there was a projected need for 100 new secondary teachers per year during the next five years to meet present deficits and expansion requirements; but after that requirements would decline steadily to only 400 new teachers per year to meet replacement needs and to support a slower rate of expansion. Hence, the permanent demand would be for about 400 new teachers a year, but for the time being there was an additional temporary demand of 600 per year.

The strategy had two prongs. One was to provide lasting solutions for permanent needs, but less costly provisional solutions for temporary needs. Thus, for example, the construction of new teacher training facilities would be limited to an output capacity of only 400 teachers per year, while provisional and less satisfactory quarters (e.g. old army barracks, estate houses, etc.) were adapted and borrowed professors were used to train an additional 600 teachers to meet the peak demand.

The second prong of the strategy involved the "accordion principle." In some neighborhoods where demand for primary and secondary education was expected to grow steadily over the years, new "modular" schools were built to which additional modules could later be added. This required buying and developing larger sites than were needed in the short run, but avoiding the premature construction of school space. Over the years this would save on capital costs. Conversely, in areas where the school population was expected to decline, demountable classrooms were installed.

These were sturdy prefabricated structures, also modular in design, that could be moved by trailer from "surplus" to "deficit" areas. The initial efforts to design and develop these demountable units ran into a variety of technical problems, but once they were overcome and factory production got underway, the cost per classroom (including moving) fell below the cost of a "regular" classroom. Needless to say, many people, including many educators, at first opposed the idea of "standardized" demountable schools, considering them somehow dehumanizing and unaesthetic. But they relented as it became evident that these units were not only educationally efficient but that each could have its own distinctive personality. The modular units could be arranged differently to fit the contours and conditions of each site. Moreover, students and teachers in different villages and urban neighborhoods were soon competing in making attractive landscape designs, planting shrubs and flowers, introducing novel color schemes, fashioning outdoor sculptures, and otherwise beautifying their respective schools.

The obvious moral of this final parable applies as well to all the others: in planning educational facilities these days, unconventional thinking and great ingenuity are called for, backed up by good pedagogical judgment, alert planning, and competent cost analysis. Temporary solutions should be devised to meet temporary needs, but even to meet enduring needs, flexible solutions should be sought. For if there is to be a revolution of teaching-learning technologies, as there clearly must be, this will require a kind of architectural flexibility and ingenuity that will not suffocate new educational ideas and practices.

Appendix 1 to Chapter 9

Typical List of Basic Furniture
for General Secondary Schools
To Be Used for Estimating Capital Cost

Description (dimensions in centimeters)

DESKS—TABLES—WORK COUNTERS AND BENCHES

Single classroom table (60L x 60W)
Double classroom table (120L x 60W)
Teacher's desk (120L x 60W)
Demonstration bench (240L x 70W)
Single-sided laboratory bench with sink (240L x 60W)
Single-sided laboratory bench (240L x 60W)
Work counter/cupboard unit (100L x 60W)
Work counter with fume hood (100L x 70W)
Trolley with shelf (100L x 70W x 90H)
Seater desk unit in tiers (average per seat)
Regular rigid table (100L x 60W)
Office desk (160L x 80W)
Office desk (120L x 70W)
Typist table
Student's work table (150L x 60W)
Sewing machine table
Large work table (200L x 100W)
Reading table (150L x 80W)
Kitchen counter/cupboard (100L x 60W)
Kitchen counter with built-in sink (100L x 60W)
Small coffee table
Writing desk
Dining table
Instructor's table

Laundry bench
Drawing table (80L x 60W)
Tracing table
Multi-purpose workshop bench (single)
Multi-purpose workshop bench (double)

CLASSROOM I (Maximum: 16 students)

8 double classroom tables
1 teacher's desk
16 students' chairs
1 regular chair
1 classroom cupboard
1 blackboard
1 notice-board
Total

CLASSROOM II (Maximum: 24 students)

12 double classroom tables
1 teacher's desk
24 students' chairs
1 regular office chair
1 classroom cupboard
1 blackboard
1 notice-board
Total

CLASSROOM III (Maximum: 32 students)

16 double classroom tables
1 teacher's desk
32 students' chairs
1 regular chair
1 classroom cupboard
1 blackboard
1 notice-board
Total

Appendix 2 to Chapter 9

ILLUSTRATIVE BILL OF EQUIPMENT FOR A NEW SCHOOL (BRAZIL)

Type of school: lower-level secondary
Anticipated enrolment: 400 pupils (per session)

EQUIPMENT	NO. REQ.	UNIT COST NCR$	TOTAL COST NCR$
Desks and chairs	340	40.00	13,600.00
Chairs (loose)	280	11.00	3080.00
Teachers' classroom desks	16	60.00	960.00
Library tables	10	50.00	500.00
Conference table	1	70.00	70.00
Typewriter tables	2	45.00	90.00
Office desk	1	115.00	115.00
Revolving chair	1	35.00	35.00
Plain cabinets	15	130.00	1950.00
Cabinets with glass windows	4	130.00	520.00
Physical education equipment storage cabinet	1	100.00	100.00
Filing cabinet	1	450.00	450.00
Waiting-room furniture	1	100.00	100.00
Library bookcases	3	70.00	210.00
Library counter	1	80.00	80.00
Stove	1	300.00	300.00
Typewriter	2	800.00	1600.00
Records file	2	40.00	80.00
Green wall blackboards	16	30.00	480.00
Wall charts	10	15.00	150.00
Globe	3	50.00	150.00
Wastepaper baskets	15	2.00	30.00
Equipment for audio-visual lab	1	5000.00	5000.00
Equipment for physical science, chemistry, and natural history labs	1	12,000.00	12,000.00
Equipment for agricultural courses and/or industrial arts	2	10,000.00	20,000.00
Equipment for commercial arts	1	12,000.00	12,000.00
Shop work benches			6350.00
Total			80,000.00

Note: At the time of the case study, the rate of exchange was \$1 = 4.46 New Cruzieros (NCR \$).

10 *Checking Feasibility*

After an educational plan (or policy, project, reform, or innovation) has been carefully costed, there still remains to be answered the most crucial question of all: Can it be implemented? Is it realistic and feasible? This chapter makes some suggestions on how to answer this question, and what to do if the answer is negative. It focuses mainly on testing *financial* feasibility, but since successful implementation depends on a good deal more than money, we start with a broader view of the matter.

Prerequisites for Successful Implementation

The evidence presented to Unesco's first International Conference on Educational Planning (Paris, 1968) showed that a great majority of recent educational plans had been poorly implemented or, worse still, were gathering dust on some lonely shelf. Thus the Conference declared effective implementation to be the most urgent problem facing educational planning.

The following checklist of minimum essentials for successful implementation may help give *your* future plans a better fate.

Broad participation in plan preparation. To lift any educational plan off paper and translate it into reality requires the help of many willing hands, throughout the educational system and outside it. All these people—politicians, administrators, teachers, students, employers, parents, civic leaders, and taxpayers—must understand the plan, believe in it, and feel that they have a stake in it. It follows, then, that any plan concocted by a handful of technicians in a back room in the Ministry of Education, without benefit of a wide-ranging dialogue with all the interested parties, stands little chance of getting implemented. It will pay planners and decision-makers to go to considerable trouble to encourage wide participation and consultation in the process of preparing any plan, and doubly so if the plan involves major reforms and innovations.

Detailed action plans. General nationwide plans that establish general targets and the broad parameters for the educational system's development are highly useful as a basis for allocating national resources and other broad purposes. But until and unless such aggregate plans are disaggregated into specific action plans for each sector of the system, each geographic area, and each educational unit, they cannot be effectively implemented. Without clear and specific guidelines—and a reasonable degree of lattitude and discretionary authority—even the most willing hands down the line, who must do most of the implementing in the final analysis, lack the means for action. Over-all national education plans are rarely plans for action; they prescribe the destinations to be reached by a given future date and the price tag for the trip, but they provide no specific routes for getting there. A series of detailed roadmaps are needed to make the trip successfully. The need is especially great in federalized countries such as India and Brazil where the main initiative for implementing national education plans resides with the individual states.

Ample administrative strengths. Linked to the foregoing point is the unhappy fact that most educational systems are not yet sufficiently equipped, organizationally and administratively, to handle expeditiously and efficiently the heavier tasks imposed on them in expanding and changing education at a much accelerated pace. Even France, with all its administrative sophistication, lagged in dispersing available funds for educational construction in a number of recent years because of administrative bottlenecks.

Today's brand of educational development calls for more than the traditional supervisory and caretaker type of educational administration; it requires a much more dynamic, action-oriented administration. An understaffed, overworked central ministry, playing by archaic rules, soon becomes the major bottleneck to implementing its own plans. As papers shuffle tardily from desk to desk, accumulating signatures, action waits and plans fall behind schedule. Thus the first requirement for improving the implementation of plans in many countries is to modernize and more adequately staff the administrative system. Meanwhile, the educational planner is well advised to take careful account of the administrative system's practical limitations as he proceeds to test the feasibility of any plans.

Adequate financial resources. This imperative for successful implementation is self-evident and better known than any other (though sometimes disregarded in practice). The main problem here, which we will return to shortly, is how to determine with reasonable accuracy how much money is going to be needed, how much is likely to be available, and how to bring the two into balance. A number of our case studies shed practical light on this problem.

Adequate real resources. Having sufficient money, however, is not enough; the main point is to have enough *real* resources. Shortages of teachers, books, and classrooms resulting from physical limitations on the nation's supply of qualified manpower, land, construction capacity, publication facilities, and other basic resources can easily derail an educational plan even when it seems to have ample money. It will be recalled that Madagascar's ambitious scheme for expanding rural primary education fell behind schedule basically because of a teacher shortage; thus the program was rescheduled, using prospective teacher supply, rather than funds, as the limiting resource.

An adequate information system. Once a plan is launched, it is vitally important to monitor its progress every step of the way in order to spot unforeseen bottlenecks and act quickly to break them, and to make prompt adjustments in the plan as required. Without a well-functioning information system for this purpose, the educational managers may discover much too late that the implementation of the plan is being frustrated. Educational authorities in Chile, it will be remembered, at first thought their problem was money—money to hire more technical secondary teachers to handle larger enrolments; but when the money could not be found, they took a hard second look and discovered that their malfunctioning information system had failed to signal them that the existing supply of teachers was adequate but wrongly deployed.

The foregoing factors—the extent of participation in the planning process and of translation of macro-plans into specific action plans, the administrative capabilities of the system, the supply of financial resources and real resources, the adequacy of the information system—all these factors taken together form a framework of constraints that ultimately determines how well or poorly a given educational plan gets implemented. At any given time any one of these factors may be the principal bottleneck. Hence the planner's task is to try to anticipate where the greatest rub will come and to recommend corrective action. At best, however, there will always be, for every educational system at every stage of its career, some maximum rate at which it can absorb additional resources to expand and renew itself. To spend funds beyond that point will force costs up and quality down.

Major Considerations in Projecting Financial Resources

We cannot in this book explore the many intricacies of educational finance and the variety of methodologies for projecting revenues in different situations, but it may nevertheless be useful to note some important distinctions and to make a few practical suggestions.

Even if you happen to have economic training, and even more if you do not, you will certainly want to seek the help of well-informed financial economists in the economic planning office or finance ministry on the matter of projecting educational revenues.

This applies especially when you are seeking enlightenment on what the total national flow of revenues to education may be in coming years. This depends (as noted in Chapter 5) on a constellation of determinants that lie beyond the normal purview of educational managers—such as the growth rate of the economy and of over-all public revenues, the income-elasticity of the existing tax structure, recent or anticipated changes in tax policies, inflationary trends, the financial needs of other sectors, foreign trade balances, and general prospects for external assistance. While you may have your own judgments about these matters, it will be useful to check them with other expert opinions and against the basic assumptions and projections underlying official economic plans and forecasts. We would also suggest, however, that you do not accept these official assumptions as gospel truth or as the only possibility. You should at a minimum understand the basis on which the projections were made and discuss plausible alternative assumptions with interested economists.

Forecasting educational revenues is a tricky business at best; many uncertain variables are involved and no one set of figures will serve all your needs. Again our advice is to give your main attention to the variables that count most and waste no time manicuring minutiae. The difference, for example, between a 3 and a 6 per cent growth rate in the economy, or between a 15 and a 20 per cent share of public revenues going to education, will affect education's financial future vastly more than, say, an adjustment in student textbook fees.

Listed below are several points that are especially important to bear in mind in dealing with estimates of future revenues.

1. *The best point of departure.* As with projecting costs, the most solid ground to start from in projecting future revenues is the recent record of actual revenue behavior. You can usually dig out reasonably satisfactory evidence (or estimates) from nearby sources on such important dimensions as: (a) the total annual income of your education system over the past five to ten years, broken down by levels; (b) the division between public and private institutions; (c) the main sources of income (governmental,

private, foreign); (d) the percentage relation of educational income to the GNP and to total public revenues. When these figures are entered on a chronological table comparable to Table 8.13 in Chapter 8 (Sources of public funds for teacher costs), it will be easy to identify important shifts and trends that have been taking place and that provide useful clues to the future.

This is not to say, of course, that the future will be the same as the past; it almost certainly will not be. But trends in the recent past will very likely carry over and influence the future. In most circumstances (though not all) it can be assumed that future revenue flows will be no smaller than in the recent past. Thus the main question to be answered is: How much increase in educational revenues for various purposes and from various sources can reasonably be expected to occur in the next five years over the past five?

2. *Different time horizons.* For some purposes (such as preparing next year's budget) it will suffice to project revenues only one or two years ahead and this can be done with a relatively high degree of accuracy. For other purposes (such as testing the feasibility of a five-year plan), it is essential to make middle-range estimates. But if, for example, you want to check the feasibility of achieving universal primary education twenty years hence, you will need to make a much longer-range projection and it goes without saying that this will inevitably have a much wider margin of error.

Unfortunately, because of education's long "production cycle," it is often necessary to look considerably farther into the financial future in planning and education than economists normally do for planning the economy (typically only five years); thus you may have to go it alone on these longer-range projections. A major new educational venture launched during the next five years (e.g. a large expansion of teacher training; the introduction of two-year colleges or new technical institutes) may have relatively modest revenue requirements in the initial period that will grow much larger in the next five-year period; so you had better be clear about the longer-term implications. The Ivory Coast primary school television venture is a good case in point. When this project was being planned in the mid-1960's, projections of recurrent and capital costs were wisely made extending to 1980. When these projections were critically reviewed, side by side with revenue projections, by the IIEP team that prepared the case study on this project, the conclusion was reached that there would probably be no serious financial obstacle in the first five years but the same could not be said for the next five.

The main point is that whenever long-range targets are being set or when any major reform or innovation is being contemplated, it is imperative to examine its cost and revenue implications well beyond the usual five-year horizon.

A different point is that, even within a five-year span, it is often important to examine the year by year "phasing" of financial requirements and revenue prospects to ensure that they balance at all times. Available revenues will usually be greater toward the end of the period than at the beginning; hence it is sometimes desirable to rephrase an expansion plan so that it starts more modestly and accelerates later in the plan period. This was done in the case of Makerere University College in Uganda. A rephasing of the proposed expansion of student admissions to put more of the increase in the latter years of that period had the dual advantage of achieving a better balance between student intake and the flow of qualified secondary school finishers, and between resource requirements and prospective revenues.

3. *Differentiating revenue sources and purposes.* The most basic point to bear in mind is that the ultimate source of all educational revenues is the nation's current national income (except for support from abroad), and there is just so much to go around. A portion of the national income is diverted to education by way of the public tax structure and public borrowing; a further (and typically smaller) portion comes through private grants and payments.

Most educational systems have "mixed financing," meaning that their revenues come from the national income through a variety of channels. Moreover, the mix is likely to differ from one part of the system to another according to variations in the ratio of public to private education at each level, the respective financing roles of different levels of government, and (where foreign aid is important) the selective policies of external assistance agencies. It is important to make separate revenue projections for each main source of income and each educational sub-sector. The sources are subject to different economic and political forces and hence behave differently, with consequent differential impacts on various parts of the educational system.

Central government contributions can usually be projected with greater technical ease and accuracy because basic data are more plentiful and better analyzed. This is fortunate because the central government in most countries provides upward of 50 per cent of all education revenues; it is the major revenue collector, pre-empts the most reliable and lucrative sources of income, and is uniquely in a position to redistribute national income from rich to poor sections of the country (which, for education, is an important consideration).

Educational *revenues from state and local governments*, on the other hand, are more difficult to forecast and often can only be crudely estimated. Records and basic data at these levels tend to be poorer, less up-to-date, and less well analyzed. Revenue flows tend to be less reliable and less responsible to economic growth. Revenue-raising potential varies widely among geographic areas, as do local decisions on how much to spend on education. Nonetheless, in poorer countries especially, local government is often the most promising source of increased educational support as the pressures pile up from all directions on the overstrained central budget.

The Madagascar case study demonstrates the problems that may arise from local financing. The central government chose to leave the initiative to individual rural communities to get new schools started (which the Center would then subsidize), but community responses differed and fewer initiatives were taken than hoped—especially by poorer communities. In these circumstances it was extremely difficult to anticipate the behavior of local support.

Among the domestic sources, *private revenues* (contributions, grants, fees, etc.) are the most difficult of all to forecast. Clear records of past private revenues are typically sparse and future revenues highly unpredictable. This is not a grave problem in countries where private funds are a minor fraction of the total; here it will suffice to estimate them crudely, at least for making aggregate revenue forecasts. But where private revenues play a major role—as they do, for example, in secondary education in much of Latin America—then a more careful effort is required to gather accurate data from a representative sample of institutions.

If you lack any better basis for estimating private revenues, the safest assumption to make is that they will continue in the future at more or less their past absolute level. Thus, if total revenues are rising, the private portion will decline in percentage, with public contributions taking up the slack. This is consistent with observed trends in most countries over the past two decades.

Projecting educational *resources from abroad* calls for special caution. Many an educational plan has run afoul due to overestimating foreign aid, or expecting it to arrive sooner than it actually does. There is need to estimate not only the total value of such aid (measured in local value-equivalent) but the timing, the form it will take (e.g. capital, teachers, books, etc.), and where it will go within the system (little is likely to go, for example, into elementary education). You should bear in mind also that foreign support often must be matched by local resources, and that capital projects financed from abroad generate large future demands on domestic revenues.

For rough estimating purposes, if you have no better information to go on, it could reasonably be assumed that foreign aid over the next five years will approximately equal that of the previous five. For more refined estimating, however, you should examine the current state of project negotiations and commitments with various bilateral and multilateral assistance agencies, bearing in mind that there is usually a time lag of at least two years between the start of negotiations and the actual arrival of new assistance. Thus, anything not already under discussion is unlikely to count during the first half of your five-year period.

We strongly recommend against the facile assumption that foreign aid can be expected to fill whatever gap remains between projected requirements and projected domestic resources. This has rarely proved to be a valid assumption, at least when used to force a statistical balance for a plan that is inherently too ambitious.

Where there is mixed financing (as there usually is), it is important to make separate revenue estimates for different levels and types of education. In all cases, university revenues should be separately projected. The University of East Africa provides a particularly complicated example of financing by three different governments and a variety of external agencies. But even where only one nation is involved, it is frequently the case that the central government plays a larger role in financing technical and higher education than primary and general secondary schools, whereas the opposite is true for state and local governments.

4. *Capital vs. recurrent resources.* Even for the roughest feasibility testing it is important to estimate recurrent and capital resources separately. First, they are usually financed quite differently; for example, recurrent costs are generally covered by current tax revenues and private fees, whereas capital projects are frequently financed by borrowing and special donations. Second, recurrent revenue requirements follow a relatively smooth curve from year to year while capital requirments often fluctuate erratically.

It is well to repeat here the warning that, before any major capital commitment is undertaken, it is important to estimate what its consequences will be for recurrent costs for the next five to ten years, and what the chances are of being able to secure enough additional recurrent revenues to cover these new costs.

5. *Marco vs. micro projections.* There is a great difference in technique between testing the feasibility of a comprehensive national educational plan and testing a particular educational subdivi-

sion, reform, innovation, or individual project. The basic aim of ensuring a balance between needs and resources is, of course, the same in all cases, but micro planning requires more refined data and more precise methods than macro planning.

In most nations, over-all revenue projections are provided by the top economic planning agency or the finance ministry for about five years ahead, based on forecasts of general economic trends and the projected behavior of the national accounts. Such projections embrace the entire economy and all parts of the governmental sector and are designed to be mutually consistent. (Revenue estimates made independently by various ministries based on their own needs, on the other hand, are likely to be quite incompatible with one another and add up to well over 100 per cent of the over-all public revenues that will be available.) Educational planners will do well to look critically at centrally made projections and to understand clearly the basis on which they are made, but usually they will prove to be the best framework to use for feasibility testing.

Where systematic national economic planning exists, the educational sector is likely to be assigned a tentative "planning allocation" as a fiscal framework within which to formulate plans for the coming plan period. This tentative allocation may later be adjusted, of course, in light of revised public revenue forecasts, demonstrated additional needs of education, and inter-governmental negotiations. It would be rare, of course, for any education ministry (or any other ministry) to be fully satisfied with its assigned allocation, but in the end this method of starting with a tentative allocation is likely to prove more advantageous to education than waiting to the end of the planning process before any financial limits are imposed. Not only does it make for more realistic and disciplined planning, but it gives the educational sector more time to build a strong case for a higher allocation if one is really warranted (in light of competing national needs).

If you are unfortunate enough not to be able to receive guidance on future revenues from a central economic planning group (still the case in many countries), then the best advice we can offer is to recruit a competent general economist for your own team and make your own estimates as best you can. We also recommend that you establish a realistic financial ceiling to guide your planning from the outset. Otherwise, you may put great effort into formulating and costing a fine-looking plan that later has to be dismantled and reconstructed because it has failed a last-minute feasibility test. In short, the first step in designing a new plan is to find out, at least tentatively, what resources there will be to work with.

Let us turn briefly to what is involved in testing the feasibility of a micro plan—a specific project or improvement or innovation. As we said earlier, this requires close attention to details, but it also requires keeping a broad and balanced perspective. We can best illustrate the point by recounting a micro-planning exercise carried out by twenty IIEP interns a few years ago. These experienced educational administrators and former teachers organized themselves into small planning teams to work out solutions to several typical educational problems: for example, the redesign and improvement of teacher training for rural primary education; modernizing secondary level math-science programs; reforming a rural primary school curriculum. Each team went about its assignment with great seriousness and enthusiasm, devised a highly imaginative new model to replace the unsatisfactory old one, and then presented its "plan" to a jury of peers for critical review. Judged in pedagogical terms, every proposal won general approbation. But judged in terms of practical feasibility, every one was severely criticized.

Why so? Well, each team had focused its attention so narrowly on its own particular "problem," and became so enamored of its "solution," that it neglected to maintain the broad perspective required for good planning. Unwittingly, each team had come to assume that *its* particular problem and solution had first claim on whatever resources it needed, regardless of what disruptions and penalties might be imposed on other parts of the system. They had found an attractive solution but had not seriously examined its feasibility in the larger context. They had made no assessment of future revenue possibilities, set no tentative cost limits before designing their solution, and failed to trace the impacts their solution would have on related parts of the system. Thus their solutions, though meritorious for their ingenuity, were "academic" in the worst sense; they could not be implemented without creating more problems than they solved. The moral became clear, and it was probably the most valuable and lasting lesson of the year.

We have told this tale because the IIEP interns on that particular occasion (and most had already become competent *general* planners) were seized by a syndrome that is very common among education specialists when they tackle a particular problem or project. They tend to look at it through a narrow lens and to forget that the solution they emerge with must not only solve the particular problem but must be compatible with the interests of the rest of the system and with the over-all resources available. The world's educational landscape is fairly littered with ill-fitting projects conceived in such a manner.

Examples of Feasibility Testing

Feasibility testing should be applied in any situation where educational plans or decisions are being considered that will significantly affect future resource requirements.

Our case studies illustrate a great variety of ways that feasibility testing has been applied for different purposes in different situations. We can refer to them only briefly here, but readers desiring more detail will find it rewarding to examine the case studies themselves. They are not held up as ideal models; indeed their negative lessons, as we warned earlier, often outweigh the positive ones. But the cases do provide a realistic demonstration of the practical problems involved in the following types of feasibility testing.

Long-range targets. The "Unesco Asian Model" illustrates a useful and quite simple analytical device for testing long-range targets in a rough and general way. This analytical model can handle a substantial number of important variables and alternative hypotheses and translate them quickly into aggregate financial terms reaching a decade or two ahead. It is not intended to give precise estimates of the kind needed, for example, to test the feasibility of a specific capital project. But for the purpose of determining whether a given set of long-term expansion targets and resource input ratios affecting quality are within the plausible range of feasibility, the Unesco model is a great improvement over cruder previous methods.

In demonstrating the model to Asian educational leaders, the Unesco experts wisely assumed alternative rates of economic growth and alternative percentages of total public revenues going to education, in order to show a range of possibilities and the sensitivity of educational resource flows to changes in these critical assumptions. Had this model been available when the original "Karachi targets" were chosen in the early 1960's and when similar long-range expansion targets were calculated for Africa and Latin America, the results might have been rather different. But the basic data needed to operate the model were not available in those days.

Spain recently made good use of a modified version of the Unesco Asian Model to test the long-term feasibility of its sweeping educational reform. This "Madrid Model," programmed in a computer, played a significant role in the legislative debate leading to the approval of the Reform. A direct communication line between the legislative chamber and the central computer made it possible to answer with remarkable speed financial questions posed by legislators.

Medium-term general plans. Several of the case studies demonstrate feasibility testing of five-year national educational plans. Each has its own special features and techniques.

The Soviet and French cases involve a close integration of educational planning and economic planning and the setting of tentative financial ceilings at the outset of the educational planning process in order to minimize the adjustments needed at the end and to ensure a coherent pattern of over-all government spending.

Thailand's 1967–71 educational plan, on the other hand, was subjected to feasibility testing only after it was drawn up. The tests indicated that there would probably be sufficient resources to meet the selected enrolment targets at the pre-primary and primary levels and in vocational education and teacher training. It appeared, however, that there would be a financial shortage at the secondary and university levels, and particularly for private secondary schools. We will mention later how this imbalance was rectified.

The Uganda educational planners were given stringent financial limitations to work within from the outset and soon found that, even with extraordinary economies, the minimum expansion targets acceptable to political leaders could not be achieved within these constraints. This exercise, however, had built a watertight case for raising the initial financial ceiling and thus they later found themselves in the rare position of being asked by the top policy-makers to prepare a more expensive plan.

Annual budgets. The Hungarian case demonstrates the use of an ingenious feasibility testing model that ties annual budgets to the Five-Year Plan and differentiates between expenditures on quantitative expansion and on qualitative improvement (the latter including such factors as improved teacher qualifications, maintenance, and class size). This model appears to work quite successfully, judging from the close match between planned costs and actual subsequent expenditures.

Major reforms, innovations, and policy-decisions. Still another kind of model was used in Norway to check the economic consequences and feasibility of several alternative ways of reforming and extending primary education. The model was used to help educational authorities and legislators make better-informed choices.

Rather more sophisticated models were used in Toronto, Canada, to help university authorities to choose intelligently among several alternative ways of reforming medical education within prescribed financial limits. The "customers"—the administrators who had to decide—were evidently pleased with the help it gave them.

A simpler method was used in Poland to compare the costs and feasibility of alternative ways of reforming teacher training. In the end the authorities rejected the cheapest way in favor of a higher-cost one that had greater attraction on other grounds, but they had the benefit of knowing the comparative costs and that the one they finally chose was economically feasible.

We hesitate to mention the Ivory Coast television case once more, but it stands as one of the best examples of a serious effort to examine both the short-range and long-range feasibility of a far-reaching educational innovation. In a similar view, but using a very different method, the Barbados case presents an ingenious technique for determining the economic feasibility of extending a limited experiment in team teaching to the whole school system.

University expansion. The Uganda case on Makerere University College, and one of the cases from the U.S.S.R., demonstrate different approaches to arriving at financially feasible university plans and budgets. The Uganda case involved a pragmatic "cut and fit" approach and a confrontation between two independently conceived proposals—one made by a university staff preoccupied with pursuing excellence, the other by central government planners concerned with getting the most from scarce resources. In the end a compromise was reached which seemed financially feasible.

The U.S.S.R. case, by contrast, illustrates a much more highly developed system of university planning—working from the individual institution upward and from the central government downward. At both levels, however, the detailed planning and budget-making is done within financial limitations set by the top economic planning authorities.

This does not exhaust the examples of feasibility testing provided by our case studies, but perhaps it will suffice to underscore two basic points: first, feasibility testing is an indispensable step in planning any future educational action, and, second, it can take many forms in many kinds of situations.

Ways To Balance the Equation

The moment of truth arrives for the planner and the policy-maker when the two sides of the equation are confronted—the resource requirements side and the resource supply side. More often than not, on the first time around, the equation turns out to be seriously out of balance, with requirements far outweighing prospective resource supplies. What can be done about it?

It is sometimes tempting to let the imbalance stand, or to make it disappear with statistical magic. This is no solution at all, however; it simply postpones the agony, permits the problem to fester, and virtually guarantees that the plan will not be fully implemented. Unrealistic plans can be worse than useless; they can mislead policy-makers and the public at large, frustrate the educational hopes of young people and their families, and cause serious waste of scarce resources.

There are basically three ways to remedy a financial imbalance: (1) by reducing the size of the plan—stretching the targets over a longer period; (2) by achieving major economies; and (3) by finding additional sources of revenue. All three ways appear in the case studies.

In the French case, expansion targets in the draft Five-Year Plan were cut back substantially to stay within the revised financial allocation, but they were not cut back uniformly or arbitrarily; internal priorities were applied and some levels were cut much less than others.

In Ceylon the educational planners in 1964–65 tested the feasibility of achieving 90 per cent participation in primary education by 1971. They concluded that recurrent costs alone would have to equal 7 per cent of the projected GNP by then, and, beyond this, the nation's building potential was too small to handle the task. It was clear that achievement of this ambitious goal would have to be postponed.

The "search for economies" approach is particularly well illustrated in the Uganda educational planning case. Economies of many sorts were explored—some of them quite conventional and others very unconventional and controversial—to avoid having to reduce the targets. Actually only a few of the proposed economies were accepted; the government chose instead to raise education's allocation.

In the Barbados case, policy-makers were shown a series of potential trade-offs within a fixed financial ceiling. By cutting out one item they could add another, possibly to greater educational advantage. But they could not have both and yet stay within the limit.

We must confess some disappointment, however, in finding so few cases where major steps were taken to achieve new economies in the use of limited resources, compatible with educational quality and effectiveness. This, of course, is not surprising. The natural impulse of most busy educational administrators when faced with a financial imbalance is to press as hard as they can for a larger budget, and, if this fails, then to cut the program goals as a last resort, or to spread the available resources over more students, accepting a decline in effectiveness rather than a cut in enrolment targets. But the internal methods and practices of the system are not essentially altered by such adjustments; they are simply watered down. The implicit assumption is that there is no other way —or at least no better way—to run the system and to attain the desired results.

There is good reason to believe, however, that there are in fact some better ways, if one looks for them hard enough and is willing to risk temporary discomfort and inconvenience to try them out. Indeed, if this were not the case, if it were a fixed fact of life that educational plans could only be brought into balance by cutting them back or by getting more money, then the outlook for most of the world's educational systems would be extremely bleak. Virtually all these systems are going to have to live with tighter resource constraints in coming years, but at the same time be subjected to mounting pressure to serve more students and to serve them better. The only way out of this dilemma is to find new and better ways of getting larger and improved results from the limited resources available. This requires improving the internal efficiency and effectiveness of existing educational processes, which in turn requires changing the traditional ways of doing things.

Obviously this will not be easy; there never seems to be a good time to change, even when change is admittedly needed. We suggest, however, that the best time to make these hard decisions and to get them accepted and into effect is precisely when a widely desired plan or policy is subjected to the test of feasibility and found wanting. At that point the options become clear for all to see. Either cut back the goals and educate fewer students, or reduce quality and effectiveness and keep the numbers rising, or economize and innovate in ways consistent with educating more and educating them better. We hope that the earlier pages of this book have suggested a number of ways in which progress toward the latter option can be made.

We do not mean to imply, however, that the planners and leaders of financially hard-pressed educational systems should give up trying to find greater financial resources. On the contrary, we recommend an innovative approach here, too. A number of systems have found that it pays to seek out unconventional ways and untapped potential sources for supplementing the revenues from normal sources.

As this book is being written, the IIEP is making a wide search for unconventional financing measures being used in some countries that might provide encouragement and useful guidance to others. No one expects to find any panaceas, nor any totally painless ways for channeling more resources into education. Someone always has to sacrifice when resources get redirected, and often a new type of revenue-raising measure requires the violation of one or another politically sacred principle. Thus it takes a combination of ingenuity, courage, and compassion to solve the problem.

In some Latin American countries, to take an example, the burden of financing technical education has been shifted from the public purse to local industries that benefit from such education by getting a more competent manpower supply. But it is a two-way arrangement. Representatives of these industries participate in determining the types of training and how it will be accomplished, to ensure that it is relevant and useful to the students and employers alike. The arrangement seems to be working quite well.

In some countries, such as Kenya, parents whose children cannot get into the regular secondary school have created schools of their own and financed them with their own money. To be sure, such schools often do not fit the official "standards" and thus are looked upon by educational officials as a "problem." In fact, however, they may be less a problem than an opportunity; they represent a way to channel more resources into education beyond what the public coffers can afford. The main problem, if any, is to find ingenious—and flexible—ways to help them improve their performance.

Quite a number of poor countries have succeeded in harnessing this great desire of parents, particularly in rural areas, to give their children an educational change, by encouraging the village to build the school and the parents to buy the books, with the understanding that the government will help supply the teacher. The contributions of parents and neighbors, far from being a diversion of national resources from other needs, often add additional productive efforts to the GNP.

It is apparent in most developing countries that the central budget is becoming so severely strained that there is little choice but to count more heavily on local governments to assume a larger share of education costs. This poses difficult problems of politics and of possible geographic inequalities of educational opportunity, but it may be an unavoidable necessity if education is to go forward.

It seems clear, too, that until their public economies grow stronger, many of these countries must look to increased private educational payments, as unpleasant a prospect as this may be. Obviously, it would be ideal to have free education for all, at every level, but this ideal is still far beyond the reach of poorer nations, and for that matter most richer ones. The real issue, then, is not private fees vs. free education, but how to expand the private sharing of educational costs and at the same time avoid widespread social injustice. The answers will not come easily, but they must come. Ironically, quite the opposite of social justice occurs today where free university education is clung to in the name of social justice while private fees continue to be charged for primary and secondary education. The net effect oftentimes is that lower-income families are subsidizing, through the taxes they pay, the higher education of the children of more fortunate people who attend the university in disproportionate numbers and are acquiring an education that will later give them distinct economic advantages.

The foregoing are merely illustrative of the complex issues and stubborn problems to which all nations must find solutions in the coming years if they are to fulfill their educational needs and aspirations and to make continued progress toward their broader development goals.

Cost analysis can be an important tool for helping to clarify and solve many of these issues and problems, though obviously it cannot by itself provide the solutions.

11 *A Brief Look at the Future*

Despite the substantial gains of the past decade, educational cost analysis is still in a very rudimentary state compared to what will be needed in the years ahead. If the increasingly complex problems and choices confronting educational systems are to be dealt with intelligently, if these systems are to get the most from their severely limited resources, if they are to adapt speedily enough to important changes in their environment and extricate themselves from a deepening crisis, then educational systems must have far better information about themselves and their environment than they now possess, and better analytical instruments for applying this information to decision-making.

Improved cost analysis will help considerably, but as we noted earlier, costs standing alone have limited value for the planner and decision-maker. It is only when costs are juxtaposed with educational objectives, outputs, and ultimate benefits that the performance of an educational process can be intelligently assessed and rational choices made among alternative ways to improve it.

The sorts of analysis and evidence required to confront costs with results raise greater difficulties than cost analysis alone. The matter at that stage extends well beyond the domain of economics into complex issues of pedagogy, sociology, psychology, and even politics. As baffling as these issues are, however, there is no alternative but to penetrate them as well as possible and to get the best obtainable picture of costs in relation to results. Otherwise, educational systems are condemned to flying blind.

The bright side of the matter is that the intellectual frontiers of this whole field are alive today with fresh ideas, experimental efforts, research, and wholesome controversy. The best way to get a look at what the future may hold is to survey some of these frontier developments, including some that may still be far from ready for practical application. This final chapter undertakes to do this briefly. So that no one will have any illusions, however, it begins with a reminder of some of the intrinsic difficulties that will inevitably condition the pace of progress in this field. And to assure today's practitioners that they can make important progress on their own without awaiting the results of future research, the chapter suggests a few useful steps that any educational system can take right now to diagnose and improve the ratio between its costs and results.

An examination of the relationship between educational costs and results, both past and prospective, is essential to a variety of important purposes. It is essential, for example, to deciding how much of a nation's resources to allocate to education and how best to allocate these resources within education. It is essential to assessing how effectively present resources are being utilized and to determining how they might be put to more effective use. It is essential above all to planning the future, to weighing the comparative advantages and feasibility of alternative courses of action, and to determining whether the prospective benefits of a proposed new program or project are likely to justify the costs.

Different combinations of data and analytical techniques are needed for these different purposes, but the same underlying logic and principles of systems analysis, already discussed in Chapter 4, apply to all of them. Applying these principles to real-life situations, however, can be a complex and messy affair.

It is no activity for people who insist on easy answers, or for perfectionists. Only stouthearted, critically-minded pragmatists, willing to settle for results that are useful yet far short of ideal, are likely to get very far on this rough terrain.

Intrinsic Difficulties

Any effort to apply the principles of cost effectiveness and cost-benefit analysis to education is guaranteed to produce a chorus of discouraging warnings that educational objectives are too undefinable, learning attainments too unmeasurable, and educational benefits too imponderable to make any such analysis feasible. There is much truth to these warnings, but not enough to conclude that all such efforts should once and for all be abandoned. There is too much evidence to the contrary to warrant such a pessimistic view.

This much is unquestionably true. Educational objectives, stated in their most general form, are usually too vague to provide an operational yardstick against which to evaluate performance. But as one narrows his focus to specific sub-systems—such as teaching reading or arithmetic at a given grade level, or training for specific agricultural or industrial skills—it becomes increasingly feasible to define objectives in operationally meaningful terms and to gather relevant evidence by which to measure achievement. This is not to say that it will be easy or that ideal results can be secured, even in such limited areas of the whole educational system. It is far more difficult to cope with the non-cognitive objectives (relating, for example, to the development of critical thinking, problem-solving ability, or various desirable attitudes) than with the cognitive ones (to which most student tests are still confined). Fortunately, however, the frontier developments mentioned earlier include a variety of promising efforts to develop more adequate instruments for measuring such elusive educational outcomes.[1]

Much of the difficulty of defining objectives stems from the innately complex nature of learning and human behavior, but much of it also stems from failure to give sufficient attention to clari-

1. For a summary of recent significant research in this field, see Nathan Kravetz, "The Evaluation of Educational System Outputs: An Exploratory Study," IIEP (Mimeo.), October 1970.

fying objectives and priorities and to designing examinations and other evaluation instruments that really fit the avowed objectives. If neither teachers nor students are clear about what they are trying to accomplish and why, the results can hardly be expected to be very good. And if their joint efforts are dominated by examinations that bear very limited relation to the presumed objectives, the results are bound to be disappointing. This, unhappily, is the way most schools and higher educational institutions seem to function, but they are not condemned to function that way forever.

If educational objectives are hard to define clearly and learning outcomes very difficult to measure, the assessment of the ultimate benefits presents even more intractable problems. These benefits, of course, take a variety of forms—economic and non-economic, social and private. In principle at least, it is relatively easier to gauge the economic benefits (such as higher lifetime earnings resulting from additional years of education), since these can be measured in standard monetary units, compared against the educational costs stated in similar units, and the relation between the two expressed as a percentage yield on the investment. This is essentially what the economists have been trying to do with their "rate-of-return" studies. (See below.) But what about the non-economic benefits? In the first place, what are they? Can they be defined in sufficiently precise terms even to prove they exist, not to mention measuring them by some common unit? Even assuming that these non-economic benefits could be measured, how much of the credit should be given to education for producing them and how much to a host of other influential factors outside the educational system?

Merely to pose the questions in this form is to indicate the virtual impossibility of ever answering them fully and precisely. But one does not need perfect answers; half a loaf is far better than none. The best hope lies in finding some incomplete yet useful indicators. This, in fact, is how the medical profession gets along; it has far from perfect understanding or answers, yet it does much good, and it does far better today than a century ago. If medical doctors refused to attempt a diagnosis until all the means were available for getting a full and precise picture of what is going on inside a patient, health care would still be in a medieval state. But doctors are content to use the best indicators available, as limited as they are. And medical research has steadily given them better ones.

Educators can take heart from this experience of the medical profession, for they need better indicators to help diagnose and improve the health of educational systems. Research can and undoubtedly will help to find them. Meanwhile, however, there is much more that educators can do right now with the crude indicators already available, as we will attempt to show below.

Cost-Effectiveness Tests

Earlier we defined cost effectiveness as the relationship between the inputs and corresponding immediate educational outputs of any educational process, and cost benefit as the relationship between the inputs and resulting benefits that accrue thereafter. The first relationship is a measure of internal efficiency, the second a measure of external productivity. There is no disputing the basic logic and utility of these concepts; the only real issue is how to apply them in practice.

Perhaps the most salutary progress lately in this regard has been not so much in the realm of new methodologies as in the fact that responsible educators have more and more been thinking in these analytical terms. Inevitably this has whetted their appetite for more cogent facts and estimates, sharpened their powers of observation, and caused them to question conventional practices and assumptions long taken for granted.

A case in point is the more sophisticated consideration now being given to the whole matter of "educational wastage." Dropout and repeater rates have been of increasing concern to educators in many countries, but the available data were often so crude as to conceal the true dimensions of the problem and to encourage simplistic thinking about how to solve it. Conventional wisdom held that the only way to reduce these rates was to increase expenditures per pupil—in other words, to do more of the same only better.

An international study carried out in 1969–70 by Unesco and the International Bureau of Education, using more refined methods of data collection and analysis, put the problem in a clearer light and showed it to be even more shockingly wasteful of human and economic resources than had previously been realized.[2] No educator can seriously examine these new figures without having grave doubts about the adequacy of attacking the problem by simply doing more of the same. New research is clearly needed to get at the real causes of the phenomenon and to suggest new ways of approaching it.

Dropouts and repeaters, of course, are only one indicator of educational inefficiency. Waste can take a variety of forms. A school system or university, as we saw earlier, even with a good record on dropouts and repeaters, can under-utilize available space and equipment or pay too much for them to begin with. It can waste the precious time of teachers and students by using archaic and educationally inefficient teaching methods and technologies. It can deploy its resources in an unbalanced way, such as spending too little on textbooks and other learning aids relative to what is spent on teacher salaries.

Some of these inefficiencies can be detected and remedied without applying a full cost-effectiveness test. But in the final analysis the acid test of an educational system's internal efficiency is what the students carry away from the experience beyond what they brought to it, and what it cost to provide that "educational value-added."

Economists, as we have seen, can usually manage to piece together at least a rough picture of the cost side of the equation, but getting a picture of the output side (other than the number of students dropping out or finishing) is far more difficult. Traditional academic exams, intended to test the performance of in-

2. "The Statistical Measurement of Educational Wastage," Unesco: International Bureau of Education (Mimeo.), June 1970.

dividual students and not of the system itself, are of limited help; moreover, they do not give a before-and-after picture, even for the individual. Until fairly recently, pedagogical-measurements experts concerned themselves mainly with testing at the point of admission or at the point of completion, but not with the relation between the two. Fortunately, a variety of new research efforts are now being applied to this gap, and to devising new instruments to measure important educational outcomes that escape detection by conventional academic tests. Equally important, other social scientists have been probing into the out-of-school environmental and family influences that strongly condition a child's school performance. Their findings thus far show that these out-of-school factors have a greater bearing on a child's overall education than schooling itself, and that for many children what happens in school is the wrong thing. This is especially the case for culturally deprived children from uneducated homes who attend schools designed for middle-class children.

More research along these lines is greatly needed, but no one should be surprised if it reveals even greater inefficiency and ineffectiveness on the part of conventional schooling than is already suspected. It should not be forgotten that unit costs are themselves a very simple and useful indicator of cost effectiveness. If unit costs rise steadily and substantially over a period of time, with no demonstrable improvements in the quality and amount of learning per student, there is a *prima facie* case of declining efficiency.

New Approaches to Educational Budgeting

The cost-effectiveness concept and the cost-benefit concept, dealt with below, can be usefully incorporated in the budgetary process. It is not there now. Conventional budgets and accounts, though useful for certain purposes (particularly to help auditors guard against misappropriation of funds), are of limited help to analysts and evaluators trying to measure and improve the efficiency of educational systems. They typically lump expenditures by such categories as administrative salaries, teacher salaries, supplies and materials, repairs and maintenance, and so forth, but this fails to reveal how these funds are allocated or used in terms of specific educational functions and objectives. How much, for example, goes into teaching reading, social studies, general science, and so forth? Until one knows how the resources are actually used, he has no basis for comparing costs with corresponding educational results. Several new approaches to budgeting—bearing such labels as "program budgeting," PPBS, performance budgeting—have been suggested as a way of making the budget a more effective instrument for analysis, choice-making, and evaluation and are being tested in a few places.

Each of these approaches has its own distinguishing features which we will not go into here, but their basic common characteristics are to gear expenditure allotments directly to specific educational targets and to apply performance criteria by which progress toward these targets can be periodically tested. The application of these principles forces attention to the weighing of educational priorities and to the choice of the best among alternative action plans for pursuing the selected targets. The process could work approximately as follows:

First, an initial estimate is made of the over-all resources likely to be available for the new budget period (which could be a single year or a longer period).

Second, the priority program objectives to be achieved within these resource limits during the period are chosen and specified as concretely as possible, along with specific criteria and types of evidence to be used in monitoring progress and assessing achievements at the end of the period.[3]

Third, alternative plans of action for achieving each objective are designed and costed in order to select those with the best cost-effectiveness rating. At the same time, alternative "fall-back plans"

3. The objectives at the primary level, for example, might include: specified increases in participation rates and average daily attendance; specified improvements in the profile of student attainments in reading, arithmetic, etc. at given grade levels; an increase in student participation in individual group social studies projects, etc.

are chosen to be used in the event that total resources prove to be less than originally estimated.

Fourth, once approved and funded, the program budget is put into action. During the period, but especially near the end, the achievement criteria are applied, using selected evidence that has been accumulating along the way. Short-falls and over-achievements are diagnosed, causes identified insofar as possible, and the resulting operational lessons fed back into the process to benefit the next cycle.

In effect, program budgeting translates longer-term macro-educational plans into more concrete action and budgetary terms for shorter periods and for particular sub-systems.

The practical problems involved are much the same as those already discussed that arise in any effort to apply cost-effectiveness principles to education. The difficulties should not be underestimated, but neither should they frighten anyone away from trying. Early experience suggests that a considerable time should be allowed to make the full transition to program budgeting and that the best way to get there is by limited, manageable stages.

This can be illustrated by an exercise carried out for the Los Angeles, California, school system on the objective of reducing the high dropout rate (28 per cent).[4] The goal for the exercise was a sharp reduction of the dropout rate for a specific cohort of students entering the seventh grade, to be accomplished by an action program involving intensified counseling, supplementary teaching, and other special program inputs. This program was then costed for the full period during which the cohort would progress from the seventh through the twelfth grade. These projected costs could be differentiated from the amalgamated normal budget and matched against the statistical evidence or dropout rates over the entire period, thereby giving a measure of cost-effectiveness. If the goal were not achieved on schedule, there could be only two explanations: either the required resources

4. Werner Z. Hirsch, "The Budget as an Instrument for Medium- and Long-Range Planning and Programming in Education" (unpublished OECD paper DAS/EID/68.9, April 1968.)

were not forthcoming and the action program had been frustrated, or else it was based on faulty premises to begin with. By starting with a goal of this sort against which progress can be rather easily measured, it is possible to take the first steps toward program budgeting without getting encumbered with far more complex goals and measurements.

A somewhat similar partial approach to program budgeting is illustrated by our Ceylon case study. There, it will be remembered, the planners recommended a separate budgetary provision (on an ascending annual scale) for a series of actions to improve the quality of learning in certain subjects. In this instance the costs could be identified but progress toward the goal would be more difficult to demonstrate. Nevertheless, the Ceylon approach did have the virtue of identifying a specific priority goal and a corresponding action program for which incremental funds could be specifically earmarked. This was in marked contrast to the traditional budgetary approach in Ceylon which concealed even the breakdown between primary and secondary teacher costs.

Educational systems can draw useful inspiration from the general concept and principles of program budgeting, even if they are not ready to adopt it. One useful initial exercise which any school could carry out, for example, would be to estimate roughly, by a sample of classroom observations, how much relative time teachers and students at different grade levels actually spend on different subjects (learning objectives). On this basis a rough estimate could be made of how the primary school budget is in fact allocated according to educational objectives, and what the unit cost per pupil is for each of these objectives. Possibly for the first time the system would see how it was actually using its resources in terms of various educational purposes (and this might be quite an eye-opener!).

It should be emphasized that experimentation with program budgeting does not require abandoning the traditional budget with which everyone is familiar. The two types of budgets simply show the same operation from different vantage points and each has its own particular advantages. It is probably desirable, in fact, at least for some years, to treat program budgeting as a supplement to the "normal" budget.

Our case studies suggest a number of other kinds of innovations, apart from program budgeting, that can make the budget more useful for decision-making and for translating long-term plans into yearly action programs. The Hungarian case study, for example, shows how a national budget, applied in conjunction with cost norms and standards, became an important decision-making tool. The Canadian and Ugandan case studies illustrate some useful techniques for using institutional budget data to compare the costs of alternatives. And experience in Denmark shows that a multi-year budget, involving little more work than the traditional style budget, provides a broader perspective for decision-making.

As every experienced administrator knows only too well, there is little leeway for redeploying over-all resources in any one year. Any major redeployment must usually be achieved by a cumulative series of marginal budgetary shifts in the same direction over a period of years. The shift can come more quickly if the budget is growing rapidly; it can be painfully slow when the budget remains stabilized. But the main point is that a *desirable* redeployment can be accomplished only if the priorities and objectives are clearly defined, and only if they are doggedly pursued over a good period of time. A type of budget and budgetary process that reveals the deployment of resources in terms of objectives and not simply by expenditure categories can be a powerful instrument for enabling an educational system to get where it wants to go, assuming it knows where it wants to go.

Applying Cost-Benefit Tests

Many people apparently believe, mistakenly, that the cost-benefit approach to educational planning and decision-making is synonymous with "rate-of-return" studies. The latter are merely one among many species of the larger genus. Actually, prudent administrators have used the cost-benefit approach for a long time, but like the man who discovered that he had been using prose all his life, they did not realize it. No smart administrator, for example, would consider advocating an expensive new educational program or project without first satisfying himself—and being prepared to satisfy others—that its ultimate benefits would amply justify the costs. Nor would any smart administrator choose Route A to a given objective if he had reliable facts showing that you could get there at least as well via Route B at half the cost. This hard-headed logic illustrates the cost-benefit approach to decision-making.

In applying this approach, however, educational administrators have usually been forced to rely largely on intuitive judgment and persuasive rhetoric, having few hard facts or solid analysis to go on. Many times, for example, they have argued for a new vocational secondary school on the grounds that teenagers not going on to college should have an opportunity to acquire some salable skills that could benefit both them and society. The goal was undoubtedly good, but if more facts and comparative analysis had been available, they might have shown that the same benefits could be achieved by a quicker and cheaper method.

These days educational decision-makers are finding it increasingly necessary to undergird their decision-making with more facts and better analysis. If they do not ask the tough and searching questions themselves, someone else is sure to. Most of the questions are fairly obvious and they all relate to cost benefit. Is there a real demand for such vocational training on the part of students? On the part of employers? What skills are most likely to be needed and to afford the best employment opportunities? What is the best way to provide these skills? Is a full-time formal vocational secondary school the best answer, or are there alternative ways that might have a much better cost-benefit ratio?

Questions such as these can never be answered with precision and certainty, if only because they involve the future. Yet they still need to be asked and thought about hard, drawing on the best facts and estimates one can assemble, for to make an important decision in any other manner leaves much greater room for serious error.

The greatly increased attention being given these days by educational planning to demography, costs, manpower and employment factors, economic growth rates, and the like, and the steadily improving supplies of facts on these matters, enable educational decision-makers to apply—even if crudely—much better cost-benefit tests than they could earlier. They can be greatly helped in this by social science analysts, whether on their own staffs, in the university, or elsewhere, who can undertake revealing sample surveys and other limited pieces of research.

One important piece of self-analysis which almost any educational system or institution can undertake with modest effort (though surprisingly few have tried it) is to run a sample survey of previous students to determine how they have made out, how *they* in retrospect appraise the various aspects of their education, and what lessons all this suggests for improving the cost-benefit ratio. Some jolting discoveries may result from such a survey, pointing to the need for some drastic changes, but it is better for educational institutions to make such discoveries themselves and take action to improve the situation than to wait to be pushed into it by someone else.

Another important and feasible form of self-appraisal is to make a candid and realistic review of the curriculum—preferably with the help of a few wise and judicious but tough-minded friends of education from outside the system. The aim would be to determine how much of the present curriculum really makes sense and merits a continuing claim on scarce resources and, similarly, what of importance is missing from the curriculum that might be substituted from lower-priority things without boosting costs. Nothing depresses educational benefits in relation to costs so much as teaching the unimportant, the outmoded, and the inappropriate.

A third helpful self-diagnostic exercise for improving the cost-benefit ratio (particularly where costly technical or other training is involved) is to examine the pattern of student distribution by fields of study to see if it makes sense in relation to prospective national manpower needs and employment opportunities. Highly detailed manpower forecasts are not needed for this; quite rough and general ones will suffice. If, for example, in an agrarian country where rural development is lagging badly, the statistics of higher education enrolments show that only 3 or 4 per cent of the students are preparing for careers in agriculture and rural development whereas about 30 per cent each are majoring in law or the humanities, this is fairly convincing evidence that the benefits derived from higher education will be much lower in the future than they could or should be, and that drastic changes in the enrolment proportions are needed.

By acting forcefully on the telltale clues that can be readily obtained from surveys of alumni and employers, critical curriculum reviews, and from data on student enrolment patterns relative to employment prospects, any educational system can lift, perhaps dramatically, the future benefits it is helping to generate from the scarce resources it is using.

Improvements in the cost-benefit ratio must also be vigorously sought on the cost side by finding ways of using available resources more fully and effectively, but since we have traversed this ground before we will not return to it here.

Rate-of-Return Studies

We have left to the end our discussion of rate-of-return studies because this most sophisticated (and more controversial[5]) method of cost-benefit analysis is difficult for many educational systems to apply without specialized outside assistance. Moreover, this method still must undergo years of further research and development before it can be considered a practical tool in the hands of decision-makers. Meanwhile, however, whatever else one may

5. See the chapter by John Vaizey and John Sheehan, "The Productivity of Education", in M. Ferreira Leite, P. Lynch, J. Sheehan, and J. Vaizey, *The Economics of Educational Costing: Inter-Country and Inter-Regional Comparisons*, Vol. II, Lisbon, Instituto Gulbenkian de Ciência, 1968.

feel about it, it is an extraordinarily effective device for forcing one to think hard about the many variables and relationships that should be taken into consideration in any cost-benefit approach.

Three such rate-of-return examples are included in our case studies (applying to Chile, Colombia, and India).[6] Each describes in some detail the methods and data used in each instance and the conclusions reached, and includes a critical commentary by the International Institute for Educational Planning staff. Readers interested in probing more deeply into the rate-of-return methodology are advised to read these case studies and also the useful IIEP booklet by Maureen Woodhall, *Cost-Benefit Analysis in Educational Planning.*

Few educators, we suspect, have yet tried to penetrate the mysteries of rate-of-return studies, but this is the more reason for them to understand what these studies are generally about, and what they can and cannot do for educational policy-makers.

Economists themselves are sharply divided on the efficacy of rate-of-return studies in education, even though, paradoxically, all agree that a cost-benefit approach is essential to any planning or decision-making question involving the allocation and use of scarce resources. Thus, the controversy centers on the particular methods employed in rate-of-return studies, not on the basic logic of the cost-benefit approach.

The main object of such studies is to provide decision-makers with a better picture of the comparative advantages of putting additional investments in alternative educational directions or possibly outside of education instead. For this purpose, the cost-benefit ratio is expressed as a per cent yield on the particular educational expenditure. Thus, for example, if a rate-of-return study showed that the expected yield on an additional expenditure on primary education compared favorably with the going

6. A fourth case we had hoped to include, but it was not available in time, is the most illuminating of all and well worth reading. It is a study of Kenya by Hans Thias and Martin Carnoy, and was prepared for the World Bank (Report N° EC-173).

rate of interest in the economy at large, whereas the yield on additional investment in university education would be much lower, then decision-makers would be prompted to channel new funds into expanding primary rather than university education.

This approach to allocating educational resources among alternative uses conforms to the classical economics textbook principle which says that the way to maximize over-all output from a given set of resources is to allocate each type of resource (land, labor, capital) among competing uses in such a way that its marginal productivity (yield) becomes equalized in all different uses. This is done by constantly allocating increments of each resource to its "highest marginal use," which in theory has the effect of expanding the supply of that type of production relative to demand, thereby lowering its price (or raising its cost of production) and reducing its marginal yield to a parity with alternative uses.

The practical application of this theory, of course, requires that the allocators have a fairly clear idea of what marginal productivity an increment of any resource would have in its various alternative uses (e.g. in education vs. industry vs. health, or within education as between, say, primary, secondary, and post-secondary). This is what rate-of-return studies seek to determine, by equating the costs and cumulative future benefits of an incremental investment in one or another type of education. The methods for estimating costs are similar to those discussed elsewhere in this book and present no special problems, save the criticism of other economists that it is improper to include some "opportunity costs" (i.e. the earnings foregone by students).

The main problems and controversy arise with respect to the calculation of benefits. Private benefits, to the student himself, are measured in terms of the additional lifetime earnings he receives as the result of additional education (*after* taxes, and discounted over time). These private benefits are compared with private costs of education to determine the private rate of return.

Public benefits are estimated by using private benefits as a proxy measure (*before* taxes, since the taxes go to the public).

These public benefits (discounted over time) are then compared with *public* costs of education (which are usually higher than the private costs) to determine the public rate of return (this being of primary concern to public policy-makers). An important underlying assumption here is that relative wages are a reasonable measure of the relative productivity of persons in different types of employment.

This is a highly ingenious methodology whose application calls for extraordinary statistical skill, particularly when the basic data needed to apply it are extremely scarce and of dubious reliability (as they usually are, particularly in developing nations). While it is technically a very sophisticated approach, the accuracy of its final statistical results is inevitably open to serious question.

This has led some of the less generous critics of rate-of-return studies to dub them a "statistical house of cards." A more generous appraisal, however, would caution strongly against taking the specific statistical conclusions too seriously for policy-making purposes, but at the same time would note that, as an intellectual exercise and educational device, rate-of-return studies have the great merit of forcing attention to the critical variables and relationships that should be taken into account in formulating a cost-benefit judgment of any educational situation.

As better statistics become available, the present large margin of potential error in rate-of-return studies can certainly be reduced, but many critics will still not be satisfied because they see more fundamental defects in the basic assumptions underlying the methods now in use. The main criticisms can be briefly summarized as follows, at some risk of oversimplification.

1. *At best, only part of the total educational benefits are measured; but nobody knows how large or small a part this is.* Rate-of-return studies measure only the *direct economic benefits* (reflected in the extra lifetime earnings to the individual and extra production for the nation created by additional education). The *indirect economic benefits* (for example, the beneficial effects that a supervisor's training may have on the productivity of his subordinates) and the *non-economic benefits* (for example,

increased personal satisfactions, improved family welfare, contributions to civic leadership and national unity, cultural advancements, etc.) are explicitly ignored. These in some instances might be more important than the direct economic benefits, but thus far there is no way to measure them.

2. *The use of current "age/education/earnings differentials" to project future benefits is logically unsound.* This method, the critics say, treats current wage differentials as if they would remain constant, whereas they will undoubtedly change over time in response to changes in manpower supply-demand conditions. Indeed, increasing educational investment in the presently high-yield areas (reflecting relative shortages of particular types of manpower) will itself contribute to altering wage differentials.

3. *Measuring public benefits in this manner assumes that differences in wages reflect reasonably accurately differences in real productivity, whereas there is abundant reason to believe that in reality this is far from the truth.*

4. *Earnings differentials reflect not only differences in education but in individual ability and motivation, family background, and other endogenous factors, and there is no sound basis for determining what portion is due to education.* Authors of rate-of-return studies allow for this by discounting the computed earnings differential before crediting education with the balance; the discount rate they use (often 50 per cent) is basically arbitrary.

5. *At best, rate-of-return studies only tell the decision-maker in what direction to invest but not how much to invest—which is just as important.* As indicated above, the basic theory behind such studies is limited to *marginal* increments of investment and assumes that anything more than that will alter the rate of return.

6. *The rate-of-return method ignores the question of internal efficiency and educational relevance; it measures education simply by years of exposure—to the kind of education given in the past, not the kind that might be given in the future.* The implication is that the only options open are to expand or not to expand the

existing system as it is, thus ignoring all the important possibilities of raising educational benefits by changing the content and methods of education.

Faced with the above criticisms, most proponents of rate-of-return studies readily admit that there is some validity to them. But they express faith that with more research and better facts these shortcomings can be reduced. The more evangelical ones go on to assert that there are serious defects in all approaches, but fewer in this one than others, particularly the "manpower approach" and the "social demand approach" to educational planning, which they regard as competitors.

The latter assertion, it seems to us, presents a false issue. The truth of the matter, as we see it, is that no one of the approaches is sufficient in itself. Each has useful insights to contribute, but each is limited and, taken alone, has severe shortcomings.

If policy-makers, for example, become the slaves of rising social demand for education, using this as their only guideline, they are bound to make irrational decisions and get into impossible situations as demand outstrips resources and as educational output outstrips employment possibilities. But, on the other hand, they cannot totally disregard the burgeoning popular quest for education for it is a hard fact of political and social life which policy-makers and politicians can ignore only at their peril. The manpower approach likewise has serious limitations, one of which is that it disregards the cost side of the equation. Moreover, like the rate-of-return approach, it is blind to the non-economic benefits of education. Yet to plan educational development without careful regard to future manpower needs and employment prospects can lead to disastrous results. Ironically, the more aggressive advocates of the rate-of-return attack vigorously these shortcomings of the manpower approach, yet find it essential as a foundation of their own approach.

What all this comes down to is that there is not yet—and probably never will be—any single methodological approach that will tell educational decision-makers all they need to know to make rational and wise decisions. Each of the three "classical" ɩaches mentioned above has useful insights to contribute, but ꞇally all three share a profoundly serious flaw. They implic- ake the existing educational system for granted—its structure, content, and methods—at a time when every serious student of education knows full well that existing education urgently requires drastic reform and innovation. No one of these methods gives the educational planner the guidance he needs in how to effect these changes, or even any loud signals that change is needed.

To get at this whole problem of education change and innovation, new types of planning are needed that penetrate beneath the outer "macro" dimensions of educational systems to their internal affairs (which economists, perhaps understandably, have hesitated to grapple with). Unlike most educational planning to date, this new generation of planning, yet to be elaborated, must extend beyond the goal of linear expansion of the educational *status quo* and become a positive force for redesigning entrenched and now inappropriate educational processes. Its emphasis must be on systems design—on educational processes designed to fit relevant objectives for each place and time and learning clientele in an efficient and effective manner. To achieve this sort of "design approach" to educational planning, economic research and analysis must join hands with pedagogical and sociological research and analysis. Only then will the vital concepts of cost effectiveness and cost benefit acquire their full meaning and receive more realistic application.

Appendix I
A Selected Reading List

Becker, G. S. *Human Capital: A Theoretical and Empirical Analysis with Special Reference to Education*, New York, Columbia University Press, 1964.
This is the classic example of cost-benefit analysis of formal education: not only does Becker calculate both social and private rates of return using data for 1939 and 1949, he discusses in detail the methodology of the approach, possible objectives, the application of the approach to on-the-job training, etc.

Benson, C. *The Economics of Public Education*, Boston, Houghton Mifflin Company, 1968.
The author discusses the various economic aspects of public education by examining the costs and the means of financing education with special reference to the United States.

Blaug, M., Layard, P. R. G., and Woodhall, M. *The Causes of Graduate Unemployment in India*, London, Allen Lane, Penguin Press, 1969.
A study of the problem of unemployment among matriculates and graduates in India with an attempt to apply cost-benefit analysis. This analysis shows that there has been over-investment in general university education in India.

Botti, M., *et al. Recherches sur les coûts de l'enseignement primaire à Madagascar et dans huit pays francophones d'Afrique*, Paris, SEDES, 1967 (three volumes).
An interesting methodology for analysis of budgetary expendi-

tures and the projection of future costs and expenditures. It also gives a comparative study of the costs of primary education in Madagascar and eight French-speaking African countries and their likely evolution in the future.

Bowles, S. "The Efficient Allocation of Resources in Education," *Quarterly Journal of Economics*, Cambridge, Mass., May 1967. A linear programming model for educational planning using data for Nigeria, with an attempt to investigate the economic efficiency of different patterns of resource allocation both within the educational sector and between education and the rest of the economy.

Bowman, M. J., *et al.* (eds.), *Readings in the Economics of Education*, Paris, Unesco, 1968.
A collection of sixty-six papers on various aspects of the economics of education. Includes contributions on the theory of human capital and on techniques of cost-benefit analysis.

Burkhead, J., Fox, T. G., and Holland, J. W. *Input and Output in Large City High Schools*, Syracuse, New York, Syracuse University Press, 1967.
An attempt to examine input-output relationships; inputs are measured in terms of per-pupil expenditures and a variety of school quality factors; outputs are measured in terms of test-scales, retention rates, etc.

Chesswas, J. *Methodologies of Educational Planning for Developing Countries*, Paris, Unesco:IIEP, 1969 (two volumes).

Coombs, P. H. *The World Educational Crisis: A Systems Analysis*, New York, Oxford University Press, 1968.
Using a broad analytical and diagnostic method, the author examines the conditions of the educational crisis of the world, making use of a wealth of evidence. The major issues facing educational systems are identified and priorities in dealing with them are suggested.

Edding, F. *Methods of Analysing Educational Outlay*, Paris, Unesco, 1966 (Statistical Reports and Studies).
A useful technical discussion of the methods of analyzing educational expenditures with some illustrative data by one of the foremost authorities in the field of cost and financing of education.

El-Ghannam, M. A. *Financing Education in the Arab States: A Survey of Recent Trends and Future Prospects*, Paris, Unesco: IIEP, 1970 (Occasional Papers 20) (mimeo.).

Hallak, J. *The Analysis of Educational Costs and Expenditure*, Paris, Unesco:IIEP, 1969 (Fundamentals of Educational Planning, 10).
An examination of some critical problems in the concept, the estimates, the analysis, and the use of unit costs in educational planning. Includes useful illustrative data with analysis of the experience of France and Tanzania in testing the financial feasibility of educational plans.

Hallak, J. *Coûts globeaux et coûts unitaires dans la planification de léducation*, Paris, Unesco:IIEP, 1968 (Lectures and Discussions, 24) (mimeo.).

Hallak, J. *The Role of Budgets in Educational Planning*, Paris, Unesco:IIEP, 1969 (Lectures and Discussions, 44) (mimeo.).

Harris, S. E. *Economic Aspects of Higher Education*, Paris, OECD, 1964.
A collection of papers from a conference organised by the OECD study group in the Economics of Education led by Professor Harris, a top-level specialist in the financing of education.

Hirsch, W. Z. *Analysis of the Rising Costs of Public Education*, Study Paper No. 4, in materials prepared in connexion with the Study of Employment Growth and Price Levels, Joint Economic Committee, U.S. Congress, Washington, 1959.
An analysis of the determinants of educational expenditures which concentrates on the level of teachers' salaries, the pupil-teacher ratio, the proportion of pupils in high school, the proportion of pupils in urban areas, etc.

IIEP. *Educational Development in Africa*, Vol. II, *Costing and Financing*, Paris, Unesco:IIEP, 1969.

IIEP. *New Educational Media in Action: Case Studies for Planners*, Paris, Unesco:IIEP, 1967 (three volumes).

Jolly, R. *Costs and Confusions in African Education: Some Future Implications of Recent Trends*, University of Sussex, Institute of Development Studies, 5 November 1968 (Mimeo No. 18).

A broad discussion of the patterns of African education with a special emphasis on the determinants of costs by a most experienced international student of educational planning.

Kershaw, J., and MacKean, R. *Teacher Shortages and Salary Schedules,* New York, McGraw Hill Book Co., Inc., 1962.
An interesting proposal for a change in the type of salary schedule used in American high schools, the existing unified salary schedule failing to reflect shortages of particular skills. The chapter "Future Costs Under Alternative Policies" attempts to cost the recommendation and compare these costs with present expenditures on salaries of teachers in the United States.

Knight, J. *Earning, Employment, Education and Income Redistribution in Uganda,* Bulletin of the Oxford University Institute of Statistics, 1968.
This is an interesting attempt to study on the basis of factual data the relationship between the earning structure, the employment conditions, and the cost of education in the specific case of one African country.

Leite, M. F., Lynch, P., Sheehan, J., and Vaizey, J. *The Economics of Educational Costing: Inter-Country and Inter-Regional Comparisons,* Lisbon, Instituto Gulbenkian de Ciência, 1968.
A research report by a group of authors who examine unit costs of education in a number of countries and try to establish a basis for a genuine international comparison. Includes some interesting contributions on the determinants of educational costs and on cost behavior with useful illustrative data.

Machlup, F. *The Production and Distribution of Knowledge in the U.S.,* Princeton, N.J., Princeton University Press, 1962.
This is an attempt to cost all forms of personnel and informal education in the United States in 1956 and 1958. There is a section, "Neglected Cost Items," which discusses how to measure earnings foregone, the cost of tax exemptions, imputed rent, etc. The book is notable for its attempt to calculate the total cost of education in the widest sense, including informal instruction in the family, churches, industry, etc.

Miner, J. *Social and Economic Factors in Spending for Public Education,* The Economics and Politics of Public Education No. 11, Syracuse, N.Y., Syracuse University Press, 1963.
This book provides a useful review of studies of the determin-

ants of educational expenditures in the United States. It also presents the results of study of variations in level of expenditure in twenty-three American states with estimates of the income-elasticity of educational expenditures, etc.

Oddie, G. "School-Building Resources and Their Effective Use," *Education and Development*, Paris, OECD, 1966.
Gives a detailed conceptual framework of planning of school facilities. It includes a systematic analysis of the determinants of school-building costs, methods of comparing space utilization with unit cost, with several useful suggestions for improvement.

OECD. *Budgeting, Programme Analysis and Cost-Effectiveness in Educational Planning*, Paris, 1968.
A collection of papers of a seminar devoted to studying the application of PPBS and related techniques in educational planning. It is a notable contribution to the study of the difficulties in using cost benefit and cost effectiveness in decision-making.

Palm, G. *Compiling Statistics in Educational Expenditure and Finance*, Paris, Unesco:IIEP, 1967 (Lectures and Discussions, 19) (mimeo.).

Poignant, R. *Education and Development in Western Europe, the U.S. and the Soviet Union*, New York, Teachers College, Columbia University Press, 1968.
A provocative picture of the comparative post-war growth of education enrolment and expenditure in a selected group of countries from the industrialized world, with an attempt to identify the main trend.

Poignant, R. *Financement et dépenses d'enseignement*, Paris, Unesco: IIEP, 1966 (Lectures and Discussions, 2) (mimeo.).

Robinson, E. A. G., and Vaizey, J. *The Economics of Education*, London, Macmillan, 1966.
This volume sums up the proceedings of a conference held by the International Economics Association; Part IV of the volume is devoted to the cost and financing of education. Four chapters by Bowman, Vaizey, Mushkin, and Okigh discuss some useful aspects.

Schramm, W., *et al. The New Media: Memo to Educational Planners*, Paris, Unesco:IIEP, 1967.

Summary and conclusions of a worldwide research project on the over-all feasibility of using new media by educational systems. The authors give a useful method for costing an instructional new media project.

Schultz, T. *The Economic Value of Education*, New York, 1963.
An interesting review by a distinguished economist whose research and writing have excited economists and educators for several years.

Strumilin, S. "The Economics of Education in the U.S.S.R.," *International Social Science Journal*, 1962 (No. 4).
One of the most well-known studies in the field of economics of education by a Soviet economist who was one of the pioneers in estimating the contribution of education to economic growth.

Vaizey, J., and Chesswas, J. D. *The Costing of Educational Plans*, Paris, Unesco:IIEP, 1967 (Fundamentals of Educational Planning, 6).

Vaizey, J., and Sheehan, J. *Resources for Education: An Economic Study of Education in the United Kingdom, 1920–1965*, London, Allen and Unwin, 1968.
One of the most interesting examples of the analysis of educational expenditure trends with useful sections on private expenditures, measurement of expenditures in real terms, with the aid of specially constructed price indices and an analysis of shifts in the distribution of resources.

Wasserman, W., *Education Price and Quantity Indexes*, Syracuse, New York, Syracuse University Press, 1963.
A basic study concerned in particular with methods of pricing and weighting educational inputs in order to compile education price and quantity indices. Includes some useful illustrative reference data.

Woodhall, M. *Cost-Benefit Analysis in Educational Planning*, Paris, Unesco:IIEP, 1970 (Fundamentals of Educational Planning, 13).

Woodhall, M. *Financing Students in Higher Education: Educational, Social and Economic Implications of Alternative Methods of Finance*, Paris, Unesco:IIEP, 1969 (Lectures and Discussions, 42) (mimeo.).

Woodhall, M. *The Investment Approach to Educational Planning,* Paris, Unesco:IIEP, 1968 (Lectures and Discussions, 32) (mimeo.).

Woodhall, M., and Blaug, M. "Productivity Trends in British Secondary Education," in J. Hallak (ed.), *Educational Costs and Productivity,* Paris, Unesco:IIEP, 1967 (mimeo.).
An attempt to construct an index of total factor productivity for British secondary education, with a discussion of the theoretical and practical problem of measuring inputs and outputs. It shows the decline in productivity in the United Kingdom over the period studied, with some interesting conclusions.

Appendix 2
IIEP Cost Analysis Case Studies

The twenty-seven case studies carried out in connection with this project are being published separately by Unesco:IIEP under the title *Educational Cost Analysis in Action: Case Studies for Planners,* in three volumes as follows:

VOLUME I

1. *Tanzania: Planning for Implementation* by Nicholas Bennett
2. *Tanzania: Factors Influencing Change in Teachers' Basic Salaries* by John D. Chesswas
3. *Ceylon: Costing First- and Second-Level General Education* by Jinapala Alles, W. D. Fernando, D. P. Wijegunasekera, D. Guanaratus, M. A. deSilva, and C. Hettiarachchi
4. *U.S.S.R.: Economic Planning and the Financing of Higher Education* by D. Chuprunov and L. Tul'chinskii
5. *U.S.S.R.: Estimating the Annual Budget Requirements of the Educational System* by Vasilii Ivanovich Basov
6. *France: The Use of Capital Costs in Educational Planning—the Case of the Fifth French Plan* by Claude Tibi
7. *Thailand: Educational Cost Analysis* by H. W. Reiff
8. *Thailand: The Use of Cost Analysis in Estimating the Total Cost of an Educational Plan and Testing Its Feasibility* by H. W. Reiff
9. *Asia: Cost Analysis in an Asian Model of Educational Development* by J. Auerhan and E. S. Solomon
10. *Chile: Evaluating the Expansion of a Vocational Training Programme* by Lucila Arrigazzi

VOLUME II

11. *Ivory Coast: The Cost of Introducing a Reform in Primary Education* by Ta Ngoc Châu

12. *Madagascar: The Role of Cost Analysis in the Introduction and Implementation of the 1962 Reform of Primary Education* by Ta Ngoc Châu
13. *Norway: The Use of Educational Cost Models in Planning the Extension of Compulsory Education* by Olav Magnussen
14. *Barbados: Marginal Costs for Marginal Decisions—the Case of Team Teaching* by Richard M. Durstine and Barclay M. Hudson
15. *Poland: The Role of Cost Analysis in Planning a Teacher-Training Programme* by K. Podoski
16. *Brazil: Costing an Expansion Programme for Secondary Education in Rio Grande do Sul* by R. C. Fachin
17. *India: The Use of Cost-Benefit Analysis as a Guide to Resource Allocation in Education* by Maureen Woodhall
18. *Colombia: The Use of Cost-Benefit Analysis To Compare the Rates of Return at Different Educational Levels* by Maureen Woodhall

VOLUME III

19. *Uganda: Educational Cost Evaluation* by Nicholas Bennett
20. *Uganda: Behaviour of Non-Teacher Recurring Expenditures* by John Chesswas and Jacques Hallak
21. *Uganda: The Use of Cost Evaluation in the Planning of Makerere University College* by Nicholas Bennett
22. *United Kingdom: The Use of Cost Analysis To Improve the Efficiency of School Building in England and Wales* by Maureen Woodhall
23. *Canada: Comprehensive Analytical Methods for Planning in University Systems—Planning a New Health Sciences Education Complex* by Jack B. Levine, Richard W. Judy, and Richard Wilson
24. *Morocco: Costs of Public Secondary Education—Analysis of the Results of a Governmental Survey* by J. Proust
25. *Chile: Improving Efficiency in the Use of Teachers in Technical Education* by Lucila Arrigazzi and José de Simone
26. *U.S.S.R.: Comparative Costs and Efficiency of Full-time and Part-time Education* by V. Zhamin and B. Remennikov
27. *Hungary: Programming Annual Current and Capital Expenditures During the Planning Period* by L. Faluvégi

Sample of IIEP case studies by level and type of education.

COUNTRY		PRIMARY	SECONDARY	TECHNICAL	HIGHER	TEACHER TRAINING	NON-FORMAL	ALL LEVELS
Africa	Ivory Coast	X						
	Madagascar	X						
	Tanzania (Plan)							X
	Tanzania (Salaries)	X						
	Uganda (Plan)							X
	Uganda (Higher)				X			
	Uganda (A/cs)		X					
Latin America	Barbados	X						
	Brazil		X					
	Chile (Inacap)						X	
	Chile (Tech.)			X				
	Colombia	X	X		X			
Arab State	Morocco		X					

Asia	Asian Model							X
	Ceylon	X	X					
	India	X	X	X	X			
	Thailand (1)							X
	Thailand (2)							X
Eastern Europe	Hungary	X	X		X			
	Poland				X	X		
	U.S.S.R. (1)				X			
	U.S.S.R. (2)	X	X					
	U.S.S.R. (3)				X			
OECD Countries	Canada				X			
	France							X
	Norway	X						
	U.K.	X	X					

Sample of IIEP case studies by type of purpose, region, and country.

COUNTRY		COSTING AND TESTING THE FEASIBILITY OF PLANS	EVALUATING AND IMPROVING THE ALLOCATION OF RESOURCES	WEIGHING THE COMPARATIVE ADVANTAGES OF ALTERNATIVE WAYS TO PURSUE THE SAME OBJECTIVES	DETERMINING THE SHORT-RUN COST DIVERSIONS AND LONGER-RUN COST IMPLICATIONS OF PROJECTS AND INNOVATIONS	IMPROVING EFFICIENCY AND PRODUCTIVITY	CHECKING THE ECONOMIC IMPLICATIONS AND FEASIBILITY OF SPECIFIC POLICY DECISIONS
Africa	Ivory Coast				x	x	
4 countries	Madagascar				x		x
(7 studies)	Tanzania (Plan)	x					
	Tanzania (Salaries)						x
	Uganda (Plan)	x				x	
	Uganda (Higher)			x	x		
	Uganda (A/cs)		x				
Latin	Barbados			x	x		
America	Brazil		x				
4 countries	Chile (Inacap)		x				
(5 studies)	Chile (Tech.)					x	
	Colombia		x				

Arab State	Morocco		x			
(1 study)						
Asia	Asian Model	x				
3 countries	Ceylon	x				
(5 studies)	India		x			
	Thailand (1)					x
	Thailand (2)	x				
Eastern	Hungary			x		
Countries	Poland					x
3 countries	U.S.S.R. (1)	x				
(5 studies)	U.S.S.R. (2)		x			
	U.S.S.R. (3)			x		
OECD	Canada			x	x	
Countries	France	x				
4 countries	Norway			x		
(4 studies)	U.K.				x	

Index